THE HEART'S FOREST

THE HEART'S FOREST

A Study of Shakespeare's Pastoral Plays

by David Young

New Haven and London: Yale University Press

1972

Published with assistance from the foundation
established in memory of Amasa Stone Mather of
the Class of 1907, Yale College.

Designed by John O. C. McCrillis
and set in Baskerville type.
Printed in the United States of America by
The Colonial Press Inc., Clinton, Massachusetts.

Published in Great Britain, Europe and Africa by
Yale University Press, Ltd., London.
Distributed in Canada by McGill-Queen's University
Press, Montreal; in Latin America by Kaiman & Polon,
Inc., New York City; in Australasia and Southeast
Asia by John Wiley & Sons Australasia Pty. Ltd.,
Sydney; in India by UBS Publishers' Distributors Pvt.,
Ltd., Delhi; in Japan by John Weatherhill, Inc., Tokyo.

for Chloe
pastora fida

Contents

Preface

This is a study of four of Shakespeare's plays—a comedy, a tragedy, and two late romances—in terms of their structural, stylistic, and thematic relations to the pastoral mode and to each other. Pastoral was among the liveliest and most attractive channels of artistic expression from the early Renaissance through the eighteenth century, and it has long been acknowledged that Shakespeare knew of it and resorted to it on more than one occasion. Several recent critics have commented most perceptively on the implications of pastoral for certain aspects of certain plays; and interest in the pastoral in its own right seems to have grown steadily during this century. But there has as yet been no comprehensive study of Shakespeare as a writer of pastoral.

One problem with pastoral, of course, is that it is no longer alive to us in the form known to Shakespeare; it lacks the familiarity and immediacy that comedy, tragedy, and even history seem to retain when we approach Shakespeare from a generic point of view. One effect of this book, then, might seem to be to remove Shakespeare further from us and our present concerns and preoccupations. Yet this, I have found, is not at all the case. On the contrary, I think its effect is to draw us closer, and for two significant reasons.

First, while we may have lost the exterior conventions of pastoral—the shepherds, sheephooks, and love declarations among groves and meadows, all the misunderstood decorum that eventually stifled pastoral as a serious mode of expression —we have not lost the impulses that gave rise to the genre, first in the ancient world and again in the Renaissance, and nourished it for so long. Shakespeare, as I shall try to show, was scarcely more concerned with the trappings of pastoral than we. What drew him to the convention was its essence, the interlocking subjects which continue to preoccupy us in new forms and configurations and which we could scarcely escape

if we wished to: man's relation to the natural world; his search
for harmony with his environment; his tendency to idealize,
alternately, the life of the city and that of the country; his
dreams of escape, retirement, and a self-contained life hospitable both to sensual gratification and to spiritual fulfillment;
and the origin of good and evil in terms of the opposition between the civilized and the primitive. None of these subjects is
exclusive to the pastoral, nor were his pastoral plays the only
occasions when Shakespeare's imagination engaged them. But
pastoral was the literary mode in which these questions were
most immediately and significantly raised for his contemporaries, and it is scarcely surprising, under the circumstances,
that Shakespeare made use of that fact. In a time when we are
faced with the need for a searching reexamination of our own
attitudes toward our environment, and with the question of
its, and our, survival, Shakespeare's dramatic expression of the
same preoccupations through the pastoral mode can scarcely
be said to lack interest.

Second, insofar as a study like the present one clarifies some
of the aims and interests of the plays discussed, and to the extent that it manages to reveal their subtleties and intricacies,
it ought to help us to read and produce Shakespeare—at least
the plays in question—more effectively and with greater understanding. To aim at accomplishing such ends is not, it
seems to me, to relegate Shakespeare to the past but to help
restore him to the present; and it is a much more useful activity, I would maintain, than distorting his works, by commentary and production, to a kind of specious and short-lived
contemporaneity. To make my intentions clearer in this respect, I have included a short appendix in which I discuss the
ways by which some of my findings about the plays might be
implemented by actors, directors, and designers. I do not consider myself an expert in these matters. But it seems to me that
an interaction between those who study Shakespeare and those
who labor to bring his plays to a new life on the stage is not
only vital to the success of both endeavors, but likely to enhance the enthusiasm and creativity that deserve to surround
his name and work.

Much of the work on this book was made possible by a Junior Fellowship from the National Endowment for the Humanities and a Research Status Appointment from Oberlin College during 1967–68. To both institutions my grateful thanks, with these further acknowledgments: to Philip Silver, who greatly stimulated my interest in the pastoral and who extracted from me, for a humanities course on pastoral that he organized and taught in 1966, a lecture on *Lear* and *The Tempest* which was the genesis of this study; to Robert Pierce, my colleague, who read most of the manuscript and offered valuable advice and suggestions, and to whose own work on *As You Like It* I am considerably indebted; to William Carroll, who, first as a student and later as a colleague, exchanged ideas with me about Shakespeare in general and *The Winter's Tale* in particular; to Wayland Schmitt, initially my editor at Yale, who helped me with revisions of the first chapter and the appendix and who prodded me into writing the Epilogue; to John Hobbs and David Bevington for additional advice about the manuscript; and to my students at Oberlin, whose abilities and insights have kept me from feeling that there was any divorce between scholarly work and classroom study.

D.Y.

Oberlin
January 1972

Note on the Texts

Citations from the plays have been drawn, wherever possible, from the New Arden editions (London and Cambridge, Mass.): Kenneth Muir's of *King Lear,* F. D. Hoeniger's of *Pericles,* J. M. Nosworthy's of *Cymbeline,* J. H. P. Pafford's of *The Winter's Tale,* and Frank Kermode's of *The Tempest.* The important exception is *As You Like It,* for which no Arden edition was available; citations from this play, and other incidental citations, are drawn from Hardin Craig's *Complete Works of Shakespeare* (Chicago: Scott, Foresman, 1951).

1

A Singular Gift in Defining

A Pastoral of a hundred lines may be endured, but who will hear of sheep and goats and myrtle bowers and purling rivulets through five acts?

Dr. Johnson, *Life of Gay*

> But that no style for Pastoral should go
> Current, but what is stamped with Ah! and O!
> Who judgeth so, may singularly err,
> As if all poesie had one character
> In which what were not written were not right.
>
> Ben Jonson, *The Sad Shepherd*

It is certainly true that pastoral was a convention. . . . But to establish the occasion, and even the fashion, of a work of art is not to explain its significance. The more conventional it is, the more likely it is to have some central core of meaning from which individual treatments may originate. "Originality" cannot be estimated until we know what the convention meant to the writers working in it.

Hallett Smith, *Elizabethan Poetry*

It may seem ominous to begin in the footsteps of Polonius, but the fact is that his list of genres and their permutations—whether read off the players' handbill or his own exuberant invention—constitutes a fascinating reference to dramatic types, one of the very few to be found in Shakespeare:

> The best actors in the world, either for tragedy, comedy, history, pastoral, pastoral-comical, historical-pastoral, tragical - historical, tragical - comical - historical - pastoral, scene individable, or poem unlimited: Seneca cannot be too heavy, nor Plautus too light. For the law of writ and the liberty, these are the only men. [2.2.415–21]

1

The passage is usually cited as an illustration of Shakespeare's contempt for literary species, and a warning to commentators that it is hardly profitable to treat his work in terms of purity of genre. It should not, however, serve to close off considerations of genre altogether. For the traditional picture of Shakespeare as a writer unaware of categories and ignorant of rules deserves to be replaced, as for the most part it has been, by a conception of him as a spirited experimenter, intensely aware of genres without in any way being confined by them, more interested in "poem unlimited" than in "scene individable," committed to "liberty" but with no lack of knowledge of the "law of writ." He had in fact observed, early in his career, the traditional categories of Senecan tragedy and Plautine comedy, but even *Titus Andronicus* and *The Comedy of Errors,* for all their academic propriety, show a certain restlessness at the idea of close imitation of models: in both cases the author exploits the given mode to the limit, as if to discover its confines. And he never resorts to such "purity" again.

Further evidence of Shakespeare's independence is provided in those early stages of his career by his experimentation with a new genre, the history play, which recent commentators have come to feel he was instrumental in establishing, furnishing, and defining—always, of course, by practice rather than by theory.

Three of Polonius' categories are thus easily touched on in discussions of Shakespeare's practice. But what of the fourth? Pastoral, which crops up four times in the list, is more difficult to account for. We need not, fortunately, rely on Polonius' testimony for its existence as a genre. A number of contemporary plays, lost and surviving, were described as pastorals.[1] And the document appointing Shakespeare's com-

1. Plays actually designated as pastorals (on title pages, in court records, or in Stationer's Register entries) include the following: "A Greek Maide" (lost, anon.; played by Leicester's men at Court, 1579); "Phillyda & Choryn" (lost, anon.; played by Queen's men at Court, 1584); *The Arraignment of Paris* (George Peele, ca. 1584; also his lost *The Hunting of Cupid,* ca. 1591, described as a pastoral by Drummond of Hawthornden); *Love's Metamorphosis* (John Lyly, ca. 1590); *Robin Hood and Little John* (lost,

pany as the King's Men (19 May 1603) authorizes them "freely to use and exercise the Arte and faculty of playinge Comedies, Tragedies, histories, Enterludes, moralls, pastorals, Stage plaies, and Such others like as theie have alreadie studied or hereafter shall use of studie." [2] If pastoral was a recognized dramatic type, then, did Shakespeare have any interest in it beyond such casual references as Polonius' list? Did he make serious use of it? Did it play any significant part in his experimentation with the possibilities of his art? This study is grounded on the assumption that these questions can be answered affirmatively and that they have not previously had the attention they deserve.

Shakespeare's awareness of the pastoral mode has never been in dispute. He makes use of it as early as *3 Henry VI*, in the emblematic scene at the battle of Towton, when the forlorn king, who has already invoked the shepherd "blowing of his nails," as part of a comparison, sits on a molehill and imagines a different existence for himself. The passage is worth quoting because it demonstrates Shakespeare's early awareness of the tensions and contrasts—between court and country, active and contemplative, fortune and nature, complex and simple—which are the basis of the pastoral design.

> O God! methinks it were a happy life,
> To be no better than a homely swain;
> To sit upon a hill, as I do now,
> To carve out dials quaintly, point by point,
> Thereby to see the minutes how they run,

---

anon.; S.R., 1594); *A Pastoral Tragedy* (George Chapman; lost or unfinished; payment by Henslowe, 1599); *The Fairy Pastoral, or Forrest of Elves* (William Percy, 1603); *The Queen's Arcadia* (Samuel Daniel, 1605); *The Faithful Shepherdess* (John Fletcher, ca. 1608; described in preface as a "pastoral tragicomedy"); *Hymen's Triumph* (Daniel, 1614). Dates are drawn from E. K. Chambers, *Elizabethan Stage* (Oxford, 1923), and Alfred Harbage, *Annals of English Drama*, ed. S. Schoenbaum (Philadelphia, 1964). This list should in no sense be taken as a guide to Elizabethan pastoral drama. It is simply evidence of the use of "pastoral" as a generic term.

2. Chambers, 2:208.

How many make the hour full complete;
How many hours bring about the day;
How many days will finish up the year;
How many years a mortal man may live.
When this is known, then to divide the times:
So many hours must I tend my flock;
So many hours must I take my rest;
So many hours must I contemplate;
So many hours must I sport myself;
So many days my ewes have been with young;
So many weeks ere the poor fools will ean;
So many years ere I shall shear the fleece:
So minutes, hours, days, months, and years,
Pass'd over to the end they were created,
Would bring white hairs unto a quiet grave.
Ah, what a life were this! how sweet! how lovely!
Gives not the hawthorn bush a sweeter shade
To shepherds looking on their silly sheep,
Than doth a rich embroider'd canopy
To kings that fear their subjects' treachery?
O yes, it doth; a thousand-fold it doth.
And to conclude, the shepherd's homely curds,
His cold thin drink out of his leather bottle,
His wonted sleep under a fresh tree's shade,
All which secure and sweetly he enjoys,
Is far beyond a prince's delicates,
His viands sparkling in a golden cup,
His body crouched in a curious bed,
When care, mistrust, and treason waits on him.

[2.5.21–54]

Henry's shepherd is not outside of time, but he is in harmony
with it as it exhibits itself in the rhythms of nature—"to the
end they were created"—and thus free of history as Henry
knows it. He is not so much longing to escape from reality
as arguing the case for a reality which is, paradoxically, at
once more lowly and more exalted than the one in which he

finds himself. The passage is a momentary but full-fledged invocation of the meanings and conventions of pastoral.[3]

There have, of course, been other attempts, none of them very recent, to explore Shakespeare's relation to the pastoral and describe his use of it.[4] The difficulty most commentators have had in getting very far with the subject has risen from a deplorable tendency to limit discussion of the genre to its "pure" examples, to a degree which they would never think of employing in, say, studies of tragedy. Perhaps nowhere has the unimaginative assumption that a genre does not exist outside certain codifications been more disastrously imposed than in considerations of pastoral drama by the generations since Guarini, whose *Il Pastor Fido* has been taken, along with Tasso's *Aminta,* as the model of its kind. Guarini, who was certainly his own best apologist, managed to foster the impression that his brand of pastoral tragicomedy was the only legitimate form of pastoral drama, thus blocking from view a great deal of interesting work that had preceded him and a great deal more that was to follow. Ultimately, perhaps, the "version" of pastoral he helped to found and codify can be said to have played its part in the death of the convention— or, rather, the lapse in our understanding of it—in the eighteenth century. To anyone who surveys the peculiar history of criticism of the pastoral, William Empson, whose *Some Versions of Pastoral* (1935) widened and revived the subject, must appear as a genuine, if somewhat erratic, savior. If Empson's work did not reverse the common tendency to as-

3. Other early glances at the convention include the two songs at the end of *Love's Labour's Lost,* the song "Who Is Sylvia" in *The Two Gentlemen of Verona,* and *A Midsummer Night's Dream,* 2.1.66–68.

4. Perhaps the most significant is Edwin Greenlaw, "Shakespeare's Pastorals," *Studies in Philology* 12 (Jan. 1916):122–54. Greenlaw describes a typical plot, of which he lists seven elements. The basic model, he argues, is *Daphnis and Chloe* rather than Italian and Spanish pastorals. He traces parallels through the *Arcadia* and *The Faerie Queene,* which he then links to *As You Like It, Cymbeline,* and *The Winter's Tale.* The Florizel-Perdita episode he finds "the most exquisite and satisfying pastoral in Elizabethan literature" (p. 146).

sume that Shakespeare had only one brush with the pastoral as such—*As You Like It*—in which he was mainly concerned to satirize the convention, it made possible, by a drastic alteration of attitude toward the strength and inherent meaning of pastoral, the lines of approach on which the present study is based.

The terminological problem—getting straight just what we mean, or what was at any given time meant, by the word pastoral—stems in part from the fact that formal and generic terms can be used to denote a number of different aspects of a literary work.[5] Perhaps a list would be useful.

> *External characteristics* (E.g., a sonnet has fourteen lines, a rhyme scheme, etc.)
>
> *Structure* (E.g., a sonnet usually has two parts or movements.)
>
> *Subject* (E.g., at one time the sonnet was a love poem.)
>
> *Emotional focus,* a term which must cover both the author's attitude and the effect on the reader, the function (E.g., the Petrarchan sonnet not only dealt with love but dealt with it in certain prescribed ways which covered such matters as the author's attitude toward his mistress; at the same time the sonnet was meant to relieve the writer's passion and to serve as an instrument of courtship or seduction. The presumed power of tragedy to produce catharsis is another example.)

A firmly understood term might seem to embrace all four categories, as "sonnet" at one time did, or as neoclassical definitions of tragedy tried to do; but a firm genre is not necessarily a healthy one. For the fact is that a good artist is apt to question any or all of the four categories and to "meddle" with redefinitions, as both Donne and Shakespeare

5. The discussion that follows is partly based on some suggestions in Allardyce Nicoll's "Tragical-Comical-Historical-Pastoral: Elizabethan Dramatic Nomenclature," *Bulletin of the John Rylands Library* 43 (1960–61):70–87. Nicoll shows how terms like "tragedy" and "history" tended to fluctuate in meaning, and discusses Shakespeare's innovations. He does not touch upon the pastoral.

did with the sonnet. And hybridizations are the rule rather than the exception. Insofar as *The Faerie Queene,* for example, partakes of epic, allegory, and chivalric romance, it must do some violence to the purity of each generic term.

It is also worth noting that we have learned, especially with the larger genres, to put more emphasis on subject and emotional focus than on external characteristics and structure. Where a neoclassicist might have hoped to identify a tragedy in terms of external features (did it have a chorus and observe a certain decorum of language and action?) and structural techniques (did it observe the unities and follow the five-act structure?) we would be more inclined, so as not to have to dismiss *Hamlet* and *Lear* from consideration, to put stress on the subject and on a somewhat intangible quality called "tragic vision," which would seem to belong under the fourth heading, emotional focus. The writer of tragedy, we would surely argue, ought to be free to experiment with, transform, and even violently alter the previous features of the genre, in the interests of promoting its essential vision, despite the fact that this must entail a loose and impermanent definition. The dialogue between works of art and critical categories is, and ought to be, an endless one.[6]

If these observations smack of the obvious, it is nevertheless remarkable how seldom they were brought to bear in older discussions of the pastoral. The first three of the above categories were variously favored; the crucial fourth was virtually ignored. Thus we find Homer Smith, in an 1897 monograph, working on the assumption that a pastoral must be about shepherds, and shepherds only, with all the trimmings found in certain Italian and classical examples, and having to reject

6. This view of literature and literary categories, while radical in the Renaissance, was not unknown to Elizabethan writers. Even so strict a writer as Jonson could call on it when it suited his purpose, as the quotation heading this chapter indicates. And it had been vigorously expressed as early as 1585 by Giordano Bruno, in the first dialogue of his *De gli Eroici Furori,* written and published in England and dedicated to Philip Sidney. For a discussion of this dialogue see John Buxton, *Sir Philip Sidney and the English Renaissance* (London, 1964), pp. 165–67.

from consideration examples which have admixtures of such
other elements as the mythological and the supernatural.[7] His
survey of pastoral drama is accordingly a woeful catalogue
of dreadful but untainted examples. W. W. Greg, whose
immensely learned and comprehensive *Pastoral Poetry and
Pastoral Drama* is the standard work on the subject, shows
considerable irritation at Smith regarding the mythological
elements, but in other respects is similarly bound by a definition which lays most of its stress on the trappings of pastoral
and tends to miss, again and again, its essential vision. Greg
knows perfectly well that Elizabethan dramatists did not feel
constrained to work within the limits of the Guarinian model,
but he is not really prepared to forgive them this heresy. "The
idea of pastoral current among the playwrights," he remarks
at one point, "and no doubt among the audience too, was
largely derived from novels such as the Arcadia, and, as we
have seen, the tradition of these works was one rather of polite
chivalry and courtly adventure than of pastoralism proper." [8]
The trouble is that "pastoralism proper" seems to have little
or nothing to do with viable drama—it constrains Greg to
give little more than a nod in the direction of *As You Like It*
and to putter around such molehills as Abraham Fraunce's
adaptation of the *Aminta* and Samuel Daniel's *The Queen's
Arcadia*—and that it does not begin to account for the power
and popularity of a mode of artistic expression that swept
across Renaissance Europe in the sixteenth century and fired
the imaginations of poets, painters, musicians, novelists, and,
not least, dramatists.

The tendency to identify pastoral with sheep and sheephooks (and the goats, myrtle bowers, and purling rivulets
which so exasperated Dr. Johnson) was, as I have suggested,
abruptly reversed by Mr. Empson. He accomplished this, in
terms of the above categories, by studying pastoral in terms
of emotional focus which led in turn to a reworking of subject

7. Homer Smith, "Pastoral Influence in the English Drama," *PMLA* 12
(1897):355–460.

8. W. W. Greg, *Pastoral Poetry and Pastoral Drama* (London, 1906), p.
337.

and structure. That is, he set out to identify the motives an artist might have for writing pastoral and the interest it might hold for the reader or spectator, and this resulted in a new understanding of the subject matter of pastoral, and, to a lesser extent, its typical structure. The following passage is crucial:

> The essential trick of the old pastoral, which was felt to imply a beautiful relation between rich and poor, was to make simple people express strong feelings (felt as the most universal subject, something fundamentally true about everybody) in learned and fashionable language (so that you wrote about the best subject in the best way). From seeing the two sorts of people combined like this you thought the better of both; the best parts of both were used. The effect was in some degree to combine in the reader or author the merits of the two sorts; he was made to mirror in himself more completely the effective elements of the society he lived in. This was not a process you could explain in the course of writing pastoral; it was already shown by the clash between style and theme, and to make the clash work in the right way (not become funny) the writer must keep up a firm pretence that he was unconscious of it.[9]

There are questionable assumptions here, such as the one about not becoming funny. But the excerpt should serve to demonstrate Empson's talent for getting at the function of pastoral (what he later sums up as "putting the complex into the simple"),[10] its aim at universality, and the way in which this leads to a reconsideration of subject (strong feelings, the social microcosm) and of a feature ("the clash between style and theme") which can be seen to be related both to structure and to external characteristics. Reading such a passage, one can begin to discover the relevance and interest of "the old

9. William Empson, *Some Versions of Pastoral* (Norfolk, Conn., 1935), pp. 11–12.
10. Empson, p. 23.

pastoral," and the purling rivulets can be allowed to go their way.

The problem presented by Empson's work is that he did not so much open a door as knock down a wall and proceed toward the horizon. He was concerned, as his title suggests, to show how the vitality of the pastoral, its essential vision, had worked to produce conscious and unconscious analogues, or "versions," both in its own time and in such recent examples as *Alice in Wonderland* and the socialist myth of the worker. As he himself admits, "Probably the cases I take are the surprising ones rather than the normal ones," [11] and that is something of an understatement. In the case of Shakespeare it means a discussion of *Henry IV*, for the way in which it deploys contrasting worlds somewhat analogous to the pastoral worlds of court and country, rather than of any of the plays which might be claimed to have a stronger link to the convention as Shakespeare knew and practiced it. The net result of his study is to leave virtually unchanged the traditional assumption that Shakespeare was either unaware or contemptuous of the possibilities presented by the pastoral as such.

In the years since Empson's study there has been some excellent work on the Renaissance pastoral in general [12] and on its manifestations in the work of particular artists such as Sidney and Spenser.[13] But the question of Shakespeare's use of and interest in the convention remains, except for some incidental work on particular plays, largely undiscussed. It is this area which I propose to explore in the present study, and

11. Ibid.

12. See especially Hallett Smith, *Elizabethan Poetry* (Cambridge, Mass., 1952); Frank Kermode, *English Pastoral Poetry* (London, 1953); Renato Poggioli, "The Oaten Flute," *Harvard Library Bulletin* 11 (Spring 1957): 147–84; and Edward William Tayler, *Nature and Art in Renaissance Literature* (New York, 1964).

13. Walter R. Davis, *A Map of Arcadia: Sidney's Romance in Its Tradition*, in *Sidney's Arcadia* (New Haven, 1965); John Arthos, *On the Poetry of Spenser and the Form of Romances* (London, 1956); Donald Cheney, *Spenser's Image of Nature: Wild Man and Shepherd in The Faerie Queene* (New Haven, 1966).

my task is to find a place to settle between the stools of Empson and Greg: to treat the pastoral as it existed in Elizabethan England and as Shakespeare was able to develop it,
that is, as a definable convention, and at the same time to
recognize, with Empson, what an extraordinarily fluid and
adaptable thing a literary convention is apt to be in the hands
of a great artist. We know already how freely Shakespeare
handled comedy and tragedy, and to what effect. We have
begun to discover, and are still discovering, the originality of
his work in the history plays. About his treatment of pastoral,
for the reasons given above and because of its uncertain status
as a genre, we know very little. But if we are simply willing
to assume that his handling of pastoral may have been consistent with his treatment of Polonius' other categories, we
will find opening before us a largely unexplored and immensely interesting territory, an Arcadia that is partly traditional, mostly unique.

It is hardly necessary to demonstrate the widespread popularity of the pastoral in sixteenth-century Europe and Elizabethan England, or to trace the history of the convention
from its classical origins to its revival in the Renaissance.
What is required before undertaking a detailed look at the
four plays with which this study deals is to say something
about the European, and in particular the English, context
of the pastoral as it existed both in its dramatic and nondramatic forms when Shakespeare took it up; to outline the
meanings and extensions of the pastoral, the possibilities that
it presented to the working artist; and to say something about
my reasons for grouping these four plays together as "pastorals," temporarily displacing their traditional generic desig-
nations, and excluding other plays which might well be
thought to have a claim for consideration too.

❧

The rapid spread of pastoral from Italy to Spain, France,
England, and the rest of Europe in the sixteenth century made
its influence felt in all the literary modes, but its marked suc-
cesses were always nondramatic to begin with; it was only

after the fashion for pastoral had been established in poetry
and narrative romance that dramatists took it up, although
they were by no means slow to do so. The reason for this pattern had surely to do in part with the existing classical
models, which were poetic—the idylls and eclogues of Theocritus and Virgil—and narrative—the *Daphnis and Chloe* of
Longus. When it came to ancient precedents in the drama,
theorists were reduced to speculation. No one was sure what
a satyr play ought to be, but conjecture linked it to tragicomedy and a pastoral setting.[14] Beyond that dramatists had
to be content to adapt pastoral for the stage from other
literary forms and to imitate each other.

Two aspects of Renaissance pastoral have traditionally been
identified as containing the seeds of its eventual growth in
drama: the conversational and dialectical form of the eclogue
and the popularity of pastoral as a framework for court entertainment. Both, however, can be said to have had their draw-
backs, if only because they suggested drama where it did not
in fact exist. The implied dramatic relationships of the
eclogue—the overheard complaint, the singing contest, the
disputation about court and country—become both artificial
and static when transferred directly to the stage. The problems inherent in stretching the eclogue's features for stage
presentation can be seen in the operatic tendency of much
Italian pastoral drama, which was characteristically built
around set pieces, lyrics, and choruses, and often lacked forward movement and genuine tension.

Nor was the static quality of pastoral drama discouraged by
its other root in court entertainment, where a discursive,
presentational style was the order of the day. The additional
danger of court entertainment was its relatively narrow perspective. It was aimed, inevitably, at a small, select audience,
and since its chief aim was flattery (of a special kind, in the
case of pastoral, based on the allegation of simplicity and
humility), it could hardly be said to have much dramatic

14. For an account of this and of Giraldi Cinthio's *Egle* (1545), see
Marvin T. Herrick, *Tragicomedy* (Urbana, 1955), pp. 10–14.

range. It is one thing to please a king or queen with shepherds who dance, sing, and turn compliments to the royal patron; it is quite another thing to please an audience of diverse tastes expecting to see a play.

With these two slippery footholds in the pastoral, then, the dramatist had a good deal to overcome. The eclogue proved that shepherds conversed, sang, gossiped, suffered, and mourned; but it hardly provided useful dramatic models. And the popularity of pastoral in court entertainments offered the possibility that the dramatist who could combine it with elements that had a wider appeal might simultaneously capture a larger audience and attain to literary respectability; but whoever used it ran the risk of falling victim to a specialized genre, more lyric than dramatic, reflecting court needs and values alone. The solution, which came gradually, proved to be a combination of the features of the narrative romance and the pastoral, an amalgam which could be traced back to *Daphnis and Chloe*—surely a respectable and promising ancestry—and which had achieved both popular and critical success in three romances combining prose and verse, Sannazaro's *Arcadia* (1504), Montemayor's *Diana* (1545), and Sidney's *Arcadia* (1590), as well as in two great narrative poems, Tasso's *Gerusalemme Liberata* (1576, 1581) and Spenser's *The Faerie Queene* (1590, 1596).[15] It is the manifestation of pastoral represented by these works, I would maintain, that, with the exception of some individual songs and eclogues, produced the most significant and lasting achievements of Renaissance pastoral; and if I am right, then it is plays like *The Winter's Tale* which belong to the main line of development rather than plays like *Aminta* and *Il Pastor Fido*, so long thought to represent the central accomplishment of pastoral drama.

It is in the years immediately preceding *The Shephearde's Calendar* (1579) that we begin to find evidence of the use of

15. The dates are of publication. In many cases the work in question was begun much earlier (e.g. Sidney's first *Arcadia*, 1580), and circulated in manuscript before publication.

rustic and pastoral motifs in the entertainments arranged at
court and during the progresses of the Queen.[16] A mask of
"Six Shepherds" had been presented at the Scottish court in
1563. At Greenwich, in 1573, Elizabeth was presented with
"a mask of wild men." There is good evidence that the Italian
players who entertained on Elizabeth's Progress in 1574 played
pastorals of some kind or other.[17] For the famous Kenilworth
entertainment of 1757 Gascoigne wrote a dialogue between a
wild man and an echo and dressed himself up as "Sylvanus,
god of the woods," to hold a conversation with a voice from
a bush. At Wanstead, in 1578, the Queen heard a piece by
Sidney involving the "Contention of a Forrester and a Shepherd for the May-Lady." In 1579 Leicester's men played "a
pastorall or historie of A Greek maide" at court. And so it
goes, with royal entertainments featuring pastoral characters
and situations continuing past the death of Elizabeth and on
into the reign of James.

Just when someone first made the step of producing a full-
fledged pastoral drama for the delectation of the court cannot be said with certainty; perhaps it was the "historie" of
the Greek maid mentioned above. The earliest such surviving
play, and a likely candidate for the original attempt, is George

16. The information in this paragraph is variously drawn from Nichols,
The Progresses and Public Procession of Queen Elizabeth (Edinburgh,
1799–1823), Harbage and Schoenbaum, *Annals of English Drama*, and A.
Feuillerat, *Documents Relating to the Office of the Revels in the Time of
Queen Elizabeth* (Louvain, 1908). An account covering most of these
events may be found in A. H. Thorndike, "The Pastoral Element in the
English Drama Before 1605," *MLN* 14, no. 4 (1899):228–46. Thorndike's
account is, on the whole, more useful than Greg's.

17. "Hookes," "Lamskynnes," and "staves" for "shepperds" are among
the properties listed in the Revels Accounts for February 1573 to Novem-
ber 1574 as charges "ffor the Ayrynges, Repayryngs, Translatynges, pre-
paring, ffytting, ffurnishing, Garnishing, Attending & seeting foorth of
sundry kyndes of Apparell properties & ffurnytyre for the Italyan players
that ffolowed the progresses & made pastyme fyrst at Wynsor & after-
wardes at Reading." Also included in the list are "Horstayles for the
wylde mannes garment" and "A Syth for saturne." Feuillerat, p. 225, pp.
227–28. See also K. M. Lea, *Italian Popular Comedy*, vol. 2 (Oxford, 1935),
p. 353.

Peele's *The Arraignment of Paris* (ca. 1581). Predictably it is a curious mixture of pageantlike effects, with deities thronging the stage, and an attempt to wind the inevitable flattery of the Queen out of a genuine plot conflict. Although Paris may not seem to us a very likely hero for a pastoral, to the Renaissance he was, as Hallett Smith has suggested, an archetypal figure of the shepherd.[18] But the *Arraignment* is best viewed as a sophisticated and successful example of court entertainment rather than as a wedding of pastoral conventions to the drama.

John Lyly, another court dramatist, was, without any very clear-cut or programmatic commitment to pastoral drama, happy to fill his plays with gods and goddesses, nymphs and shepherds in the same Ovidian-Golden Age setting of the *Arraignment*. While his *Love's Metamorphosis* is in many ways close to Italian pastoral drama, the play by Lyly which strikes me as the most interesting in the development of pastoral drama, more for the direction it points in than for any full accomplishment of its own, is *Gallathea* (ca. 1585). The bulk of the action is spent in the woods, and its preoccupation with amorous confusion against a sylvan setting links it in interesting ways with *A Midsummer Night's Dream* and Fletcher's *The Faithful Shepherdess*. What is of particular interest is the way in which the play begins to sketch out the pastoral romance pattern of extrusion from society—the characters choosing disguise and a rustic existence until justice and equilibrium are restored—which was to become the basis of English pastoral drama. Significant too is Lyly's casual freedom in handling pastoral motifs. He is probably aware of Italian models (although he is exactly contemporary with Guarini), but he does not seem to have felt bound by them. Lyly needed some safe and convincing means of treating the life and interests of his courtly audience, and his primary solution was his continual use of the Ovidian-mythological tradition. But the pastoral, associated with the Golden Age and familiar and fashionable at court, made a convenient and

18. Smith, p. 6.

easily blended second ingredient, having equally to do, in his view and presumably his audience's, with the two favorite subjects of love (as sexual infatuation) and metamorphosis.

Lyly's drama was, at any rate, merely a partial step in the creation of a viable dramatic structure around the pastoral. For all its interest and skill it was still primarily court entertainment, and as likely to point the way to Samuel Daniel's stiff imitations from the Italian as to Shakespeare's supple variations. What was needed was the intervention of a more popular form, and that came through the marriage of pastoral and romance, first hazarded (if we except Longus) by Sannazaro, in his *Arcadia,* continued by continental writers like Tasso, Montemayor, Gil Polo, and Cervantes,[19] and in England by the pastoral novels of Sidney, Greene, and Lodge, and by the sixth book of *The Faerie Queene.* The plot structures shaped by these writers, their characters and situations, and, not least, the impressive popularity they achieved, were to provide valuable precedents for the dramatist.

The history and development of the romance has never really been fully told, and the task would be a formidable one, so many and so varied are its permutations. But most would agree, I think, that the episodic, the melodramatic, and the spectacular are essential features of the basic romance pattern. S. L. Wolff's description of Greek romance is helpful here:

> As the links of Cause are broken, and Fortune takes direction of the affairs of men, events are no longer calculable, as they had been in any imaginative work based, like the Attic drama, for example, upon the ancient myths, and exhibiting "the laws of the gods"; indeed, their interest comes to lie in their very incalculableness. The reader's pleasure no longer consists in seeing law work

19. Gaspar Gil Polo wrote the *Diana Enamorada,* a continuation of Montemayor's *Diana.* Cervantes' first published work was a pastoral romance, *Galatea* (1585), the work by which he expected to be remembered by posterity. There is also a liberal use of pastoral episodes in *Don Quixote.*

itself inexorably out, but in being surprised, shocked, made to "sit up," by the unexpectedness, the queerness of the turns things take. The paradoxical, the bizarre, the inconsistent, the self-contradictory—these were stock in trade with the writers of Greek Romance.[20]

It is perhaps necessary to add that mixed with surprise at the unexpected shifts of fortune is the reader's confidence that things will in fact turn out for the best, that some sort of inscrutable destiny or equilibrium is at work; the hero will be reunited with the heroine, their noble parentage will be revealed, and so forth. But the general impression of a mysterious and terrifying reality is not thus nullified, for the anticipated happy ending is more apt to be felt as an imposed fiction, counterbalancing the exaggerated disasters, than as an illustration of "the laws of the gods."

The chivalric tradition had provided the basic material for medieval and early Renaissance romances, and it was not so much displaced by the pastoral in the writers listed—at least in the cases of Tasso, Sidney, and Spenser—as mixed with it. The two traditions could be blended readily enough, for they had much in common: both were associated with the dream of the Golden Age,[21] both were insistently fictive, given to fantasy; and the mysterious forests where enchanters and monsters lurked were the more interesting when juxtaposed to the peaceful regions, equally remote, where literary shepherds grazed their flocks.

It was not the pastoral's kinship with the chivalric that attracted writers of romance, however, so much as its differences, the new possibilities it offered. It had, to begin with, the prestige of the classics. In addition, it had novelty. Chivalry was growing obsolete. It offered a fairly simple confrontation between good and evil, with a background of divine providence; in pastoral one could lay more stress on the exigencies of Fortune and thus steer closer to the basic

20. Samuel Lee Wolff, *The Greek Romances in Elizabethan Prose Fiction* (New York, 1899), pp. 4–5.
21. See Arthos, p. 52, who cites *Don Quixote*, I, xx.

pattern of the Greek Romances. Personal and lyric elements could be introduced. A good deal more attention could be paid to the subject of love in the pastoral, since it tended to show the lovers united (whatever their difficulties) instead of, as in the chivalric romance, largely separated. In the place of heroism and its vicissitudes the pastoral could substitute the domestic and the daily, social norms, peace and quiet, the possibility of a model community, and a chance for the characters to discuss and debate favorite topics. In fact, the pastoral invited more intellectualizing and less sheer adventure; the writer who blended it with the chivalric romance had available a kind of sliding scale from pure event to pure discussion. Thus the social and psychological interests not served by the chivalric but made possible through the pastoral must have made the latter seem an important opportunity to ambitious writers. The bulk of chivalric writing was entertaining trash, and the success of a writer like Spenser in transforming the tradition into serious literature, while not unprecedented, was rare. Even Spenser, who had renounced pastoral in favor of more heroic subjects in the first book of *The Faerie Queene*, found himself drawn back to it in Book VI.

These generalities have been offered in lieu of a detailed account of the growth of pastoral romance in the sixteenth century; they may also serve to introduce the English examples of the genre, the most important of which is easily Sidney's *Arcadia*. The *Arcadia* was enormously popular in its time, and the high regard in which Sidney was held, as both a writer and a model human being, made his work a kind of touchstone of what good pastoral ought to be. It is well to remember, however, that most of the features of pastoral romance are not original to the *Arcadia*; they simply exist there in a considered combination that makes it a masterpiece of its kind.

Perhaps the most important single innovation exemplified by the *Arcadia* was the concept of the *sojourn*, the experience of the pastoral world as a part of a larger set of circumstances, both spatial and temporal, often as a segment of a journey. Two radical changes in the character of the pastoral were thereby accomplished: the characters dealt with could be visitors to Arcadia as well as inhabitants, pseudo-shepherds as well as shepherds; and the pastoral experience became sequential, giving rise to more opportunities for plot.[22] In the first instance, something more than simple variety of characterization was brought about; a shift in point of view was also allowed to take place. In the pastoral lyric or eclogue, the urban or sophisticated is likely to exist only in the writer's treatment or the reader's reaction, as an implied point of view; in the pastoral story it is objectified and dramatized among the characters, and that step was an essential one if pastoral was to come to life on the stage.

As for the sequential aspect, it stands to reason that if you want to present not merely the static ideal of man in harmony with nature, or the static error of man out of harmony with nature (for purposes of satire or lament), but some image of the process whereby man succeeds or fails in the attempt to achieve this harmony, becoming rather than being, you need some such pattern as that of the romance, which was, it is well to remember, just about the only narrative procedure available to the Renaissance writer. If the chivalric romance—with its tripartite structure of separation, wandering, and reunion which so easily corresponded to the movement into and return from the green world—had not existed, it would probably have been necessary to invent it in order to get the pastoral from the lyric to the narrative and dramatic modes.

The concept of the pastoral as sojourn can be traced to the bucolic episodes which often interrupt the action of epic or chivalric poems. Poggioli calls these "pastoral oases" and finds them in the *Aeneid*, the *Commedia*, *Orlando Furioso*, the *Lusiad*, *Gerusalemme Liberata*, *Don Quixote*, and *As You*

22. These features were not altogether foreign to the eclogue. As Walter Davis points out, "The Renaissance pastoral romance seems as distant in character as in time from Virgil's *Gallus*; yet most of its seeds are there—the change of life a sojourner would experience in Arcadia extended to a plot, Gallus' imagined pastoral double multiplied into reflecting episodes, and so forth. What the pastoral romance in fact did was to implement the pastoral vision of the concord between man and his environment by a plot, an action" (*A Map of Arcadia*, p. 44).

Like It.[23] A case might be made for their origin in the
Odyssey, and certainly the listing of examples could go on
and on. What is important to note is that the pastoral as interlude or interruption came to exist not only as an episode in
a larger work of a different kind, but in its own right. In
both cases a similar effect is achieved; what was implicit in
the eclogue becomes explicit in a narrative frame: a continu-
ous reality, historical, epic, urban, or courtly, from which
characters arrive and to which, more often than not, they return. But there is obviously a great difference between a pastoral interruption, whether as brief as the passage from *Henry
VI* quoted above, or as extensive as the one in Book VI of
The Faerie Queene, and works such as the *Arcadia* or *As You
Like It.* In the latter cases the conjunction of realities, and
the reciprocal illumination it provides, is still important, but
the pastoral experience, with its specialized meanings and
values, has become the central subject. Whatever turns the
action takes—and Sidney can be said, in his expansion of the
romance, to have made the fullest possible use of the reverse
possibility of "chivalric oasis"—the arrival and sojourn of the
characters in the bucolic setting remains the basic plot stratagem of the work as a whole.

The pattern of pastoral romance, then, as developed by
Sidney and as practiced by other English writers, begins with
one or more groups of characters who leave the normal world,
usually from necessity, to take up residence in a rural or
wilderness setting, and ends with their restoration and return.
The pastoral sojourn, necessitated while society adjusts itself,
usually entails some psychological adjustment in the characters, most frequently their fulfillment, even purification,
through love. The natural setting acts as a mirror to the
action and a highly developed symbol of the social and psychological harmonies aimed at and attained. The vicissitudes
of Fortune as obstacles to the achievement of these harmonies
are stressed, with the result that the action swings curiously
between intellectual discussion and spectacular event. A pas-

23. Poggioli, pp. 155–57.

sage in praise of the quiet life is interrupted by a fight with
a savage bear. Charming scenes of rural peace alternate with
onslaughts of rapine and warfare. Characters are swept by
sudden, unaccountable passions. If love flourishes, it is in the
face of every known obstacle: rejections, enchantments, cross-
wooings, disguises, abductions, apparent deaths.[24] Almost anything is possible in this heightened, imaginary world, where
the single, overriding subject nonetheless remains the relations between man and the natural world, the "compenetra-
tion," as one critic puts it, "of nature and the lover." [25]

Just how seriously a writer wished to take himself within
this framework was a matter of considerable flexibility, as can
be discovered by a comparison of Sidney's novel with the pastoral romances of Robert Greene, *Pandosto* and *Menaphon*.
While the *Arcadia*, as a number of critics have been at pains
to show, has a high moral purpose, no such claims are likely
to be put forward for Greene, whose chief purpose is to entertain. He is handy with the common features of pastoral, and
he indulges, much more than Sidney, in towering passions and
extremes of behavior. His novels are likable enough, except
that the need to top himself in providing spectacular situations generally lands him in difficulties toward the end. Incest
is his trump card, and in *Menaphon* this device really gets out
of hand. The heroine is wooed, unwittingly, by both her
father and her son, having meanwhile become engaged to her
husband without recognizing him; grandfather stirs up father
to fight son, then throws both in prison in order to get his way
with his daughter, and so it goes. Like a pornographer, Greene
was doomed by his need for variations to run his subject
resolutely into the ground. In Sidney the device of mistaken

24. Fortune's habit of producing errors which disrupt normal ties
between lovers, friends, and members of families is usually demonstrated
in Sidney by mistaken identity, e.g. in the first book of the *Arcadia*,
Musidorus and Pyrocles, fighting in battle, do not recognize each other
because they are wearing armor; a little later the same confusion develops
because Pyrocles is disguised as an amazon. Both the main plot and the
various subplots are built around errors of this kind.

25. Bruce W. Wardropper, "The *Diana* of Montemayor: Revaluation
and Interpretation," *Studies in Philology* 48 (April 1951):129.

identity is linked to the theme of achieving self-knowledge and the progress toward perfect love; in Greene it becomes a mechanical device for complicating the plot.

It was natural, perhaps inevitable, that the public theaters should attempt to capitalize on these fashionable and popular works of fiction. Chivalric romances had already been brought to the stage with considerable success, and it was no difficult thing, given the various precedents, to dramatize the pastoral romances. In the years following Lyly and Peele a kind of play grew up, belonging to the playhouses and in general written by hacks, which contained the basic plot and common features of the pastoral romance. Three examples of the genre —*The Maid's Metamorphosis, The Thracian Wonder,* and *Mucedorus*[26]—are all of unknown authorship and uncertain date, but they seem to represent the dramatized pastoral romance at a fairly early stage of development, and it is reasonable to suppose that all three may predate *As You Like It.*

The Maid's Metamorphosis, published in 1600 as "sundrie times acted by the Children of Powles," bears enough marks of Lyly's influence—particularly in the handling of the clowns —to have been once attributed to him. In fact, however, it is stylistically remote from Lyly, and it follows more closely than any of his plays the romance pattern described above, of exile, pastoral sojourn, and return. The heroine, Eurymine, is forced to take to the woods and adopt the pastoral life. A ranger and a shepherd offer her refuge, and fall into a controversy about the respective merits of their occupations. Silvio holds out for the dignity of hunting:

> I marvell that a rusticke shepherd dare
> With woodmen thus audaciously compare?
> Why, hunting is a pleasure for a King,
> And Gods themselves sometimes frequent the thing.

26. An earlier play (ca. 1582) which follows the basic pattern is the crude *The Rare Triumphs of Love and Fortune.* See W. Carew Hazlitt, ed., *Dodsley's Old English Plays,* vol. 6 (London, 1874), pp. 143–243.

He then cites Diana, Acteon, and Atalanta as evidence. Gemulo, the shepherd, is not to be outdone:

> So did Apollo walk with shepheards crooke,
> And many Kings their scepters have forsooke:
> To lead the quiet life we shepheards know
> Accounting it a refuge for their woe.[27]

This is a typical version of the pastoral predilection for discussion and debate, and it is not surprising that it leads not to blows but to a singing contest between a chorus of woodmen and a chorus of shepherds. The play has its share of action, however. Eurymine, hotly wooed by Apollo, tricks him into changing her into a man, and must, at the end, be changed back again. As in Lyly, gods and goddesses abound, and their intervention is more than once necessary to direct the plot. Another characteristic figure is the hermit Aramanthus, a Prospero-like sage given to prophecies. He is a ruler, as it turns out, who has been exiled by his wicked brother, and Eurymine, to the surprise of no one familiar with romance conventions, is eventually revealed as the daughter whom he had thought drowned.

No claim is made here for the quality of this piece, which is simply a lively example of Elizabethan hack-work. It is not, however, as the above excerpt indicates, without its touch of literary sophistication. The point is to identify its connection with English pastoral drama, and enough has been said, I think, to indicate the way in which it combines pastoral and romance features along the same lines as the narratives described above.

The Thracian Wonder was not published until 1661, but probably dates from around 1600, which would make it coincide with the pastoral revival of those years. A dramatization of Greene's *Menaphon*, it dispenses with the Lylyesque features—the gods are replaced by an oracle—and sets its outcast characters, by means of the familiar romance device of ship-

27. Lyly, *Works*, ed. Bond, vol. 3 (Oxford, 1902), p. 318.

wreck, in the traditional pastoral landscape. The play has
a remarkable kinship with *The Winter's Tale*: an irrational
and impetuous king (three of them, actually, to *WT*'s two),
an oracle, a shepherds' festival and masque, shepherd clowns
(father and son), a coastline scene, and a summarizing chorus.
Both plays are, after all, adaptations of pastoral novels by
Greene. But the resemblance is confined to external features.
After some competently handled and promising early scenes,
The Thracian Wonder degenerates in much the same fashion
as its source; toward the end it is almost, but not quite, as
ridiculous as *Menaphon*.

The lively printing history—seventeen editions—of *Mucedorus* is clear indication of its enormous popularity. It was
first issued in 1598, and an expanded version in 1610 revealed
that it belonged to Shakespeare's company.[28] About this time
Shakespeare's name was linked with it, and the attribution
persisted through the seventeenth century. If we cannot imagine Shakespeare writing it, or even doctoring it, it is interesting to contemplate him acting in it, something he very
well may have done. And we could not have better proof of
its status as a favorite for amateur theatricals than the mention in *The Knight of the Burning Pestle* (ca. 1607) that
Ralph has played Mucedorus "before the Wardens of our
Company."

Mucedorus has customarily been dismissed in surveys of
pastoral drama as insufficiently linked to the convention to
deserve discussion, an odd conclusion when one considers that

28. "Amplified with new additions, as it was acted before the Kings
Maiestie at White-hall on Shrove-sunday night. By his Highness Servants
usually playing at the Globe." The additions are new to the printed text;
whether they were new to the play in 1610 is another question. Chambers
comments, "As the play had been in print since 1598, it must not be
assumed that, because the King's revived it in 1610–11, it was originally a
Chamberlain's play. It may have belonged to the Queen's or some other
extinct company" (*Eliz. Stage*, 4:36). Chambers suggests that the bear was
a reflection of Jonson's *Mask of Oberon* (1611), apparently forgetting that
the bear (or at least his head) had been in the 1598 edition. The original
play probably falls between the first and second editions of the *Arcadia*,
i.e. 1590–93.

the plot is based on a simplified version of Sidney's *Arcadia*.[29]
The title itself would instantly invoke Sidney's romance to an
Elizabethan, and it seems likely the play is the first—though
by no means the last—attempt to capitalize on the *Arcadia*'s
popularity by putting it on the boards. It remains, nevertheless, an extremely free adaptation, involving a hero who disguises himself as a shepherd and arrives in a forest just in
time to save the heroine from a bear after she has been
abandoned by her cowardly fiancé. Further complications include the exile of hero and heroine, her abduction by a wild
man of the woods, Mucedorus's second disguise, as a hermit,
and the traditional reconciliation and return at the conclusion. Pastoral features, moreover, crop up in interesting and
unexpected places in this play, as when the traditional invitation to the rural life (the "Come live with me and be my
love" of the Passionate Shepherd in Marlowe's lyric) is placed
in the mouth of Bremo, the wild man:

> If thou wilt love me, thou shalt be my queen;
> I will crown thee with a complet made of ivory,
> And make the rose and lily wait on thee . . .
> Thou shalt be fed with quails and partridges,
> With blackbirds, larks, thrushes, and nightingales.
> Thy drink shall be goats' milk and crystal water,
> Distill'd from the fountains and the clearest springs . . .
> The day I'll spend to recreate my love
> With all the pleasures that I can devise. . . .[30]

Bremo is an interesting forerunner of Caliban (whose version
of this speech, addressed to a drunken butler, may be found
in *The Tempest*, 2.3.161 ff.), and a close cousin, of course, to
those wild men who kept cropping up in pastoral entertainments for the Queen, and who proved so interesting to
Spenser.

Mucedorus is hardly superior in quality to the other two

29. E.g. Greg: "Beyond Mucedorus' disguise there is absolutely nothing
pastoral in the play" (p. 325).

30. Hazlitt, ed., *Dodsley's Old Plays*, 7:241–42.

plays cited above, but its undeniable popularity emphasizes
the fact that Elizabethan pastoral drama, as it existed rather
tentatively when Shakespeare turned to it, was not a courtly
and elegant genre based on Italian models, but a rough-hewn
and ramshackle affair, dressed in the hand-me-down literary
respectability it could claim through its ancestry in Sidney
and Spenser.

This throws a new light on Fletcher's complaint about the
misunderstandings which existed at the first performance of
The Faithful Shepherdess. He had provided, in his view, a
genuine pastoral tragicomedy, based on the best Italian
models and having its own decorum. The audience, however,
"having ever had a singular gift in defining," expected "a
play of country hired shepherds in gray cloaks, with curtailed
dogs in strings, sometimes laughing together, and sometimes
killing one another; and missing Whitsun-ales, cream, wassail,
and morris-dances, began to be angry." [31] These remarks have
always been thought to reflect the fact that Fletcher's audience had no idea of what pastoral drama was and therefore
expected real shepherds and English rural customs. But this
conclusion does not fit very well with our knowledge of a
Blackfriars audience around 1608. The difficulty probably
arose not out of the ignorance of the audience, but out of
their expectations of seeing a play along the lines of *Mucedorus, The Thracian Wonder,* or *The Maid's Metamorphosis,*
a thumping romance. Those gray cloaks were not to be new
to the stage; they hung in the wardrobe of Henslowe's company.[32] Fletcher's disagreement with his audience rose from
the difference between his idea of what a play about shepherds
ought to be like, based on Italian practice, and their own,
based on previous theater-going and their reading of books
like *Pandosto* and the *Arcadia.*

Fletcher's dislike of the popular stage pastorals was very

31. "To The Reader" in Francis Beaumont and John Fletcher, *Works,*
ed. A. H. Bullen (Cambridge, 1904–12), 3:18.

32. E.g. the "ij whitt sheperdes cottes" in the 1598 inventory. See
Philip Henslowe, *Diary,* ed. R. A. Foakes and R. T. Rickert (Cambridge,
1961), p. 319.

likely centered on the same features that had endeared them to such a wide public: a tremendous variety of incident that included love, fighting, disguising, clowning, singing and dancing, shipwrecks, wild animals, shepherds, savages, and kings. Audience appeal was insured in the popular theater, and genuine literary achievement, whatever Fletcher may have thought, was not out of the question. What was wanting was the hand of a master, someone who could do for the dramatic what Sidney had done for the narrative. And that, of course, is where Shakespeare comes in.

❦

Four of Shakespeare's plays—*As You Like It, King Lear, The Winter's Tale,* and *The Tempest*—have precisely in common a story concerned with the exile of some of its central characters into a natural setting, their sojourn in that setting, and their eventual return. All four exhibit, moreover, the themes which had become attached to this structural pattern in earlier pastoral writings. In addition, certain external features, mainly stylistic, which had become part of the pastoral tradition can be found in each of the four.

The fundamental appeal of pastoral to an artist like Shakespeare is difficult to isolate, given the variety of possibilities open to writers who chose to work with it. The relation between subject and audience, however, provides an important clue. Pastoral was about rustic life, but it was not for rustics.[33] The man who wrote it might pose as a shepherd, but everyone knew he was not. Arcadia, or its equivalent, was always elsewhere—often in time as well as space. Pastoral offered an *alternative* to the complex, hectic, urban present, but it was an imaginary alternative. For if pastoral writers sometimes appealed to a historical Golden Age, or praised the life in a known, accessible region, there was generally a shared understanding that the pastoral novel, poem, or play was to be held

33. Lyly must have had his tongue in his cheek when he wrote in the prologue to *Midas*, "At our exercises, souldiers call for tragedies, their object is blood: courtiers for comedies, their subject is love; countrimen for pastorals, shepheards are their saints."

to fictive standards only. Our own attitude to science fiction is perhaps analogous; most of us suspect or believe that there is life on other planets, but we do not expect science fiction writers to document it. They must rear their imaginative structures, we understand, out of the here and now.

If pastoral was an alternative, it could not help but be, in one way or another, a criticism of life.[34] As a member of the family of myths based on "human resentment at the conditions and struggles of life," [35] it tended to branch off toward idealism on the one hand and satire on the other. But its idealism was of a special sort, based not so much on perfection and abundance as on retrenchment, renunciation, and retreat. Take less, the pastoral writer seemed to suggest, and you will have more; reduce your needs to the only legitimate one, harmony with nature, and you will experience fulfillment. William Empson puts the general point this way:

> The feeling that life is essentially inadequate to the human spirit, and yet that a good life must avoid saying so, is naturally at home with most versions of pastoral; in pastoral you take a limited life and pretend it is the full and normal one, and a suggestion that one must do this with all life, because the normal is itself limited, is easily put into the trick though not necessary to its power.[36]

As Empson suggests, and as the experience of sojourn in plays as different as *As You Like It* and *Lear* confirms, the degree of pretense is variable. He goes on to point out that the sense of life's inadequacy may itself be felt as a pretense, "intended to hold all our attention and sympathy for some limited life." Despite these shifts of attitude, pastoral's function as an alternative, born of dissatisfaction, remains constant.

Renato Poggioli identifies the "psychological root of the pastoral" as "a double longing after innocence and happi-

---

34. This phrase is especially used by Hallett Smith, e.g. pp. 2, 57, 61.

35. Kermode, p. 15. He uses the phrase to describe the "primary impulse" of the Golden Age myth.

36. Empson, pp. 114–15.

ness." [37] The literary shepherd, he says, is a "witness," who
bears testimony to the superiority of a solitary life, in communion with nature. One thinks of the affectionate treatment
of innocence in *Daphnis and Chloe,* the hymn of praise to a
Golden Age of unfettered pleasure in the opening chorus of
the *Aminta,* and the entire second half of *The Winter's Tale.*
Poggioli invokes the insights of Freud:

> the task of the pastoral imagination is to overcome the
> conflict between passion and remorse, to reconcile inno-
> cence and happiness, to exalt the pleasure principle at
> the expense of the reality principle.[38]

The reality principle suggests that "erotic happiness cannot
be fully attained in our civilization," [39] and the pastoral imagination accordingly constructs its alternatives.

The dual concern with innocence and happiness helps to
explain why love stories again and again form the central
subject of pastoral literature, why it tends to value chastity
on the one hand and sexual fulfillment on the other, and why
it generally equates unhappiness with unrequited love. Critics
have balked over the curious mixture in Fletcher's *Faithful
Shepherdess* of exalted chastity and downright lasciviousness
in the female characters; but Fletcher was at least in that
respect working squarely in the tradition by providing a spectrum, comically observed, of pastoral alternatives of innocence
and fulfillment. The same sort of spectrum is provided in *As
You Like It,* and both Shakespeare and Fletcher find much
of the comic potential of pastoral in the clash of reality and
pleasure principles in a setting where they are supposed to be
resolved.

Another dream behind the pastoral—or rather another version of the same dream—is the desire for spiritual peace and
personal fulfillment through a contemplative existence in
communion with nature. A hermit could hardly be expected
to achieve sexual fulfillment, but he might hope to arrive at

37. Poggioli, pp. 147–48.
38. Ibid., p. 159.
39. Ibid., p. 160.

an ideal of the good life nonetheless, "the state of content and mental self-sufficiency which had been known in classical antiquity as *otium*." [40] The self-contained and isolated life of the shepherd and the pastoral community was a kind of symbol for an equivalent state of mind, and Renaissance pastorals customarily contain an old man, hermit or shepherd, who is a spokesman for this insight. Corin is such a figure, and Prospero and Lear may be seen as significant variations. Meliboe, in the Sixth Book of *The Faerie Queene*, draws on his years as a courtier for comparison in constructing his apology for the simple life:

'Surely, my sonne,' (then answer'd he againe)
If happie, then it is in this intent,
That having small yet doe I not complaine
Of want, ne wish for more it to augment,
But doe my selfe with that I have content;
So taught of nature, which doth little need
Of forreine helpes to lifes due nourishment:
The fields my food, my flocke my rayment breed;
No better doe I weare, no better doe I feed.

Therefore I do not any one envy,
Nor am envyde of anyone therefore:
They, that have much, feare much to loose thereby,
And store of cares doth follow riches store.
The little that I have grows dayly more
Without my care, but onely to attend it;
My lambs do every year increase their score,
And my flockes father daily doth amend it.
What have I, but to praise th'Almighty that doth send it?
                                              [6.9.20–21]

At the basis of such passages lies the assumption that interior peace and harmony are inextricably bound up with exterior peace and harmony; that man in society fails to come to terms with himself and his world because he imposes on himself order and rhythms different from those of the natural world

40. Hallett Smith, p. 2.

to which he inevitably belongs. This is the point at which the concerns of pastoral and the concerns of lyric poetry tend to merge. Both are concerned to relate human experience to the great rhythms of the natural world. Hence their binding together of such elements as human love, weather, seasons, fertility, sex, and birth and death. The territory of the lyric cuts across the forests, heaths, pastures, and islands of Shakespeare's pastorals. And the vision of human experience as an expression of the rhythm of events in nature gives rise to a concern with the nature of time that is especially evident in *As You Like It* and *The Winter's Tale.*

Another consequence of the special link between the inner and outer worlds in pastoral is its subjectivity; its landscapes are as often as not landscapes of the spirit, recording mental events and psychological states. Whether this takes the form of "sermons in stones," of Lear in the storm, or of Prospero's masque hardly matters; the point is that the pastoral had from the start an expressionistic tendency, and that, of course, helps to explain why writers of pastoral were not held to realistic, objective criteria; subjectivity, artificiality, and mannerism were their stock in trade. Nature was a glass that, rightly held, gave access to the regions of the mind.

No wonder, then, in light of its subjective features and its relation to the lyric vision, that Arcadia became a kind of poets' country, a realm of the imagination where the composing of verses and songs was a natural activity, and where poetic values were taken for granted. Arcadia harbored many other ideals as well, of course; as something that predated or avoided human degeneration it could be linked to the legend of Eden on the one hand and the classical Golden Age on the other. But it was natural for poets to assume that poetry had an ideal status in such times and places too. Orpheus, the first poet, was thus depicted as a shepherd. Nature and art were represented as in complete harmony, and art became a leading subject of the pastoral. For someone like Spenser, this art about art implied poems about poetry; he turned to pastoral when he wanted to treat the problems and ideals of his profession. Shakespeare, likewise, makes his pastoral dramas ex-

aminations of their medium, exploring the implications of
fiction, artifice, convention, genre, and of the impulses that
give rise to art. His work reveals to the fullest Renaissance
pastoral's tendency toward self-consciousness, toward a stressing of the connections between aesthetic values and the
dreams of contentment and fulfillment. If the pastoral could
not be true to life, it could be true to the imagination, and
that in turn enhanced the meaning and value of art.

To be a credit to art, however, pastoral had to avoid the
limited accomplishments of escape and wish-fulfillment,[41] and
had to face the issues it raised. In its function as an alternative it was to be dialectical, a kind of discourse between reality and the imagination. This process quite naturally called
for continual recourse to antithesis, a favorite stylistic device,
and it should be obvious, even to the most casual reader of
pastoral, that it is founded on a series of tensions and oppositions.

The social antitheses are perhaps the most obvious: urban
versus rural, court versus country. They could deal variously
with manners (polished versus rustic), with class divisions
(aristocrat versus commoner), and with economic differences
(rich versus poor). Disguise a prince as a shepherd and set
him among real shepherds, and these contrasts begin to make
themselves felt.

Psychological tensions rose from an associated topic, the
active life versus the contemplative, a Renaissance favorite
that seemed almost designed to fit the pastoral pattern.
Worldliness and innocence were another standard pair, and
they were related, as were most of the contrasts between complicated and simple forms of existence, to the great antithesis
of nurture and nature, which raised moral and educational
issues as well: was a man better for the training and refinements of his civilization—his "nurture"—or did he come
naturally by his goodness, even if he were a "salvage" or a
wild man? This had a historical dimension, as we have seen,

41. Poggioli's comment that "the pastoral ideal shifts on the quick-
sands of wishful thought" (p. 148) does not really do it justice.

in its relation to the issue of human degeneration, a problem that could be posed as an opposition of present and past, or, when pastoral grew Utopian or, as in *Lear*, contemplated the end of the world, present and future.

Perhaps the most pervasive and important of all the pastoral contrasts, however, is the famous Art–Nature opposition. It could be narrowly conceived to deal with aesthetic issues, but it could also be posed so comprehensively (the two terms having so many meanings) as to take in any or all of the above contrasts. For that reason it probably deserves to be described, as Kermode suggests, as the philosophical basis of the pastoral.[42] But Nature has another dichotomous relation in pastoral as well, through its pairing with Fortune. This contrast raises metaphysical questions, and it seems to have formalized the wedding of pastoral and romance. That Shakespeare had a deep and abiding interest in both antitheses, Art and Nature and Nature and Fortune, will be evident in the chapters to follow.

May we not suppose that it was the pastoral's habit of employing such antitheses—and my list is by no means exhaustive—rather than the use of speakers in the eclogue or the fashion for shepherds in court pageants, that attracted the real interest of the dramatist? Conflict and opposition are the stuff of drama, and those of the pastoral simultaneously provided intellectual interest as well. To an artist like Shakespeare, who was fond of organizing his plays in terms of polarities and contrasts, they were a natural area for exploitation. The romance plot, with its introduction of outsiders into the pastoral world and its taste for dramatic events, had already accomplished the initial step of embodying contrasts which had been implicit or oblique in the eclogue. The playwright's opportunities were clear.

It should also be stressed that there was nothing rigid or doctrinaire about the oppositions employed by pastoral. They were capable of infinite variation. If you wanted to contrast nurture and nature, it made a great deal of difference, obvi-

42. Kermode, p. 37.

ously, whether you chose to stress overrefinement, corruption, or genuine courtesy (in Spenser's sense of the word) on the one side, and simple honesty, stupidity, or out-and-out brutality on the other. Nor were you limited to single choices. Spenser's Calidore, who has met several wicked knights, encounters in the pastoral world such diverse representatives as Colin Clout, Coridon, and the Salvage Man. Nature in *The Tempest* means Caliban, but it also means Ariel, just as nurture means Ferdinand as well as Antonio and Sebastian.

One can go further than this, however, in describing the use of oppositions in pastoral, and say that there was something fundamentally equivocal in pastoral which, from the start, tended to undermine and invert its familiar antitheses. Here I part company with a number of commentators who feel that the introduction of the equivocal in pastoral is a clear sign of decadence.[43] But a tendency to paradox is evident as early as Theocritus and Longus.[44] It is inherent in the initial contradictions of the genre. The Spenser passage quoted above, it will be noted, employs paradox rather than straight contrast. So do the euphuistic cadences of Robert Greene:

> Sir, what richer state than content, or what sweeter life than quiet? we shepherds are not born to honor, nor beholding unto beauty, the less care we have to fear fame or fortune. We count our attire brave enough if warm enough, and our food dainty if to suffice nature. . . . We are rich in that we are poor with content, and proud only in this, that we have no cause to be proud.[45]

43. Greg is typical: "Like the garden of the Rose which satisfied the middle age before it, the Arcadian ideal of the renaissance degenerated, as every ideal must. The decay of pastoral, however, was in this unique, that it tended less to exaggerate than to negative the spirit that gave it birth" (p. 52).

44. Tayler finds in Longus an "unequivocal attitude toward Nature and Art" (p. 69), which he summarizes as follows: "Virtue in Longus, then, consists in conformity to Nature, and corruption is the result of Art" (p. 67). But this ignores the beginning of *Daphnis and Chloe* in which the author says he first saw the story in a series of paintings, as well as the tone of the romance as a whole, especially its comic aspects.

45. *Pandosto*, ed. P. G. Thomas (London, 1907), pp. 50–51.

Pastoral values the simple, but is itself apt to be complex. It praises the rustic, but it does so for a sophisticated audience. "Take less, have more," is its paradoxical advice. It affects to prefer nature to art, but is itself highly artifical and turns out to have art as one of its major subjects. It confounds the exterior and the interior, transforming landscape to mood and back again. Like the imagination from which it proceeds, it is elusive, unstable, protean. "He who cannot attract Pan," wrote Pico della Mirandola, "approaches Proteus in vain." [46] For pastoral the motto can be reversed.

If not every artist who has practiced pastoral has seen fit to exploit these peculiarities, or indeed had the wit to, they are nevertheless native to it and present in the genre at its best. Moreover, they help to account for the fact that pastoral had no sooner been introduced in the Renaissance than it began to be travestied and burlesqued. This is not, as might be thought, so much a sign of its vulnerability as an indication that its full potential was being sought out. Pastoral was a form in which you could have something both ways, and thus was potentially comprehensive and resonant. The possible effect is instanced in Marlowe's famous lyric. "The Passionate Shepherd to his Love," when it is paired with Raleigh's point for point retort, "The Nymph's Reply to the Shepherd." Raleigh's lyric does not cancel out Marlowe's or annihilate the meaning of pastoral; rather, the two taken together suggest the range of pastoral, its tendency to take in opposites and deal in paradoxes and contradictions. Raleigh is picking up something already implied by Marlowe. All this makes it a difficult convention to deal with adequately, and while that may be an excuse for the artist who tries it and fails, I am not sure it should be an excuse for the critic.

In any case, I shall not be concerned solely with the structural, thematic, and stylistic features which the four plays I have chosen for analysis have in common. Their differences, as I hope to show, hold a particular interest. Some are of course due to the influence of other genres and to different

46. See Edgar Wind, *Pagan Mysteries of the Renaissance* (London, 1948), pp. 158 ff.

stages of Shakespeare's career. But others—and these I expect to concentrate upon—will be due to variations in the
pastoral design introduced by Shakespeare's experimentation.
In other words, I shall be concerned to show that these four
plays are indeed "versions" of pastoral in a sense more literal
than that used by Empson.

The merits of my argument can be judged, in the case of the
inclusions, by the individual analyses which follow. I suppose,
however, that my exclusions also deserve some explanation
here. Certainly there are a number of plays in the canon
which can be said to show some influence of the pastoral
design. *Two Gentlemen of Verona,* based on a story from
Montemayor's *Diana,* ends in the woods. *Love's Labour's Lost*
places its characters in a scholarly retreat which is partly
pastoral in character. And a number of plays make convenient
use of alternative worlds—Belmont in *The Merchant of
Venice,* Eastcheap in *Henry IV,* Cyprus in *Othello,* Egypt in
Antony and Cleopatra—in a way that is strikingly similar to
that of pastoral. But this is neither a survey of Shakespeare's
every brush with or glance at the pastoral tradition, nor an
investigation of his use of analogous patterns. It is a study of
his direct use of a tradition that came to him through the pastoral writers of his age.

Nevertheless, three plays, *Timon, Cymbeline,* and *A Midsummer Night's Dream*—have a better claim to inclusion, so
extensively do they partake of the pastoral sojourn and its
accompanying themes. Seven plays instead of four would
have been unwieldy, but not impossible. In each case, however, certain factors argued for exclusion. *Timon,* for whatever reason, does nothing very remarkable with its natural
setting once it has sent its hero there. There is very little to
be said about it that would not apply to *Lear* as well, and
separate treatment of *Timon* would be wearying, I think, both
to writer and reader. Since two late romances are treated fully,
an extensive analysis of *Cymbeline* seemed likewise superfluous, but that play will be discussed in the chapter on *The
Winter's Tale. A Midsummer Night's Dream* I have excluded
with some hesitation, but for three reasons. First, I have

treated the play in considerable detail elsewhere, and can refer the reader to that discussion.[47] Second, an important difference between the *Dream* and the plays to be discussed in this study involves the amount of time spent in the natural setting. One night does not seem to me to amount to a sojourn. Finally, it seemed best to begin the study with the play that is most clearly Shakespeare's first direct engagement with the pastoral tradition, *As You Like It,* and to proceed to later variations. This entails more emphasis on late plays than on early ones, an arrangement which seems to me just in light of the fact that, as the very late plays suggest, Shakespeare's interest in the pastoral tended to increase rather than diminish as he grew older.

The way ahead, then, leads through the Forest of Arden, across the wind-swept heaths of English legendary history, along the seacoast of Bohemia that so resembles the South Downs, to Prospero's echoing island, somewhere in the Mediterranean. The subject is Shakespeare's variations on a significant Renaissance theme. The goal is new knowledge about four great plays, a sense of the continuity and development of Shakespeare's art along one line of interest, and a clearer understanding of his attitudes toward that art, especially in its relation to reality. May Nature and Fortune, those veiled goddesses who may be one and the same, smile kindly on the enterprise!

47. David P. Young, *Something of Great Constancy: The Art of "A Midsummer Night's Dream"* (New Haven, 1966).

2

Earthly Things Made Even: *As You Like It*

In the hinder part of the Pageant did sit a Child, represent-
ing Nature, holding in her hand a distaffe, and spinning a
Web, which passed through the hand of Fortune and was
wheeled up by Time, who spake as followeth.
> The while my wheele with ever turning gyres,
> At heavens hie heast serves earthly mens desires,
> I wind the Web that kinde so well beginnes:
> While Fortune doth enrich what Nature spinnes.
> George Peele, "Descensus Astraeae"

> Let Art and Nature goe
> One with the other;
> Yet so, that Art may show
> Nature her mother.
> The thick-brayn'd Audience lively to awake,
> Till with shrill Claps the Theater doe shake.
> Michael Drayton, "The Sacrifice to Apollo"

Sometime around 1588 a courtier and poet named Thomas
Lodge, on a voyage to the Canaries, set himself to the task of
writing a pastoral romance. The result, published in 1590,
was *Rosalynde: Euphues' Golden Legacy,* easily the most successful, after Sidney's *Arcadia,* of the Elizabethan pastoral
novels. Lodge's method was typical: on to an old romance
called "The Tale of Gamelyn" (then thought to be Chaucer's),
he grafted the setting, characters and conventions of pastoral.
The narrative was cast in the elaborate euphuistic style then
popular, and interspersed with a great deal of very mediocre
poetry.

When Shakespeare undertook to adapt *Rosalynde* for the
stage, in the midst of a revival of interest in pastoral some ten

years later, it must have seemed to him, as it does to us now, that the story was begging to be released from the chains of its mannered style and the narrow cage of its decorum. Lodge had produced a clever and charming romance, with a great deal of potential humor, but his commitment to a consistent, moralistic, and mannered treatment of it had allowed him little opportunity to exploit diversities, develop characters, or release, by comic juxtaposition and the clash of style against style, the wonderful humor that envelops *As You Like It*. The point is that Shakespeare does not seem to have been bent on demolishing or ridiculing his source, but to have set about perfecting it, releasing it "To liberty and not to banishment."

Indeed, it is probably no longer necessary to argue this point. For if there existed at one time what we might call the "silvery laughter" conception of the play, which stressed its mockery of the pastoral and its satire of the literary conventions associated with Silvius and Phebe, this has been largely replaced by a recognition that Shakespeare wrote *As You Like It* out of a sympathetic interest in pastoral, which he undertook to explore more fully than Lodge had done. The play is not a series of jokes at the expense of literary fashions and ideals, but rather, like all Shakespearean comedy, a survey of the wonderful diversity and folly of human life and an affirmation of its ability, despite all shortcomings, to retain its resilience and renew itself. The achievement is channeled, in this particular instance, through the fertile possibilities of the pastoral design. Bullough sums up this view:

> It is incredible that *As You Like It* would have been the play it is had [Shakespeare] been contemptuous of his material and his audience. . . . The play is not a "satire" on the pastoral play, though it contains some satire through the deliberate invention of Jaques and Touchstone. It is a humorous fantasy on several levels of pastoral manner popular at the time.[1]

1. Geoffrey Bullough, *Narrative and Dramatic Sources of Shakespeare* (London, 1957), 2:157.

We might, then, profitably compare Shakespeare's handling
of the pastoral ideal in *As You Like It* to Cervantes' treatment
of chivalry in *Don Quixote,* or to Chaucer's of the pilgrimage
in *The Canterbury Tales.* What is involved in each case is
not a dismissal through mocking and parody, but a more
searching look at the ideal through an intensive examination of its distance from the real, the distance providing an
infallible source of comedy. The *Quixote* is a serious work,
finally (and to say this is to expand rather than reduce its
comic scope), because the needs and ideals that inform the
quest cannot be totally dismissed. A similar approach governs
As You Like It. And just as it would be ridiculous to refuse
to discuss *Don Quixote*'s relation to the chivalric because of
its "impurity," so it seems a piece of folly to turn away from
a consideration of how the pastoral mode informs *As You
Like It.*[2]

In fact, it has already been observed elsewhere that Shakespeare increased rather than reduced the pastoral content of
his source by making *As You Like It* a sort of survey of the
tradition.[3] It is not quite fair, perhaps, to argue that Silvius
and Phebe represent the extent of what Lodge has to offer,
but certainly they "belong to the conventional love pastoral" [4]
and suggest the limitations of the vein Lodge was mining so
determinedly. In Corin, Audrey, and William we have the
more realistic rustics who were sometimes introduced in pastoral to bring it closer to the facts of country life or to expose
its essential artificiality. Touchstone and Jaques introduce the

2. Cf. W. P. Ker, "Cervantes, Shakespeare, and the Pastoral Idea," in
A Book of Homage to Shakespeare, ed. I. Gollancz (London, 1916), "Shakespeare and Cervantes agree in certain places with regard to pastoral. They
agree in playing a double game about it. Pastoral is ridiculed in the
penance of Don Quixote; yet the story of Don Quixote is full of the most
beautiful pastoral episodes—Marcela the best of them, it may be" (p. 50).

3. The most detailed account is that by R. P. Draper, "Shakespeare's
Pastoral Comedy," *Etudes Anglaises* 11 (1958):1–17. Draper finds seven
varieties of pastoral in the play, each one "tested by the standards of
comedy" (p. 2). See also Mary Lascelles, "Shakespeare's Pastoral Comedy,"
in *More Talking of Shakespeare* (London, 1959), pp. 70–86.

4. Draper, p. 2.

satirical tradition of pastoral, as well as its most equivocal tendencies. The banished Duke, with his stoicism and his hearty foresters, introduces a romance element and a native strain—the Robin Hood motif, we might call it—that received little attention in *Rosalynde*. And in Rosalind and Orlando Shakespeare gives us the tradition of courtly love games and wit combats that Lodge had used and that had previously been associated with pastoral (as in Lyly), although never with such stunning success. All of these strands represented possibilities open to the writer of pastoral, and many of them lay unregarded in the twists and turns of Lodge's story. It was Shakespeare's opportunity, abandoning the decorum of *Rosalynde*, to set them all in the same echoing forest, give them full play, and, from their interactions and collisions, create a comedy of unparalleled verbal brilliance.

❧

Contemporary audiences of *As You Like It*, whether they knew its source or not, would have had little difficulty in recognizing, even in the rapid exposition of the opening scenes, certain typical features of the pastoral romance. Many were drawn from *Rosalynde*, but others were Shakespeare's additions. One of his changes was to make the two dukes brothers. By matching them thus with Orlando and Oliver, he strengthened the parallel between the violations of natural bonds and relationships which lead to the pastoral sojourn. He then went on to reduce the natural motives of each "bad" brother, bringing their behavior more closely in line with the arbitrary, inexplicable psychology of the romance tradition. Each villain is in fact made to confess this. Oliver says of Orlando:

> I hope I shall see an end of him; for my soul yet I know not why, hates nothing more than he. Yet he's gentle, never schooled and yet learned, full of noble device, of all sorts enchantingly beloved. [1.1.173–77]

The Duke, likewise, is forced to admit to Orlando:

> The world esteem'd thy father honourable,
> But I did find him still mine enemy.
>
> [1.2.237–38]

And he is unable, when he suddenly decides to banish Rosalind, to give any convincing reason for his action. "The Duke," Le Beau admits, "is humorous" (1.2.278).

The effect of such moments is partly to suggest the lack of self-knowledge in evil and unnatural behavior, and it is true that self-knowledge is an important theme in pastoral in general and *As You Like It* in particular; but the main purpose is surely not to increase psychological veracity or deepen characterization. The arbitrary evil and equally arbitrary conversion to good of Oliver and Duke Frederick serve mainly to emphasize their part in a pattern. They are not governed by individual will but by larger forces; we would say subconscious forces, but the Elizabethans would speak of Fortune, the blind goddess whom they so often cast as Nature's antagonist.[5] Shakespeare, by stressing this pattern, seems to have been calling his audience's attention to the theoretical and fictive aspects of his material.

This is one instance of a deliberate self-consciousness about the nature of pastoral that pervades *As You Like It*. Conventional elements are retained, and their artificial aspects tend to be emphasized rather than concealed. This is nowhere better illustrated than in the treatment of the natural world, the Forest of Arden in which the pastoral sojourn takes place. The very first reference to Arden establishes its mythic and hypothetical character. In response to Oliver's question about where the old Duke has gone, Charles the wrestler tells us what "they say":

> They say he is already in the forest of Arden, and a many
> merry men with him; and they there live like the old
> Robin Hood of England: they say many young gentlemen

---

5. Cf. John Shaw's excellent "Fortune and Nature in *As You Like It,*" *Shakespeare Quarterly* 6 (Winter 1955):45–50.

flock to him every day, and fleet the time carelessly, as they did in the golden world. [1.1.120–25] [6]

This careful linking of the forest to two traditions of literature and folklore is a good key to what is to follow. A great many burbling commentaries have been written about Shakespeare's "delightful rendering" of the native forest of his "boyhood memories." [7] But the powerful descriptions of nature for which Shakespeare is admired do not exist in *As You Like It*. What we have instead is a stylized and sparsely pictured setting, whose literary and artificial character is kept always before us.

I am not speaking of the easygoing attitude than can accommodate lions, oaks, palm trees and winter weather in the same landscape; that in itself would not be enough for, Elizabethans, to destroy the power of concrete natural detail. I am rather pointing to the fact that natural details in the play are stylized and mannered to a degree that would distance them even for Shakespeare's audiences. The opening scene in the forest is as good an illustration as any. The Duke is speaking of the pleasures of life in the woods. But how, exactly, does he characterize his place of exile? At first in terms of stylized and alliterated bad weather, "the icy fang / And churlish chiding of the winter's wind" (2.1.6–7). This leads him on, immediately, to the sweet uses of adversity, to a literary toad with a jewel in its head, and to "tongues in trees, books in the running brooks, / Sermons in stones and good in every

6. I find Poggioli's comment on this passage somewhat puzzling: "Here the 'golden world' stands for nurture and Robin Hood's green world stands for nature" (p. 180). Poggioli's tendency to impose arbitrary divisions on the play (e.g. "noblemen, shepherds, and peasants stand respectively for poetry, literature, and reality"—p. 181) makes his comments on it a great deal less valuable than his comments on pastoral in general.

7. E.g. John Dover Wilson, *Shakespeare's Happy Comedies* (London, 1962): "The forest makes the play, and the forest is a blend of two elements: (i) the delightful scenery of Montemayor, and (ii) Shakespeare's memories of the Warwickshire scenery round about his native home—his own forest of Arden, in fact. . . . the forest is a triumph of dramatic scene painting" (p. 151).

thing" (16–17). The charm of the speech is undeniable, but
it is a literary charm, a "style," as Amiens suggests, and hardly
serves to particularize an actual Arden.

Having established the artifice of the pastoral setting in
this speech, Shakespeare elaborates it with great enjoyment
through the rest of the scene. The rural is transformed to the
urban. The deer they are to hunt are "dappled fools" and
"native burghers of this desert city," with, of course, "forked
heads" and "round haunches." And the picture of Jaques which
follows, one of many set-pieces in the play, is a little masterpiece of mannered presentation. He lies "Under an oak, whose
antique root peeps out / Upon the brook that brawls along
this wood" (31–32). The "sequester'd stag" stretches its "leath-
ern coat" with groans, and "big round tears" course down its
"innocent nose" as it stands "on the extremest verge of the
swift brook / Augmenting it with tears" (42–43). Few readers
can have failed to notice how the language stirs to a different
kind of life when we suddenly jump to Jaques' satirical vein:

> Sweep on, you fat and greasy citizens. [55]

Naturally the Duke hurries off to see this picture; we would
like to go with him. But who would attempt to describe it as
a realistic scene in a realistic setting?

There is nothing in the scenes that follow to undermine or
contradict this initial artificiality of presentation. The forest
will prove changeable—hostile or pleasant to suit the moods
of its inhabitants and visitors—but its literary character will
be constant. We learn little more about Corin's world than
that it involves "flocks," "fleeces," and "pasture." Orlando and
Adam find themselves in "this uncouth forest," with its "bleak
air" (2.6.6,17), and Orlando bursts into the banquet scene
to describe its setting as "this desert inaccessible, / Under the
shade of melancholy boughs" (2.7.110–11). Later, he seems
to have picked up the Duke's style:

> O Rosalind! these trees shall be my books,
> And in their barks my thoughts I'll character.
>
> [3.25–6]

As for Orlando's encounter with the lion, another of the play's set-pieces, it too takes place in a recognizably picturesque setting:

> Under an old oak, whose boughs were mossed with age
> And high top bald with dry antiquity,
> A wretched ragged man, o'ergrown with hair,
> Lay sleeping on his back; about his neck
> A green and gilded snake had wreathed itself . . .
>
> [4.3.105–09]

If all this is, like Oliver, "most unnatural," we need not be surprised; it is the theoretical world of pastoral, forest of the heart and mind, theater of the imagination. The realistic touches will come elsewhere, in Touchstone's recollections of Jane Smile, Jaques' pictures of society, and Rosalind's plain talk about lovers; we get them as we gaze out at the real world from the hypothetical setting of Arden.

This emphasis on artifice is further supported by the play's references to feigning and counterfeiting, in literature and in life. When Le Beau starts to recount the wrestling he has seen —"There comes an old man and his three sons"—Rosalind interrupts him:

> I could match this beginning with an old tale.
>
> [1.2.128]

So she could; the opening of *Rosalynde,* as a matter of fact, or the tale of Gamelyn used by Lodge.[8] Later, as the Duke muses on "This wide and universal theater," that "Presents more woeful pageants than the scene / Wherein we play in," Jaques is happy to take him up with the famous speech beginning "All the world's a stage" (2.7.139 ff). The seven ages of man are seen in a framework of artifice, as seven acts in a play. One of them is to be acted out shortly, as Corin leads Rosalind to see "a pageant truly played" (2.4.55) between Phebe and Silvius (who is indeed "sighing like furnace"), so

---

8. Commentators have not been able to agree on whether Shakespeare knew Lodge's source or consulted it. So far as I know, this passage has not been cited as one indication that he did.

that Rosalind cannot resist becoming "a busy actor in their play" (62). A similar reminder of artifice comes from Jaques, when Orlando interrupts his conversation with Rosalind:

> *Orlando.* Good day and happiness, dear Rosalind!
> *Jaques.* Nay, then, God be wi' you, an you talk in blank verse.   *Exit.*
>   [4.1.30–32]

It is Touchstone who talks about poetry. The truest, he tells Audrey, breaking his deadpan paradoxes on her unwitting brow, is the most feigning, and so it is with lovers: "lovers are given to poetry, and what they swear in poetry may be said as lovers they do feign" (3.3.20–22). He might have added friendship too, for one of the songs has told us that "Most friendship is feigning." We have to do here with a word which meant both "to imagine, invent, create," and "to disguise, dissemble, deceive." [9] The wordplay provides a delicate bridge between the fictions of the pastoral and Rosalind's counterfeiting disguise. As Ganymede, her friendship with Orlando is indeed "feigning," but we are inclined to see it less as deception than as inspired invention, a triumphant feat of imagination. It is often when he seems to be talking the purest nonsense that Touchstone is making his subtlest commentaries on the world of *As You Like It,* and it is easy to get left behind in his linguistic mazes. There must be times when we all feel like Audrey.

I cannot help but think that the atmosphere of artifice and hypothesis is also engendered by the remarkably extensive use of "if" in *As You Like It,* as though the grammar that most suited a world like this one was the conditional. We notice it first as we meet Silvius, who cannot believe that Corin's love was ever like his:

9. Not to mention a second word, "faining," which could variously mean "affectionate," "longing," or even "fawning." "Fain" is used just after Touchstone's remarks by Jaques ("I would fain see this meeting" [3.3.46]) and by Rosalind at 4.1.59. "Counterfeit" is used several times at 5.3.168 f. and at 5.2.29.

> If thou remember'st not the slightest folly
> That ever love did make thee run into,
> Thou hast not loved:
> Or if thou hast not sat as I do now,
> Wearying thy hearer in thy mistress' praise,
> Thou hast not loved:
> Or if thou hast not broke from company
> Abruptly, as my passion now makes me,
> Thou hast not loved.
> O Phebe, Phebe, Phebe!   *Exit.*
>   [2.4.34-43]

What is both amusing and distancing here is that Silvius can manage, in his distraction and before his "abrupt" departure, to set up these conditions for true love, as is the fact that he does not really entertain them as possibilities for one moment. No one can possibly be in love the way he is.

The passage is distinctly echoed a few scenes later when Orlando bursts in upon the feasting foresters, sword in hand. "Whate'er you are," he says:

> If ever you have look'd on better days,
> If ever been where bells have knoll'd to church,
> If ever sat at any good man's feast,
> If ever from your eyelids wiped a tear
> And know what 'tis to pity and be pitied,
> Let gentleness my strong enforcement be.
>   [2.7.113-18]

This is so solemn about nature and nurture as to set up a comic reaction as the Duke carefully runs through the same list in his affirmative reply. Everyone turns out to be "inland bred," so that Orlando can sheathe his sword and go off to fetch Adam.

A moment earlier than this, Jaques, who is extremely fond of "if" clauses, has provided a new verse for Amiens' song. The original "stanzos" have been the traditional bucolic invitation: a straightforward invitation to "Who loves to lie

with me" and "Who doth ambition shun" to "Come hither."
In Jaques' hands the whole proposition becomes hypothetical:

> If it do come to pass
> That any man turn ass
> Leaving his wealth and ease
> A stubborn will to please,
> Ducdame, ducdame, ducdame.
> Here shall he see
> Gross fools as he,
> An if he will come to me.
>
> [2.5.52–59]

By this time Jaques presumably has the foresters gathered
around him, so that to Amiens' question, "What's that 'duc-
dame'?", he can snap, " 'Tis a Greek invocation to call fools
into a circle," thus demonstrating his hypothesis with a practical joke. He leaves saying, "I'll go sleep, if I can; if I cannot,
I'll rail against all the first-born of Egypt" (61–63).

The "if" constructions rise to a special pitch in the last act,
as Rosalind ends the hypothetical courtship and arranges her
finale. "If you do love Rosalind so near the heart . . . shall
you marry her," she tells Orlando, adding:

> I know into what straits of fortune she is driven; and it
> is not impossible to me, if it appear not inconvenient to
> you, to set her before your eyes to-morrow human as she
> is and without any danger. . . . Therefore put you in
> your best array; bid your friends: for if you will be mar-
> ried tomorrow, you shall, and to Rosalind, if you will.
> [5.2.72–81]

Silvius and Phebe now join them, and a chorus of love declarations develops, climaxing in "If this be so, why blame you
me to love you?" (110 f.), repeated in turn by Phebe, Silvius,
and Orlando. Rosalind hastens to cut them off:

> Pray you no more of this; 'tis like the howling of Irish
> wolves against the moon. [*To Sil.*] I will help you, if I
> can: [*To Phe.*] I would love you, if I could. To-morrow
> meet me all together. [*To Phe.*] I will marry you, if ever

> I marry woman, and I'll be married to-morrow: [*To Orl.*]
> I will satisfy you, if ever I satisfied man, and you shall
> be married to-morrow: [*To Sil.*] I will content you, if
> what pleases you content you, and you shall be married
> to-morrow. [118–26]

"If you like it, so," Lodge had told his "Gentlemen Readers," [10] and Shakespeare's title had made this more positive,
just as Rosalind now winds up with a flourish of "as's":

> [*To Orl.*] As you love Rosalind, meet: [*To Sil.*] as you
> love Phebe, meet: and as I love no woman, I'll meet. So
> fare you well: I have left you commands. [127–31]

It is, again, an amusing kind of formality, the more so because
we share with Rosalind the knowledge of which hypotheses
can come true. Rosalind runs through it all again in the wedding scene, setting out the "ifs" for each of the lovers. Then,
as she disappears to transform herself, Touchstone steps forward to deliver his own views on the uses of conditional grammar. Courtly quarreling is his subject. After running through
a sample quarrel, all cast in "if's" ("if I said his beard was not
cut well, he was in the mind it was"), he sums up with an
oblique defense of feigning and hypothesis:

> all these you may avoid, but the Lie Direct: and you may
> avoid that too, with an If. I knew when seven Justices
> could not take up a quarrel, but when the parties were
> met themselves, one of them thought but of an If as, "If
> you said so, then I said so," and they shook hands and
> swore brothers. Your If is the only peace-maker; much
> virtue in If. [5.4.100–07]

This might be the last word on the subject, except that Shakespeare, in Rosalind's epilogue, takes one final opportunity to
remind us of the world and mood of "if" and the play we have
just seen, where a boy played a girl impersonating a boy in
the imaginary landscape of the pastoral:

10. For an unintentionally ludicrous use of "if" in *Rosalynde,* see
"Saladynes Sonnet," Bullough, 2:234.

If it be true that good wine needs no bush, 'tis true that
a good play needs no epilogue; yet to good wine they do
use good bushes, and good plays prove the better by the
help of good epilogues. . . . If I were a woman I would
kiss as many of you as had beards that pleased me, com-
plexions that liked me and breaths that I defied not: and,
I am sure, as many has have good beards or good faces or
sweet breaths will, for my kind offer, when I make curtsy,
bid me farewell.

Gently, deftly, the pastoral hypothesis is dissolved, and we are
left in the theater, applauding.

❦

The tendency of *As You Like It* to keep before us the artificial basis of the pastoral design is closely linked to its stress
on the relativity and subjectivity of the experience of sojourn.
The forest is constant in its imaginary character and changeable in each contact with a separate imagination.[11] The essential subjectivity of pastoral thus emerges with considerable
force; and since each character's encounter with Arden differs,
the play offers a growing awareness of the fundamental relativity of human experience. This is much more so in *As You
Like It* than in, say, Montemayor, Sidney, or Lodge. But it
nonetheless springs from the idea of pastoral, and is a logical
extension of the tendency in the eclogues to show nature reflecting human moods, and the themes of self-discovery and
self-knowledge in the pastoral romances. It is again a case of
Shakespeare seeing the full possibilities of a subject and ex-
ploiting them with uncommon skill.

The forest of Arden, like the theater or any art, can be
likened to a special sort of mirror that reflects the subject
under the guise of objects. It is not surprising that its viewers
so seldom realize that they are seeing themselves when they

11. Cf. John Russell Brown's comments in *Shakespeare and His Comedies* (London, 1957), p. 149: "the forest mirrors one's mind; if peace and
order are found there, the forest will reflect them. . . . Contentment in
love is, like content in Arden, subjective; it is as one's self likes it."

look at it. Even as the Duke is declaring winds to be counselors and stones capable of sermons, we realize that he is finding in nature an image of his own tendency to moralize. Jaques is engaged in the same thing, and his forest differs as he himself differs from the Duke: he finds it a reflection of the world and an opportunity for invective, but the truth is nearer in his own resemblance to the sequestered stag, and the amusing mirror-image of him, "weeping and commenting / Upon the sobbing deer" (2.2.65–66), with which the scene closes. Jaques may be, as the Duke says, "full of matter" at such moments, but the matter is whatever he has brought to the forest in his own person rather than anything he has learned there. This tendency to be imprisoned in one's own nature may not destroy the ideal of contemplation which informed the pastoral (reflection and contemplation were, and are, respectable cohorts), but it certainly gives it a comic and skeptical flavor which is largely Shakespeare's own contribution.

Everywhere this world gives back to its inhabitants and visitors the images of their own selves and preoccupations. Adam and Orlando find it hostile because they are lost and hungry; when they have had a square meal its savage character vanishes, to return for as long as it takes Orlando to forgive Oliver and dispatch the lioness. Corin sees in his flock the image of his own peace and contentment, while Touchstone, exercising his fascination with sexuality, turns it all into "the copulation of cattle," with Corin as presiding pimp. Touchstone comes closest to acknowledging the subjectivity of pastoral experience. "Ay, now am I in Arden," he remarks on arrival, "the more fool I" (2.4.15). And he goes on to demonstrate this intensification of selfhood, proving a much apter and funnier clown in the forest than he ever was at court.

It is not only in nature that the characters find themselves reflected, but in each other as well. Rosalind and her party have no sooner arrived than they have an opportunity to hear Silvius on the subject of his love for Phebe. Rosalind is immediately referred to her own passion for Orlando:

> Alas, poor shepherd! Searching of thy wound,
> I have by hard adventure found mine own.
>
> [2.4.44–45]

So has Touchstone, but with a characteristic difference:

> And I mine. I remember, when I was in love I broke my
> sword upon a stone and bid him take that for coming
> a-night to Jane Smile; and I remember the kissing of her
> batlet and the cow's dugs that her pretty chopt hands had
> milked; and I remember the wooing of a peascod instead
> of her, from whom I took two cods and, giving her them
> again, said with weeping tears "Wear these for my sake."
> [46–53]

This is the funnier for being so complicated. Touchstone is
not only defacing literary landscape with genuine rusticity,
real postures in real pastures, he is also participating in and
simultaneously parodying everybody else's subjectivity. His
"wooing . . . instead" even prefigures Orlando's hypothetical
courtship of Ganymede.

Indeed, it is Touchstone, parodist supreme, who proves
the deftest reflector of others in the play, partly because it is
his professional role. Had he been merely "nature's natural,"
a clown like Bottom, Sly, or Dogberry, he could have accomplished this only in part. But Shakespeare, inspired by
his success with Falstaff and by his new clown, Robert Armin,
made him a master stylist and wit, and his verbal adaptability
gives him his astonishing range. He is as much a chameleon
as the forest, although this fact seems to have escaped the
commentators who have disapproved of him as a show-off,
cynic, and lecher.[12] Touchstone is either a grotesque reflec-

---

12. Among his "shortcomings," according to Draper, are the fact that
he is "a hanger-on of the court," his tendency to show off, and his vanity
(p. 8). James Smith ("As You Like It," *Scrutiny* 9:9–32) finds him "apa-
thetic" (p. 20) and "nasty" (p. 22); of his relations with Audrey, Smith
says: "nor does he spare an occasion, public or private, of pouring ridi-
cule on the ingenuousness of which he has taken advantage" (p. 23).
Touchstone's conversation he finds "mere playing with words" (p. 23). I
mention these views because Smith's essay is still praised and recommended.
For more useful accounts of Touchstone see Robert H. Goldsmith, *Wise*

tion of those he encounters, as with Jaques, Silvius, and Orlando, or a reflection of what they think a courtier must be like, as with Corin, William, and Audrey. He exists to score off other characters and conventional attitudes, and as such he is a source of pure, and at times extremely subtle, enjoyment. If his grounding in the lost tradition of the licensed fool makes him a difficult character for a modern actor to re-create, he is nevertheless one of Shakespeare's happiest inspirations.

It is shortly after he has treated us to the story of Jane Smile that we hear of Touchstone's first encounter with Jaques, reported by Jaques himself. The special irony of this instance of reflection, with the "deep contemplative" fool railing "on Lady Fortune" and moralizing "In good set terms," is that the resemblance never strikes the enthusiastic Jaques. He has been superbly mimicked, but his reaction is only:

> O that I were a fool!
> I am ambitious for a motley coat.
>
> [2.7.42–43]

Jaques does not fare very well in the holding up of mirrors which occupies so much of *As You Like It*. He is usually taken in. When Touchstone gives him some exaggerated euphuism, he takes it straight.[13] And when he meets Orlando, and for a moment their two kinds of melancholy mirror each other, it is Orlando who points out their difference and scores off Jaques with a stale joke:

Fools in Shakespeare (East Lansing, 1955), C. L. Barber, *Shakespeare's Festive Comedy* (Princeton, 1959), and the two excellent essays on the play by Harold Jenkins, "As You Like It," *Shakespeare Survey* 8 (1955):40–51, and Helen Gardner, "As You Like It," in *More Talking of Shakespeare* (London, 1959).

13. "As the ox hath his bow, sir, the horse his curb and the falcon her bells, so man hath his desires; and as pigeons bill, so wedlock would be nibbling" (3.3.80–83), to which Jaques's answer is, "And will you, being a man of your breeding, be married under a bush like a beggar?" This is one of those moments, incidentally, when Touchstone seems to me to bear an uncanny resemblance to W. C. Fields.

Jaques. I thank you for your company; but, good
faith, I had as lief have been myself alone.

Orlando. And so had I; but yet, for fashion sake, I
thank you too for your society.

[3.2.269–72]

Jaques. . . . Will you sit down with me? and we two
will rail against our mistress the world and all our
misery.

Orlando. I will chide no breather in the world but
myself, against whom I know most faults.

[293–98]

Jaques. But my troth, I was seeking for a fool when I
found you.

Orlando. He is drowned in the brook. Look but in and
you shall see him.

Jaques. There I shall see mine own figure.

Orlando. Which I take to be either a fool or a cipher.

[303–08]

And so they part, addressing each other as "Signior Love"
and "Monsieur Melancholy." Their encounter is, in one
sense, a contest between love and self-love, from which love,
not surprisingly, emerges victorious. The connection between
reflection and illusory self-esteem is made elsewhere by Rosalind, in her criticism of Silvius' behavior to Phebe:

'Tis not her glass, but you, that flatters her;
And out of you she sees herself more proper
Than any of her lineaments can show her.

[3.5.54–56]

The answer to excessive subjectivity and self-love is love for
another, but it too sometimes requires the kind of corrective
glass that Rosalind holds up for Orlando when, as Ganymede,
she mirrors his love as something less perfect and ideal than
"The fair, the chaste, and unexpressive she" (3.2.10) he had
posited while behaving like Silvius. Mirroring in Shakespearean comedy is always used to emphasize limitations of awareness, introducing the audience to comic resemblances the

characters tend to miss. In *As You Like It* it seems particularly linked to the subjectivity which threatens to nullify the contemplative ideal of the pastoral sojourn. What is the value, in other words, of Jaques musing all day in the forest, if he cannot see himself clearly and chide accordingly? Something else is needed, something provided by Rosalind's experience and, through her, in Orlando's.

Accompanying the emphasis on subjectivity is its natural concomitant, a sense of relativity. As the play progresses it becomes clear that blanket judgments and rigid categories will not suffice in this world; they must be adapted to the characters and situation in question. Thus, while we begin the play with two of the familiar pairs of opposites from pastoral tradition—Nature and Nurture, as an expression of Orlando's dilemma, and Nature and Fortune as Rosalind's —we are not allowed to use them for easy classification or to feel that they are immutable. Orlando, denied nurture, must fall back on nature, but his case is not that simple, as his brother, who finds him "never schooled and yet learned," admits. His blood and breeding, in this case "the spirit of my father" (1.1.21), assert themselves, and they partake, since breeding is a kind of art, of both nurture and nature.

Rosalind, in turn, may be justified in describing herself to Orlando as "one out of suits with fortune," but she has contributed to the witty disintegration of the Nature-Fortune dichotomy a moment earlier. Celia has invited her to "sit and mock the good housewife Fortune from her wheel," an image in which the mockery is already well begun.[14] Celia wants Fortune's gifts "bestowed equally," and Rosalind agrees that the "bountiful blind woman" is especially unfair to women:

> *Celia.* 'Tis true, for those that she makes fair, she scarce makes honest, and those that she makes honest, she makes very ill-favoredly.

14. The excerpt from Peele's Lord Mayor's Pageant heading this chapter is intended to suggest the iconography from which Celia's image is drawn.

> *Rosalind*. Nay, now thou goest from Fortune's office
> to Nature's. Fortune reigns in gifts of the world, not in
> the lineaments of Nature.
>
> [1.2.40–45]

But the re-establishment of the distinction is merely a prelude
to further wordplay, as Celia seizes on the opportunity provided by Touchstone's approach:

> *Celia*. No; when Nature hath made a fair creature, may
> she not by Fortune fall into the fire? Though Nature
> hath given us wit to flout at Fortune, hath not Fortune
> sent in this fool to cut off the argument?
> *Rosalind*. Indeed, there is Fortune too hard for Nature
> when Fortune makes Nature's natural the cutter-off of
> Nature's wit.
> *Celia*. Peradventure this is not Fortune's work neither,
> but Nature's, who perceiveth our natural wits too dull
> to reason of such goddesses and hath sent this natural
> for our whetstone.
>
> [46–58]

The effect of this is not to deny that there is any valid distinction between the two concepts, but to leave us feeling
that they are scarcely so hard and fast as some would like to
believe, and that heroines who can bandy them about in this
fashion are unlikely to exist merely as illustrations of their
objective truth.

An even greater relativity comes to surround the opposition of Nature and Art. Like all pastoral, *As You Like It*
celebrates the values of harmony with nature, uncomplicated
living, and love without artifice. At the same time, as we have
seen, it calls attention to the artificial character of its natural
setting, and its characters turn continually to the stratagems
of art to accomplish natural ends. Orlando hangs poems on
the trees, the foresters use song and ritual to express their
pastoral commitments, Rosalind maintains a disguise and
becomes an actor to promote a more naturalistic courtship,
and, at the end, that most artificial of forms, a masque, is
used to celebrate a series of natural truths. This blurring of

the Nature-Art distinction is hardly surprising in view of the common Renaissance ideal that Nature and Art should harmonize (cf. the Drayton passage heading this chapter), an ideal of which pastoral was the standard vehicle. Again, however, Shakespeare has gone further than other writers of pastoral in making explicit the relativity of nature and art as a precondition of pastoral; most writers preferred to maintain the pretence that they were opting for nature over art in theory, whatever they did in practice.

Characterization is affected by this unstable, mutable atmosphere as well. Several commentators have noted Rosalind's ability to embody opposing points of view, mocking love at one moment and confessing herself so deeply in love that "it cannot be sounded" the next.[15] Rather than a falsification, her disguise is a means of revelation, allowing her to avoid constraining roles and give full expression to her contradictory feelings. She is by no means the only character to do so. Touchstone, as already noted, is like a chameleon, ready to take on whatever coloration will provide the most amusement. He is no more a courtier than he is a fool, and no more a fool than he is a poet, but he is ready to impersonate all at a moment's notice.

No character is more contradictory than Jaques, a fact which has led to frequent misunderstandings. His melancholy must not be taken too literally because it is in fact an enthusiasm. No one has more zest for life than this declared solitary. He can "suck melancholy out of a song as a weasel sucks eggs" (2.5.12), an appropriate image, surely, in its suggestion of furtive pleasure. His encounter with Touchstone arouses him to a frenzy of happy excitement, and leads

15. Draper (pp. 15–16) calls her "the epitome of that fusion of irony and idealism which forms the pastoralism of Arden and the comic basis of *As You Like It*." Barber notes that "Romantic participation in love and humorous detachment from its follies, the two polar attitudes which are balanced against each other in the action as a whole, meet and are reconciled in Rosalind's personality" (p. 233). Harold Jenkins (p. 50) says, "Dominating the centre of the play, playing both the man's and the woman's parts, counsellor in love and yet its victim, Rosalind gathers up into herself many of its roles and many of its meanings."

him on to a spirited defense of satire and his Seven Ages
speech. He admits to Rosalind of his melancholy that "I
do love it better than laughing" (4.1.4). It is his own artful
compound, in which he takes great pride and pleasure, and
it would be wrong to find anything but complacent satisfaction in his account of the way his "often rumination"
wraps him "in a most humorous sadness." The Duke is surely
quite right to describe him as "compact of jars," and we may
perhaps pardon a man so largely composed of fads and fashions, enthusiastically taken up, if he is unusually lacking in
self-knowledge.

There is scarcely an element in *As You Like It* unaffected
by a sense of relativity. Sex, rank, fortune, the ages of man,
the forest itself, are all seen as variables rather than con-
stants. And so is Time, not only in the play as a whole, but
quite particularly in Rosalind's opening gambit when she
encounters Orlando in the forest. "Time," she tells him,
"travels in divers paces with divers persons," and ambles,
trots, gallops, and stands still. She goes on to a detailed account that resembles Jaques' portrayal of the seven ages. Time
ambles, for example,

> With a priest that lacks Latin and a rich man that hath
> not the gout, for the one sleeps easily because he cannot
> study, and the other lives merrily because he feels no
> pain. [3.2.336–39]

It is, in effect, Orlando's first lesson, and it is a good one, a
lesson that the play takes to heart. We may suppose that the
title is related to it, as a kind of warning against categorical
judgments. Pastoral is not always true or always false or always
anything; it is as you like it. And it is not just to pastoral
that this applies, but to Time, to Nature, to Art, and to life
itself.

❦

The emphasis on feigning and hypothesis in *As You Like It*
and its projection of the personal and variable factors in the
pastoral sojourn, can both be seen to relate to the equivocal

tendencies already present in the pastoral tradition when Shakespeare took it up. There can be no doubt he welcomed the opportunities for ambiguity and contradiction as consistent with his comic aims, and exploited them fully. To the instances of equivocal treatment of themes and characters already discussed, we can now add the play's use of paradox, its structural dependence on juxtaposition and encounter, and its adjustments and reversals of attitude. All of these elements join to produce the play's movement toward a comic reconciliation of opposites.

Enough has been said already, perhaps, to indicate the extensive use of paradox in situation and character. Jaques' melancholy makes him happy. Orlando expects to find savagery and brutality among the outlaws, but these are the qualities he has left behind at court. The fool, who is supposed to be a "natural"—innocent and stupid—turns out to be the worldliest and smartest character in the play. The forest has more to do with art than with nature. And the whole treatment of Time has a contradictory air: pastoral characters are supposed to be outside of normal time, "fleeting" it carelessly, "wasting" it, and so on. In fact, however, there can scarcely be another play in which the characters are so time conscious.[16] It is no good pointing out, as Orlando does, that "There's no clock in the forest" (3.2.319). His fellow characters are always inquiring about the time, fretting about lateness, and "moraling" on the time: how we ripe and rot from hour to hour, find time moving at diverse paces, and live out a "strange, eventful history" of seven ages. Shakespeare is interested in the pastoral's criticism of time and its commitment to a kind of timelessness, but he cannot resist the fun of pointing out how these dismissals in theory often lead to a greater emphasis in practice.

It is hardly surprising that a play so filled with contradictory moments should exhibit the use of paradox as one of its primary stylistic traits. Two examples from the third act

16. Cf. Jay L. Halio's very useful survey, " 'No Clock in the Forest'; Time in *As You Like It*," *Studies in English Literature, 1500–1900* 2 (Spring 1962):197–207.

can be used to illustrate this feature of *As You Like It*. The
first comes in Touchstone's conversation with Corin, who
has asked him how he likes the shepherd's life:

> Truly, shepherd, in respect of itself, it is a good life;
> but in respect that it is a shepherd's life, it is naught. In
> respect that it is solitary, I like it very well; but in respect
> that it is private, it is a very vile life. Now in respect it
> is in the fields, it pleaseth me well; but in respect it is
> not in the court, it is tedious. As it is a spare life, look
> you, it fits my humour well; but as there is no plenty in
> it, it goes much against my stomach. [3.2.13-22]

This is scarcely to be dismissed as nonsense, amusing as it
may be. The fact that one thing may produce two contrary
feelings is a truth that pastoral stands in need of.[17] And it
is appropriate that to Touchstone's concluding question,
"Hast any philosophy in thee, shepherd?" Corin should retort with a series of tautologies:

> No more but that I know the more one sickens, the worse
> at ease he is; and that he that wants money, means, and
> content is without three good friends; that the property
> of rain is to wet and fire to burn; that good pasture
> makes fat sheep, and that a great cause of the night is
> lack of the sun; that he that hath learned no wit by
> nature nor art may complain of good breeding, or comes
> of a very dull kindred. [24-32]

These are truths too, the other side of the coin. Touchstone
declares Corin to be "a natural philosopher," and goes on to
prove him damned for never having been at court.

Phebe is driven into paradoxes after her encounter with

---

17. "Under the apparent nonsense of his self-contradiction, Touchstone
mocks the contradictory nature of the desires ideally produced by pastoral
life, to be at once at court and in the fields, to enjoy both the fat advantages of rank and the spare advantages of the mean and sure estate.
The humor goes to the heart of the pastoral convention and shows how
very clearly Shakespeare understood it" (Barber, p. 227).

Ganymede, as her new feelings outrun her judgments of this "youth" who has been so insulting:

> 'Tis but a peevish boy; yet he talks well.
> But what care I for words? yet words do well
> When he that speaks them pleases those that hear.
> It is a pretty youth: not very pretty:
> But, sure, he's proud, and yet his pride becomes him.
>
> [3.4.110–14]

Here the humor, unlike Touchstone's, is based on Phebe's unconsciousness of what is happening to her, underlined by the fact that this boy she has begun to dote on is no boy at all. There is hardly a character in the play who is not assaulted at some point by such contradictory perceptions.

Both sets of paradoxes cited above are released by encounters between two characters, and we might take Jaques' "I met a fool i' the forest" as the motto of the play, for the encounter can be seen as the main emblem of pastoral and the primary structural device of *As You Like It*. "The manner of the play," as Harold Jenkins points out, "when once it settles down in the forest, is to let two people drift together, talk a little, and part, to be followed by two more." [18] In one sense the play is a string of comic duets, some, like Jaques' encounter with Touchstone, reported, most others overheard not only by the audience but by one or more of the other characters. [19] These casual meetings are in part used, of course, to produce the thematic juxtapositions which are the stuff of pastoral. When Touchstone woos Audrey we see the familiar contrast between worldliness and innocence; Silvius and Corin give us youth and age; Corin and Touchstone supply country and court; and so it goes. What is interesting about these en-

18. Jenkins, p. 50.

19. The fact that the witnesses are sometimes silent makes them no less important. Janet Suzman's fine performance as Celia in the Royal Shakespeare Company 1967 production showed how much Celia's reactions, despite her largely silent presence in the Rosalind-Orlando exchanges, could enrich the comic meanings of the situation.

counters in *As You Like It* is their continual tendency to
grow equivocal. Jaques no doubt thinks that he is wisdom
encountering Touchstone as folly; we are inclined to turn it
the other way around. Corin declares his adherence to honesty
and simplicity; Touchstone immediately converts his liveli-
hood to bawdry. Orlando rushes upon the outlaws, thinking
he is nurture encountering nature; it is more like the reverse.
Meeting Ganymede-Rosalind he is supposedly the lover as
poet, he-she the simple native; but we know who the real
artist is.

All of the above instances may be used to demonstrate that
equivocation is not used simply for its own sake in *As You
Like It,* to confuse issues or secure easy laughs. It is a part
of the play's vision of human experience and a corrective to
the tendency of pastoral to deal in rigid categories and simple
judgments. A further aspect of this process through which
oversimplifications are dissolved and conventional attitudes
broken down can be found in the play's habit of what Harold
Jenkins calls "readjustment of the point of view." [20] This use
of readjustment so pervades *As You Like It* that it results in
a stylistic feature whereby reduction and expansion (in rhe-
torical terms *encomium* and *meiosis*) of the supposed importance of roles, attitudes, persons, and ideas is continually
carried on.

Celia's proposal to "mock the good housewife Fortune from
her wheel," transforming the dread goddess to a spinning
peasant, is a clear instance of reduction. So is Rosalind's
declaration that "love is merely a madness," her comments
about dying for love ("Men have died from time to time, and
worms have eaten them, but not for love" [4.1.107]), her remarks about travelers, her suggestion that Phebe is little more
than a commodity ("Sell when you can, you are not for all
markets" [3.5.60]), and her censures of fickleness (4.1.146 ff.).
Touchstone's reductions scarcely require illustration; they
occur almost as often as he opens his mouth.

Expansion is equally common as a stylistic gesture. It occurs

20. Jenkins, p. 49.

when Celia argues that banishment is really liberty, when the Duke discourses on the sweet uses of adversity, and when Jaques decides that "motley's the only wear." Jaques is in fact more fond of making much of things than of belittling them, as befits his enthusiastic nature. Thus the wounded deer, the professional fool, the effectiveness and integrity of satire, his own melancholy, and the attractions of religious converts all receive more due from his expansive treatment of them than they appear to deserve.

While isolated instances of expansion and reduction are common, they occur with equal frequency in close sequence and even within the same statement. Silvius expands his love till it has no precedent, and Touchstone speedily reduces it to absurdity. Amiens' song, "Under the greenwood tree," enlarges the virtues of pastoral existence, and Jaques' new stanza deflates them. Orlando's verses elevate Rosalind to a pedestal, while Touchstone's parody and her own reaction quickly bring her down. Love and marriage are amply celebrated in the final scene, but a countercheck exists in Touchstone's suggestion that they are all so many "country copulatives," that there is swearing and forswearing in the world, and that "marriage binds and blood breaks" (5.4.57). And what of a statement like "All the world's a stage"? It is a reduction of the one and an expansion of the other. So, perhaps, is the strange and beautiful song, "Blow, blow, thou winter wind," with its contradictory assertions about life. A kind of equivocality is at work in this area, too, so that Rosalind's confession, after she has "misused her sex," that her love in fact "hath an unknown bottom, like the Bay of Portugal" (4.1.215), can be seen to have a double effect, reductive through our consciousness (shared with her) of its hyperbole, and expansive as it serves to remind us how deep and genuine her love for Orlando really is.

What is the function of this continual readjustment of attitudes by inflation and deflation? It is, for one thing, a source of comic effect, a way of insuring that the juxtapositions and collisions achieve their full potential. It can also be seen to relate to the twin branches of idealism and satire in the

pastoral tradition, neither of which, in isolation, seems to
have satisfied Shakespeare, so that he set them to a kind of
running interchange from which a synthesis could emerge.
"Take less, have more," is, after all, equivocal advice in the
first place, and it deserves a wide and thorough examination,
where practice takes precedence over theory. Hymen's pro-
nouncement in the masque, that "Then is there mirth in
heaven / When earthly things made even / Atone together"
(5.4.114–16), is, besides being a celebration of marriage, a
kind of summary of what we have been through, "atone" here
meaning "to harmonize," "to exist at one." All the possibilities and contradictions we have seen can be brought into
a kind of harmony, in Arden if not in the real world; what
proves it is that we have been able to absorb them all as parts
of the rich and unified world of *As You Like It*.

¥

One further aspect of *As You Like It* that deserves mention
in any survey of its relation to the pastoral is its generalizing
tendency, its habit of drawing back to survey the ways of the
world and the human condition. "Hast any philosophy in
thee, shepherd?" Touchstone asks Corin. The question seems
natural, and the answer is yes, not only for Corin but for
nearly everyone in the play. All the characters share the
meditative concern about the world made most explicit, perhaps, in Jaques, with the result that *As You Like It* is "contemplative" with a vengeance. Once again we have to do here
with a typical feature of pastoral, its tendency to create
microcosms and to explore, by the setting up of a hypothetical
alternative, the deficiencies and advantages of life as it is.
And, once again, Shakespeare brings this tendency more fully
into the open, demonstrating the degree to which he was con-
sciously exploring, not the external features of pastoral but
its deepest concerns, and inviting his audience to join him.
By dropping the pretense that the pastoral setting is an
escape, a world unto itself, and making its microcosmic possibilities explicit, he leads us to an understanding of the convention as a convention and to a consideration of the nature
and value of art.

Even before they take to the woods, Celia and Rosalind are finding food for light conversation in the "lineaments of Nature" and the way "Fortune reigns in gifts of the world." Such concerns will fill the play, but hardly to make it solemn; they may be as lighthearted as Rosalind's and Touchstone's spoofing of Le Beau:

> *Le Beau.* What colour, madam? how shall I answer you?
> *Rosalind.* As wit and fortune will.
> *Touchstone.* Or as the Destinies decree.
> [1.2.109–11]

Orlando, meanwhile, is holding up his end at this sort of thing. If he is killed at wrestling, he tells the ladies, he will do

> the world no injury, for in it I have nothing; only in the world I fill up a place, which may be better supplied when I have made it empty. [1.2.204–06]

"World" is in fact a favorite word in *As You Like It,* and its use generally signals the oscillation between the general and the particular which is so striking a characteristic of the play. Le Beau, having warned Orlando about Duke Frederick's wrath, hopes they will meet again "Hereafter, in a better world than this." Rosalind, out of suits with fortune and in love with Orlando, sighs, "O, how full of briers is this working-day world!" (1.3.11). Adam, warning Orlando of his brother's treachery, is moved to exclaim:

> O, what a world is this, when what is comely
> Envenoms him that bears it!
> [2.2.14–15]

And Orlando, struck by his generosity and loyalty, finds him an emblem of better times:

> O good old man, how well in thee appears
> The constant service of the antique world,
> When service sweat for duty, not for meed!
> [56–58]

They resolve to go off together in search of "some settled low content."

Thus, even before all the sojourners have reached the forest, we have been made aware not only of the pastoral's status as an alternative, but of the way in which this alternative is likely to function as a means of examining and criticizing the life that has been abandoned. In Arden this process finds its way into every corner of the forest. While the Duke is generalizing about adversity and nature, Jaques, using the wounded deer as a springboard, is "most invectively" surveying "The body of the country, city, court, / Yea, and of this our life" (2.1.59–60). Corin and Silvius are found discussing not only Silvius' passion for Phebe, but love in general, so that Touchstone's mocking response likewise moves from the grotesque particulars of his affair with Jane Smile to the conclusion that "all nature in love" is "mortal in folly." Jaques finds Touchstone consulting a watch and considering "how the world wags," and is himself moved to consider the world as a stage with a seven-act pageant of life. The song which follows this speech, like the others in the play, pushes out to such wide considerations as "man's ingratitude" and the deficiencies of "most friendship" and "most loving." Jaques later invites Orlando to sit down with him "and rail against our mistress the world and all our misery." Orlando declines; he will "chide no breather in the world but myself." Touchstone has better luck than Jaques; he converses with Corin about the general qualities of court and country, and with Audrey about poetry and love, while Audrey, who is not much of a conversationalist, has a curious habit of appealing to "the gods." She later hopes "it is no dishonest desire to desire to be a woman of the world" (5.3.4).

It is Rosalind, however, who excels at this generalizing activity, making the most effective and balanced use of it, as she does with so much else. We have already noted her survey of the relativity of time. She moves from that directly to her initial comments on love, a lunacy "so ordinary that the whippers are in love too," none more than she herself. Most of her surveys of the world are aimed at the doubtful success of love and marriage. When Orlando talks of dying for love she advises him to "die by attorney," adding:

> The poor world is almost six thousand years old, and in all this time there was not any man died in his own person, videlicet, in a love cause. [4.1.94–97]

If the stories of Troilus and Leander suggest otherwise, they are "all lies." Orlando brings her back to their case by suggesting that Rosalind's frown would kill him, to which she answers "By this hand, it will not kill a fly." A fine double consciousness invades the remark; as Ganymede's it is further harsh common sense, as Rosalind's an admission of her love, the whipper whipped. A moment later Orlando swerves again into hyperbole. He will love her "For ever and a day," and once again she uses the way of the world to check him:

> Say "a day," without the "ever." No, no Orlando; men are April when they woo, December when they wed: maids are May when they are maids, but the sky changes when they are wives. [146–49]

The difference between her surveys of life and those of someone like Jaques lies in her sense of her relevance and their limits. She steers a course between the excessive subjectivity that cuts Jaques off from the immediate situation, and the excessive objectivity in Touchstone that threatens to destroy all personal emotion.

Not all of Rosalind's general observations and surveys of life are reserved for Orlando. With Jaques she examines the kinds of melancholy and the folly of travelers, and she is provoked by Silvius' mooning to the exclamation that " 'Tis such fools as you / That makes the world full of ill-favour'd children" (3.5.52–53). But her best in this kind are saved for the central and most meaningful episodes of the play, those in which she tests her love, and Orlando's, against all that can be said to make us doubt them. The process is aimed at the reconciliation of her ideals and feelings to the hard facts of the world, so that we do not tend to notice how much she is given to generalizations. The Seven Ages of Man speech

stands out and is detachable because Jaques, in his isolation,
is really only capable of set-pieces. But when Rosalind tells
us (and Orlando) that "Men have died from time to time, and
worms have eaten them, but not for love," we know that she
is not showing off; she is engaged in the business of liberating
love from folly and pastoral from artifice, releasing in the
process much of the comic energy of the play.

In light of this, the long-standing admiration of Rosalind,
if sometimes rather extravagantly phrased, is certainly justified, for not only does she excel at the play's habit of surveying the world's shortcomings, she herself comes to embody the
ideals of love and the values of pastoral. She is what can be
salvaged from a searching examination of the lies and feigning of love and art: false friend, true lover, skilled actress, and
author of the happy ending. And if we can pardon the critics'
enthusiasm for her, then surely we might be a little easier on
Orlando's. His second poem, whatever its deficiencies, points
to the truth of the matter. It begins with its own rationale:

> Why should this a desert be?
> For it is unpeopled? No;
> Tongues I'll hang on every tree,
> That shall civil sayings show:
>
> [3.2.133–36]

The subjects of these "tongues" will be the surveys of the
world that Shakespeare recognized as typical of the pastoral:

> Some, how brief the life of man
> Runs his erring pilgrimage,
> That the stretching of a span
> Buckles in his sum of age;
> Some, of violated vows
> 'Twixt the souls of friend and friend:
>
> [137–42]

But the great subject, when the real has been taken into account, will be the ideal, and its microcosm will be Rosalind:

> But upon the fairest boughs,
> Or at every sentence end,

Will I Rosalinda write,
  Teaching all that read to know
The quintessence of every sprite
  Heaven would in little show.
Therefore Heaven Nature charged
  That one body should be filled
With all graces wide-enlarged:
  Nature presently distilled
Helen's cheek, but not her heart,
  Cleopatra's majesty,
Atalanta's better part,
  Sad Lucretia's modesty.
Thus Rosalind of many parts
  By heavenly synod was devised,
Of many faces, eyes, and hearts,
  To have the touches dearest prized.

[143–60]

We might give less credit to Heaven and Nature, and more to Shakespeare, but it seems fair to say that Orlando, like any good love-at-first-sight lover, has recognized a truth that it will take us the course of the play to discover.

❧

We may now attempt to summarize some of the conclusions made possible by the above analysis of *As You Like It* in terms of its relation to the pastoral. The first thing to be noted is that the typical plot of the pastoral romance—upon which most writers intent on adapting pastoral to the stage might be expected to concentrate their attention—held little genuine interest for Shakespeare in this play. He was content to rely on Lodge for the main events, and his treatment of the story line, as a number of critics have noted, was more than a little perfunctory. The plot of *As You Like It*, its complications and outcome, clearly exists as a means to something else that occupies most of the playwright's interest.

It is this fact, I suspect, that has led so many critics to suppose that Shakespeare had little interest in pastoral when he wrote *As You Like It*, and that it was mostly a convenience upon which his comic achievement could be reared. But a closer look suggests that his interest in pastoral was very great indeed, and that he brushed past its external trappings only in order to get at its essential themes and discover its rationale, recognizing that the appeal of pastoral lay not in shepherds, shepherdesses, or pretty songs, but in its imaginative vision of life, a vision that partook of both mythical and intellectual elements. To these elements, which included idealizations of nature and love and criticisms of society and art, he addressed his considerable powers of mind and his immense skill as a dramatist; the result was a play that deserves to be described as among his two or three finest achievements in comedy—many would say the best—and as a masterpiece in the Renaissance pastoral tradition. It is the latter emphasis that we have tended to neglect.

But there is little use in placing *As You Like It* within the pastoral tradition unless we can also account for its uniqueness. This uniqueness is surely grounded in its attitude toward the convention on which it is based. In a remark already quoted, William Empson speaks of the importance of "the clash between style and theme," in pastoral, that is to say, between the praise of innocence and simplicity and the worldliness and complexity by which the praise is accomplished. To make this work, Empson claims, "the writer must keep up a firm pretence that he [is] unconscious of it," and he adds that this also protects it from becoming funny (see above, p. 9). But Shakespeare had the wisdom to recognize that the pretense could be abandoned and allowed to grow comic without destroying the value and meaning of pastoral, just as Rosalind could be allowed to mock love without losing her status as an ideal lover. The result, in both cases, is rather an enhancing and strengthening of what can survive the tests of criticism and laughter. In *As You Like It* we are invited to view the pastoral convention simultaneously from the inside, as in Lodge, and from the outside, as a frankly artificial and illusory construction. The effect is to make the play a consideration, not only of the typical pastoral themes, but of the pastoral itself. This tendency, as I have suggested (and

Empson notwithstanding), was already present in the pastoral, which had become in part a poet's country, an art about art. But the degree of detachment and self-examination introduced to the convention by Shakespeare is quite without precedent.

The aspects of the play described in this chapter—its treatment of nature, its self-consciousness, its emphasis on relativity, subjectivity, and paradox, its continual shifting of attitudes and judgments, and its generalizing tendencies—are cited to support these claims about its relation to the pastoral tradition and its unique position therein. They also give some indication of *As You Like It*'s comic achievement, difficult to do justice to in its complexity and subtlety. If most of them have turned out to be stylistic features, it is because *As You Like It* is, in fact, almost all style, accomplishing its ends through stratagems of language, brilliant verbal juxtapositions. It is not just Duke Senior who can "translate the stubbornness of fortune / Into so quiet and so sweet a style" (2.1.19–20). Everyone is drunk with style (not, fortunately, euphuism, although that receives its glances), all sorts of styles and the roles to go with them. To speak of pastoral as "a clash between style and theme" is not really adequate here, for pastoral, as Shakespeare explores it in *As You Like It*, is really a set of styles, grouped about a life style that is most unlikely to produce them. There is never any pretence that things are otherwise.

And what is the effect of this enormous accomplishment on those who witness or read the play? I think that our discoveries about the complicated relations of Nature and Art, our growing sense of the relativity of experience, our abandonment of doctrines and categories in favor of a recognition of the equivocal and paradoxical elements of life and love, all lead to a remarkable widening of judgment, a new tolerance. Perhaps it is to this that H. B. Charlton refers in his enthusiastic claim that Arden is "an immeasurable enlargement of the universe of comedy." [21] If *As You Like It* begins with the

21. H. B. Charlton, *Shakespearian Comedy* (London, 1938), p. 279.

pastoral's criticism of life, it seems to move toward an acceptance of life, based on a realistic and amused acknowledgment of its vagaries and shortcomings. What we are offered, finally, is perspective, in the amount required to make us laugh at Fortune and take Nature on her own terms. And is it not this perspective, this prospect on life, rather than escape and wish-fulfillment, that is the best and truest aim of pastoral? So it must seem, at least, by the end of *As You Like It,* when the Olympian amusement and understanding touched on in Hymen's poem seem so close to our own:

> Then is there mirth in heaven,
> When earthly things made even
> Atone together.

3

The Natural Fool of Fortune: *King Lear*

Remember, Nature sent thee hither bare;
The gifts of Fortune—count them borrowed ware.

Thomas More, *The Book of Fortune*

Thou barrein ground, whome winters wrath hath wasted,
Art made a myrrhour, to behold my plight.

Spenser, *The Shepherdes Calender*

Tell fortune of her blindness;
Tell nature of decay;
Tell friendship of unkindness;
Tell justice of delay:
And if they will reply,
Then give them all the lie.

Sir Walter Raleigh

The scene of the forest had come to be the most memorable
of all romantic settings. Wyatt's phrase, "the hertes forest,"
is a kind of epigram for it, and whether the hart be the
lover, as in Wyatt and Spenser, or the great emperor Caesar,
as in Shakespeare, or as in Malory, Christ, the forest is the
frame *par excellence* of the action, and the tremendous simplicity of Malory's words on Tristan, "whan he was madde in
the foreyste," reach the center of desolation.

John Arthos

King Lear is the one play in Shakespeare's canon which appears to qualify for Polonius' staggering category, the "tragical-comical-historical-pastoral." That, at least, is a way of
accounting for its remarkable comprehensiveness and for
those features which set it apart from the other tragedies. Its
primary standing as a tragedy has never been seriously questioned, despite such crude reclassification as the notorious

Tate version and, more subtly, those commentaries which
attempt to account for it as a study in salvation and regenera-
tion.[1] Its close kinship with the history play is suggested not
only by the First Quarto title (the "True Chronicle Historie
of the life and death of King Lear") and its ultimate source
in Holinshed's *Chronicles,* but by the presence and handling
of certain themes, such as kingship, familiar to any student
of Shakespeare's histories. Its ties to comedy, less obvious but
scarcely less extensive, range from the double plot (unique in
Shakespearean tragedy with the exception of *Timon*) and the
Fool to the grim humor which is laced through even the most
painful scenes.[2] Commentators have noted its tendency to
verge on the ludicrous at certain points, and there is ample
testimony from those who have played and produced it of
its ability to rouse laughter.

Most discussions of *Lear,* however, if they go so far as to note
its "tragical-comical-historical" possibilities, are content to rest
there. With one important exception, there has been no attention to *King Lear's* curious and extensive relation to the pastoral.[3] The reason is not far to seek. Few, if any, surface details in the play are related to the conventional trappings of
pastoral, with the result that the investigator hardly feels
pressed to pursue the grotesque possibility that tragedy and
pastoral have been combined. The knowledge that George
Chapman set out to write a "pastoral tragedy" around 1599
can have whetted few critical appetites, and the fact that the
result was either unfinished or lost has aroused neither surprise nor chagrin. What other result can be expected from
such a rash enterprise?

Yet the association of tragedy with pastoral is scarcely surprising if we consider that the funeral elegy is among its most

---

1. See John D. Rosenberg, "King Lear and His Comforters," *Essays in
Criticism* 16 (April 1966):135–46.
2. See especially G. Wilson Knight's *"King Lear* and the Comedy of the
Grotesque," in *The Wheel of Fire* (London, 1949).
3. Maynard Mack, *King Lear in Our Time* (Berkeley, 1965), pp. 63–66.
In addition to identifying *Lear's* pastoral connections, Mack's book is,
I think, easily the finest of the book-length studies of the play.

fundamental traditions and that the famous motto, *Et in Arcadia ego* refers to death "as a law of nature";[4] if we recall that its standard dramatic vehicle was felt to be tragicomedy and that Jonson had to defend himself for introducing "mirth" in *The Sad Shepherd*; and if we remind ourselves that writers of pastoral romance were often conscious of a serious, philosophical purpose in their work. Sidney's subject came to be "The almightie wisdome evermore delighting to shewe the world, that by unlikeliest means greatest matters may come to conclusion," to the end that "humane reason may be the more humbled, and more willingly give place to divine providence."[5] And Gil Polo believed that his revelation of the workings and mutabilities of Fortune could help to teach man "to entertaine pleasure as a thing not permanent, and grief and sorrowe as things that may have an ende in time."[6] Though the subject of pastorals might be "of the coursest Woofe in appearance," wrote Drayton, "Neverthelesse, the most High and most Noble matters of the World may bee shaddowed in them, and for certain sometimes are."[7] The themes and concerns of tragedy and pastoral were closer than is apparent from a first glance.

As with *As You Like It*, however, we cannot expect to discover *King Lear*'s relation to the pastoral simply by appealing to the tradition. Its use of pastoral is submerged, eccentric, and in no way bound by conventions. The result is that a significant aspect of the play is easily overlooked. An examination of that aspect, however, can illuminate the structure, characterization, and themes of *King Lear*, as well as help to resolve some of its traditional difficulties. The danger in isolating *Lear*'s pastoral content is one of overemphasis, and I have tried to be alert to it. The reader, too, will do well to

4. Poggioli, p. 164. And see Erwin Panofsky, "*Et in Arcadia Ego:* Poussin and the Elegiac Tradition," in *Meaning in the Visual Arts* (Garden City, N.Y., 1955), 295–320.

5. From the beginning of Book IV of the *Arcadia*. This quotation and the one from Gil Polo which follows are cited by Davis, p. 50.

6. *Diana Enamorada*, Yong's translation.

7. From "To the Reader of His Pastorals" in *Poems*, 1619, p. 432.

remember that what follows is not a comprehensive examination of the play, but a look at one of the tributaries to the "vexed sea" that is *King Lear* and a consideration of its effect on the play as a whole.

☙

When we look at *King Lear* in relation to the pastoral tradition it is apparent that it follows in its outlines the pattern of the pastoral romance as developed in Spain and Italy and elaborated by English romance writers and dramatists.[8] That is, it deals with characters who are forced to leave society and undergo a period of sojourn in a natural setting, and with their eventual return. As in the more serious pastoral novels, the period of sojourn is one of psychological adjustment, with the natural setting acting as a mirror to the mind. Again typically, the emphasis on the workings of Fortune creates a curious compound of philosophical speculation and spectacular turn of event. Moreover, many of the features of such stories—disguises, unaccountable and uncontrollable emotions, errors of identity and allegiance which disrupt the normal social bonds, extensive use of opposites—are readily apparent in *Lear*. Such a description of the play is of course inadequate. To speak of Lear's "psychological adjustment" is to risk absurdity. But it will serve to remind us of the basic and familiar pattern on which the action of the play is grounded.

It is clear that Shakespeare chose to impose this pattern on the Lear story as he found it. In all the older versions the king flees straight to France when Goneril and Regan have turned him out. He is immediately welcomed by Cordelia, and they return with a conquering army to reclaim his throne and punish the unnatural daughters. In the older play of *Leir* there are one or two moments which seem to hint at the possibility of the pastoral romance pattern. The king faces a hired assassin out in "the thicket." Later he and his councilor Perillus (the Kent figure), landing in France, must ex-

8. Cf. Mack, p. 63.

change their fine clothes for "a good strong motley gabardine" and "a good sheep's russet sea-gown" in order to pay their passage.[9] Since Cordella and her husband, the Gallian king, are conveniently nearby disguised as country folk, the reconciliation scene that follows can be said to have a faintly pastoral air about it. But we discover this by reading back from what Shakespeare made of the possibility rather than from any thematic intention on the part of the anonymous author of *Leir*.

The source in which the pastoral romance pattern *was* clearly present was of course the *Arcadia*, from which Shakespeare took the subplot that became the story of Gloucester and his two sons. Sidney's protagonists happen upon the blind king of Paphlagonia and his son, unsheltered, "poorely arrayed" and "extremely weather-beaten" in the midst of a terrible storm. Having heard the story of their separate extrusions and sufferings, the Princes set about restoring them to power and then go on to other adventures. The tale is one of many such in the *Arcadia*, all echoing such Sidneyan themes as self-knowledge (through extremes of behavior and through pastoral encounters and natural living), the disproportionate misfortunes that can grow from errors and sins, and, as Irving Ribner has pointed out, "the political problems of royal authority and responsibility." [10]

The double plot of *Lear*, then, whatever it may owe to Shakespeare's experience as a writer of comedy, has strong links with the *Arcadia*, both parts following the outline of banishment, sojourn, and return. And the secondary plot, in this respect, seems to lead the way. The first banishments of the play, Cordelia's and Kent's, do not lead to pastoral sojourns. Cordelia marries the king of France and Kent reappears, disguised, in Lear's service. It is Edgar who first undertakes to transform himself to "the basest and most poorest

9. Act 4, scene 7, and act 5, scene 3, respectively in "The True Chronicle Historie of King Leir and his three daughters" (1605), ed. Sidney Lee, *The Shakespeare Library* (London, 1909).

10. Irving Ribner, "Shakespeare and Legendary History," *Shakespeare Quarterly* 8 (1956):47–52.

shape" of a Bedlam beggar and "outface / The winds and persecutions of the sky." The country, he says, gives him "proof and precedent" for this. Lear, the Fool, Kent, and Gloucester will follow in turn. The Gloucester plot, meanwhile, will trace the more normal curve of pastoral, with the ceremonious defeat of the bad brother by the good brother and the good brother's restoration to society. It is against this that we measure the terrible outcome of Lear's fortunes.

Shakespeare did not, as some have suggested, need to alter the original Lear story along these lines in order to make it tragic.[11] Other possibilities were open to him for that purpose. The particular usefulness of the pastoral romance pattern, projected in a double plot, was to emphasize and clarify certain lines of interest in the original story. The speed with which the plot develops and crises occur in *King Lear* is made possible by the pastoral romance pattern: by its predetermined structure and by its tradition of arbitrary passions and sudden blows of Fortune. Further, the story of an outcast and humiliated king is enormously strengthened by a line of action which takes him to the other end of the social scale and to the isolation of a wilderness setting, expanding the story until it involves "the stripping of man to the bone, the reduction of magnificent, proud man to the level of the 'poor, bare, forked animal.' "[12] *King Lear* becomes in the process a kind of opposite to the story of Tamburlaine, who began as a shepherd and ended as a king of kings. If Marlowe's play exemplifies the Renaissance celebration of human power and possibility, Shakespeare's balances it as a study of human weakness and fallibility. Tamburlaine, who argues from a

11. R. H. Perkinson, "Shakespeare's Revision of the Lear Story and the Structure of *King Lear*," *Philological Quarterly* 22 (1943):315–29, suggests that the structure of the play was dictated by Shakespeare's decision to make a tragedy from his source, but contradicts himself by admitting that Shakespeare could have made a tragedy like *Othello* with "a lengthy period of deception" by hewing more closely to *Leir*.

12. W. B. C. Watkins, *Shakespeare and Spenser* (Princeton, 1950), p. 107.

theory resembling Edmund's, is led inexorably to his ambition
for worldly power and glory:

> Nature, that fram'd us of foure Elements,
> Warring within our breasts for regiment,
> Doth teach us all to have aspiring minds:
> Our soules, whose faculties can comprehend
> The wondrous Architecture of the world:
> And measure every wandring plannets course,
> Still climbing after knowledge infinite,
> And alwaies mooving as the restless Spheares,
> Wils us to weare our selves and never rest,
> Untill we reach the ripest fruit of all,
> That perfect blisse and sole felicitie,
> The sweet fruition of an earthly crowne.[13]

In *Lear* this process is reversed, leading backward from the
crown toward a re-examination of what Nature does after all
have to teach. And the reversal of Tamburlaine's career is the
pastoral line from court to country, from throne to hovel and
heath.

Several critics have noted that Shakespeare appears to have
telescoped the opening sequences of his story in order to
make room for the scenes on the heath and near Dover. The
same observation has been made about *As You Like It*. What
these comments really point to is the fact that the dramatist
is drawing on a narrative sequence that, because it is based
on an early crisis followed by a series of adventures, requires
almost no groundwork. Motive is less important because the
characters are largely victims of Fortune, and their own behavior reflects its unpredictable turns. The old play of *Leir*
requires two acts to cover the material of *Lear*'s opening
scene. In it the old king formulates a "stratagem" to get

13. Marlowe, *Works*, ed. C. F. Tucker Brooke (Oxford, 1910), p. 32. It is
worth recalling that Marlowe anticipated, in *Faustus* and *Edward II*, later
reactions to the spirit of *Tamburlaine*. Both *Edward II* and *Richard II*
are interesting to consider as predecessors of *Lear*. For a good comparison
of *Lear* and *Richard*, see Watkins, pp. 75 ff.

Cordella to accept a husband. If she is tricked into admitting that she loves her father best, she will not be able to refuse his request. His action is thus, as he says, an act of "policy." Similarly, Gonerill and Regan discover his plan and act accordingly, so that Cordella is the victim of a trap by her sisters, who envy her "surpassing beauty." Everyone's motives are clear, and we follow the intrigue from its inception to its climax. The point about Shakespeare's treatment of this material is neither that he was being arbitrary nor that he was pressed for space to allow for the heath scenes; it is rather that he was recasting the story in a mould that made such matters irrelevant.

A similar observation can be made about the problem of suffering and universal justice in *King Lear*. Anyone familiar with the *Arcadia* knows that misfortune there is systematically out of proportion to any fault that could be said to have initiated it. Helen of Corinth could be held to blame, perhaps, for her initial act, but not for all of its consequences; they had to be unforeseen. Parthenia must certainly be thought of as a victim rather than a sinner. And so it goes.[14] This is that world of Greek romance described by Wolff, where "the links of Cause are broken" and "events are no longer calculable," not to be confused with classical tragedy which exhibits "the laws of the gods." [15] It helps greatly in understanding *King Lear* to realize that in partaking of the pastoral romance pattern it also partakes of the reality that pattern is intended to express. This is not to say that Lear and Gloucester are not responsible for what happens to them. It is rather to point to a tension in the play between the iron-clad cause and effect of a play like *Macbeth* and the world of a play like *Pericles,* where the buffetings of Fortune have no relation to the behavior of her victims. It also accounts for the continual questioning in *King Lear* of the nature of reality and the contradictory assertions by its characters about fate, justice, and the gods. This "tragical-pastoral" tension in the play is among its most striking and memorable features.

14. Both examples are from Book I.
15. Wolff, p. 4. See above, p. 16.

❦

Another way of measuring *King Lear*'s relation to the pastoral is to consider its curious kinship with *As You Like It*. Besides sharing the plot features of the typical pastoral narrative, the two plays can be paired by their concern with the nature of Nature. Thus the similarities of detail—the Fool, the banished ruler, the familial divisions, the disguises, the natural setting as mirror to individual dilemmas, the generalizations about the world—are scarcely coincidental. They reflect shared themes which in turn mark out Shakespeare's particular interest in the pastoral. If *King Lear* is more concerned with justice, and *As You Like It* more preoccupied with love, we can nevertheless discern, as we look back from the tragedy toward the comedy, a strong undercurrent in *As You Like It* that rises to the surface in *King Lear*. The earlier play, we realize, has shown a steady, if secondary, concern with winter wind and bitter sky, with violated vows and benefits forgot, with man's ingratitude and unregarded age in corners thrown, with the foul body of the infected world, with the strange, eventful history that ends in second childishness and mere oblivion.[16] We are tempted to hypothesize. What if Duke Senior were not in a position to speak quite so calmly about the wind and weather as "counselors / That feelingly persuade me what I am"? What if Adam and Orlando did not stumble on friendly outlaws and their convenient banquet? What if Rosalind had to face a more persistent malevolence than the whim that banished her? *As You Like It* is far from oblivious of the possibilities in its material that point toward *Lear*.

We can see this clearly if we compare the two plays' treatments of their natural settings. The forest of Arden is deliberately presented as literary and artificial. This is a way of reminding us that we are in the presence of a protective fantasy that keeps the bitter weather and the suffering of unaccommodated man at bay by its reliance on convention and

16. Helen Gardner, in her essay on *As You Like It* observes that the line "And unregarded age in corners thrown" "sums up the fate of Lear."

predetermined form. In *King Lear* such assurances are removed. If *As You Like It* showed the pastoral doubling back
upon itself, *Lear* shows it turned inside out. The pleasant and
fanciful settings of Arden are gone, and into their place rushes
a natural world that is inscrutable, unpleasant, and intensely
realized.

This does not happen all at once. We first hear Lear, as he
flourishes his map, speaking of his kingdom in sweeping,
idealized terms:

> Of all these bounds, even from this line to this,
> With shadowy forests and with champains rich'd,
> With plenteous rivers and wide-skirted meads,
> We make thee lady.
>
> [1.1.63–66]

This, as it turns out, is as far from the reality as are Lear's
self-knowledge, his assessment of his daughters, and his belief
that love can be bargained for and measured in words. Shortly
before Lear's decision to "abjure all roofs . . . / To wage
against the enmity of the air; / To be a comrade with the
wolf and owl" (2.4.210–12), we have begun to hear from
Edgar, as he shifts to his guise of Poor Tom, of a different
setting:

> low farms,
> Poor pelting villages, sheep-cotes, and mills.
>
> [2.3.17–18]

It is Poor Tom's world that we are catapulted into, the most
realistic and unadorned environment an Elizabethan audience
could know, and it is part of Edgar's function to keep it
constantly before us, as an important underpinning to Lear's
extravagant nature of fen-suck'd fogs, cataracts and hurri-
canoes, and oak-cleaving thunderbolts.[17] It can, through

17. William Empson, in *The Structure of Complex Words* (London,
1951), speaking of the contemporaneity of Edgar as Poor Tom, comments:
"The shock of the thing depended on its realism; the lunatics which can
actually be met are meant to rise in the mind as standing metaphors for
cosmic affairs" (p. 137).

Shakespeare's absolute mastery of detail, be invoked with
brevity and simplicity:

> Alack! the night comes on, and the bleak winds
> Do sorely ruffle; for many miles about
> There's scarce a bush.

[2.4.302–04]

Or it can be as amply treated as in the great description of
the cliff at Dover, a landscape that is unparalleled in the literature of its age for realism, use of perspective, and imaginative strength. Most often, however, it is brought before us
by the simple and efficient device of listing, until we are sur-
rounded: with a whole menagerie of beasts, from cub-drawn
bear and belly-pinched wolf to the dogs (eight or nine breeds
are listed) who chase beggars; with a vivid awareness of ford,
whirlpool, bog and quagmire, the cold wind in the hawthorn
tree and the mildew on the white wheat; with the rank
fumiter and furrow-weeds, hardocks, nettles, cuckoo-flowers,
and darnel with which Lear crowns himself; and with the
unpleasant realities of Tom's diet:

> Poor Tom; that eats the swimming frog, the toad, the
> todpole, the wall-newt, and the water; that in the fury
> of his heart, when the foul fiend rages, eats cow-dung
> for sallets; swallows the old rat and the ditch-dog; drinks
> the green mantle of the standing pool; who is whipp'd
> from tithing to tithing, and stock-punish'd, and im-
> prison'd; who hath had three suits to his back, six shirts
> to his body,
>
> > Horse to ride, and weapons to wear,
> > But mice and rats and such small deer,
> > Have been Tom's food for seven long year.

[3.4.132–45]

The sharply realized natural world in *Lear*, even with its
"taking airs" and "wrathful skies," cannot be said to be hostile
to man; but it is certainly indifferent and, to those who are
unaccommodated, harsh and fearsome. That such knowledge
is the lesson of this pastoral sojourn is clear when Lear speaks
of his awakening from flattery and pomp:

> When the rain came to wet me once and the wind to
> make me chatter, when the thunder would not peace
> at my bidding, there I found 'em, there I smelt 'em out.
> Go to, they are not men o' their words: they told me
> I was every thing: 'tis a lie, I am not ague-proof.[4.6.
> 102–08]

It may seem that we are so far from the norm of Renaissance
pastoral romance at such moments that there is no point in
relating the play to the tradition. But the fact remains that
if there is a narrative and dramatic convention showing man
thrust out from society to the resources of nature, then what
happens in *Lear* is one of its possibilities. Those pastorals
which burlesqued the convention with realistic details and
characters took the same direction, if with less startling results. *As You Like It,* emphasizing the artifice of pastoral,
was the natural predecessor of *Lear*; the road to the heath
had been pointed out by Touchstone.

The same process of intensification that is used in the de-
lineation of natural setting is followed in the glimpses and
portraits of society. If these were more realistic than the forest
of Arden in *As You Like It,* with mewling and puking infants,
fat and greasy citizens, civet-perfumed courtiers and wives in
neighbors' beds, they were nevertheless kept at arm's length
by the atmosphere of good humor, by the equivocality of such
purveyors as Jaques, and by their subservience to the ideal of
love as tested by Rosalind. They qualified the fiction of pastoral without disrupting it. In *Lear* they are more vivid, more
numerous, and more unrelenting. They outweigh the details
of the natural setting, partly because they begin to come to
us earlier, as in Edmund's cynicisms about "whoremaster
man" and the Fool's continual references, from his first entrance, to a topsy-turvy society, partly because of the degree
to which they come to obsess Lear's imagination.

In accordance with Lear's change of awareness, the pictures
of man as social animal amidst his institutions and occupations increase in frequency as the play moves forward. Like
the details of natural setting they are sharply realistic, drawn
from the direct experience of an Elizabethan audience. And,

again, they may come in short, sharp glimpses (the Fool's unfee'd lawyer and eel-slapping cockney, Tom's rider "on a bay trotting-horse over four-inch'd bridges" and Flibberti-gibbet-possessed chambermaids and waiting-women, Glouces-ter's "superfluous and lust-dieted man") or in the amplitude of lists and catalogues. These latter are fascinating; they range from recitals like the Fool's "prophecy," which covers priests, brewers, nobles, tailors, heretics, suitors, squires, poor knights, cut-purses, usurers, bawds and whores, to detailed portraits like Kent's outburst at Oswald:

> A knave, a rascal, an eater of broken meats; a base, proud, shallow, beggarly, three-suited, hundred-pound, filthy worsted-stocking knave; a lily-livered, action-taking, whoreson, glass-gazing, super-serviceable, finical rogue; one-trunk-inheriting slave; one that wouldst be a bawd in way of good service, and art nothing but the composi-tion of a knave, beggar, coward, pandar, and the son and heir of a mongrel bitch: one whom I will beat into clamorous whining if thou deni'st the least syllable of thy addition. [2.2.13–23]

We can understand this startling and masterful piece of abuse much better if we recognize it as part of a pattern of evoca-tive pictures of society, and if we realize that Oswald stands in much the same relation to society as Poor Tom does to nature, as a representative figure around whom these clusters of detail can be grouped. It seems to be Oswald who is meant to come to mind again when Edgar as Tom describes his earlier self:

> A servingman, proud in heart and mind; that curl'd my hair, wore gloves in my cap, serv'd the lust of my mistress' heart, and did the act of darkness with her; swore as many oaths as I spake words, and broke them in the sweet face of Heaven; one that slept in the contriving of lust, and wak'd to do it. Wine lov'd I deeply, dice dearly, and in women out-paramour'd the Turk: false of heart, light of ear, bloody of hand; hog in sloth, fox in stealth, wolf in greediness, dog in madness, lion in prey. Let not

the creaking of shoes nor the rustling of silks betray thy
poor heart to woman: keep thy hand out of plackets, thy
pen from lenders' books, and defy the foul fiend. [3.4.
85–99]

This speech, with its superb detail and rhythmic organization,
has three sections, each typical of the detailing techniques
crucial to the style of *King Lear*: a portrait of the corrupt
servant, a list of his vices and metaphoric beast transformations, and a group of aphoristic warnings or "command-
ments." It has little to do with Edgar's character, or even with
his disguise, but a great deal to do with our sense of the world
of the play, and its pastoral triad of man, society, and nature.

Most of all it is from Lear's unfettered imagination that
the vision of man as creator and victim of corrupt social institutions comes to us, in fragments and flashes. While he begins
with farfetched references to "The barbarous Scythian, / Or
he that makes his generation messes," he is soon forced, by
his rapid descent of the social scale and his growing isolation,
to reassess his knowledge of society, even as he is reassessing
himself and the heaven and earth he took so largely for
granted. The process begins in his "reason not the need"
speech, and reaches its first peak as he stops to "pray" outside Tom's hovel:

Poor naked wretches, whereso'er you are,
That bide the pelting of this pitiless storm,
How shall your houseless heads and unfed sides,
Your loop'd and window'd raggedness, defend you
From seasons such as these? O! I have ta'en
Too little care of this. Take physic, Pomp;
Expose thyself to what the wretches feel,
That thou mayst shake the superflux to them,
And show the Heavens more just.

[3.4.28–36]

The insights of this moment, as many commentators have
noted, are emphasized by their reiteration in Gloucester's
speech (4.1.64 ff.).

If Lear's experience in the storm teaches him compassion

for the wretches, the later stage of his sojourn at the height
of his madness in the fields near Dover shows his understanding of society at its most comprehensive, combining scathing
indictments of corruption and hypocrisy with a general urge
to mercy. He pardons adultery even as he exposes the simper-
ing dame with the riotous appetite. Having surveyed the
"great image of Authority," dog and beggar, justice and thief,
beadle and whore, usurer and cozener, furred gowns and rags,
he adds, astonishing us, "None does offend, none, I say, none."
And a moment later he is back to the subject of the "scurvy
politician." Even as human corruption and vice are exposed
to us, we are urged to a more comprehensive understanding
based on the fact that all of us "came crying hither," to "this
great stage of fools." Lear is very near here to the final phase
of his imaginative relation to society, his willing renunciation
of it as he goes off to prison with Cordelia, where they will
"hear poor rogues / Talk of courts news" and wear out "packs
and sects of great ones / That ebb and flow by th' moon."
When we compare this with his initial wish to "Unburthen'd
crawl toward death" while retaining "The name and all th'
addition to a king," we can see how far he, and we, have come.
The renunciation of society and espousal of nature at the
heart of pastoral have been totally redefined. And the definition has yet another stage to go, for Lear's stretchings on "the
rack of this tough world" are not yet ended.

❦

King Lear, then, while it reflects the pastoral sequence of
extrusion and sojourn, and the thematic concern with man,
society, and nature such a sequence gives rise to, subjects these
familiar elements to a treatment far more searching and
disquieting than they received in *As You Like It.* As Maynard
Mack says:

> *King Lear* alludes to such patterns, it seems to me, but
> turns them upside down. It moves from extrusion not to
> pastoral, but to what I take to be the greatest anti-pas-
> toral ever penned. Lear's heath is the spiritual antipodes
> of the lush romance Arcadias. Nature proves to be in-

different or hostile, not friendly—yet curiously expressive, as in romance, of the protagonist's mental and emotional states. The figures are not Arcadian, but the
wretched fiend-haunted villagers of Edgar's hallucina-
tions. The reflections of his condition that Lear meets are
barrenness, tempest, and alienation, the defenseless suffering of his Fool, the madness of a derelict beggar who
is "the thing itself." [18]

Just how, we might then ask, does the play work itself out
against the traditional pattern it so radically transforms? I
think it can be argued that *King Lear* moves forward in a
series of peripeties, reversals not only of action but of expectation, ours and often those of the characters, and that
these reversals, while typical of the structure and atmosphere
of romance, are usually directed against the pastoral norm.
Again and again, just as the play seems about to settle into
a familiar groove of pastoral romance, it suddenly veers
sharply in a new direction. To be effective, such moments
must have settled expectations to move against. We cannot
appreciate a wolf in sheep's clothing unless we know what a
sheep is like. Nevertheless, it is not a part of my contention
that an audience of *Lear* must be thoroughly familiar with
pastoral romance. The process takes place at an almost subconscious level, and is safely built into the play. Nahum Tate
did not need to know much about pastoral romance in order
to restore the play to more conventional lines; the features he
sought were there already, and he had only to erase peripeties
and renew broken links.

The first major instance of this process comes with Lear's
extrusion. We have foreseen the event, but not the manner of
it. Kent and Cordelia have taken the blows of Fortune calmly;
Kent's stoicism is especially marked in his "Freedom lives
hence, and banishment is here" (cf. *AYLI*, 1.3.136) and "Fortune, good night; smile once more; turn thy wheel!" He and
Cordelia stand in a familiar pastoral contrast to the king, she
accused of "plainness" and Kent resolved that: "To plainness
honour's bound / When majesty falls to folly" (1.1.148–49).

18. Mack, pp. 65–66.

Edgar's adopted disguise has been more ominous, with its stretching of pastoral extremes and its emphasis on the suffering

> Of Bedlam beggars, who, with roaring voices,
> Strike in their numb'd and mortified bare arms
> Pins, wooden pricks, nails, sprigs of rosemary.
>
> [2.3.14–16]

But nothing, surely, can have quite prepared us for what happens to Lear. Instead of the decorous withdrawals of pastoral romance, we are given a scene of astonishing emotional power, building through some three hundred lines to a crescendo from which we are immediately plunged into the stormy heath scenes, where contact with nature takes on entirely new meanings as accompaniment to the king's intense suffering, and where madness seems not a striking *coup de théâtre* but the natural psychic concomitant to the social alienation we are witnessing.

Having reached this peak, the play seems likely to turn toward pastoral again, acclimatizing the king to a recognition that he is the man who "Must make content with his fortunes fit." And, indeed, that is the direction it takes as Lear calms down to recognize his surroundings and companions:

> I am cold myself. Where is this straw, my fellow?
> The art of our necessities is strange,
> And can make vile things precious. Come, your hovel.
>
> [3.2.69–71]

If Lear here and in his "poor naked wretches" speech seems, like Duke Senior, as though he is learning to "translate the stubbornness of fortune" and recognize the sweet uses of adversity, the expectation is shortlived. The entrance of Edgar as Poor Tom precipitates another violent swing away from the norm, driving Lear over the brink of sanity and back into his obsessive concern with his daughters. He will most emphatically *not* be "the pattern of all patience," and he will accept no pastoral consolations. The mock trial in the farmhouse follows.

Edgar is more willing to seek out consolations. He ends the

farmhouse scene with a soliloquy in couplets, reassuring himself with the fellowship of suffering and the likelihood of
justice. He is in the same vein when we see him next at the
beginning of act 4, scene 1. We have, meanwhile, witnessed
the scene of Gloucester's blinding, with its own series of
smaller reversals, from "I shall see / The winged vengeance
overtake such children. . . . See't thou shalt never" and "Edmund, enkindle all the sparks of nature / To quit this horrid
act. . . . Out, treacherous villain! / Thou call'st on him that
hates thee," to the rebellion of Cornwall's servant (one of the
few heartening surprises in the play), so that we are more prepared than Edgar for what is coming. Edgar is echoing the
traditional defense of pastoral, the idea that to be brought
low is at least to be out of Fortune's way; he could scarcely
have a ruder interruption:

> The lowest and most dejected thing of Fortune,
> Stands still in esperance, lives not in fear:
> The lamentable change is from the best;
> The worst returns to laughter. Welcome then,
> Thou unsubstantial air that I embrace:
> The wretch that thou hast blown unto the worst
> Owes nothing to thy blasts. But who comes here?

> *Enter Gloucester, led by an old Man.*

> My father, poorly led? World, world, O world!
> But that thy strange mutations make us hate thee,
> Life would not yield to age.

> [4.1.3–12]

The credulousness of which Edgar is accused by Edmund
tends to persist. He has a similar shock in act 4, scene 6, just
after he has succeeded in persuading his father that the
"clearest gods" have saved him and that he must be tame to
fortune's blows:

> *Edgar.* Bear free and patient thoughts. But who comes
> here?

> *Enter Lear, fantastically dressed with wild flowers.*

The safer sense will ne'er accommodate
His master thus.
    Lear. No, they cannot touch me for coining; I am the
king himself.
    Edgar. O thou side-piercing sight!

[4.6.80–85]

It is not until the final lines of the play (which are surely
Edgar's) that his comments seem entirely adequate to what
has happened and safe from this kind of contradiction.

The most terrible peripety of the play is of course Cordelia's death, and it too is preceded by an affirmation of pastoral value that is bound to give us hope. Lear and Cordelia
are being led to prison rather than exile, but their sentiments
are nonetheless those of the pastoral ideal. Cordelia has said,
in couplets, that she can "out-face false Fortune's frown," but
is concerned for her father, who is still, we are reminded, an
"oppressed King." Lear's answer, with its renunciation of the
world, is genuine and moving:

No, no, no, no! Come, let's away to prison;
We two alone will sing like birds i' the cage;
When thou dost ask me blessing, I'll kneel down,
And ask of thee forgiveness: so we'll live,
And pray, and sing, and tell old tales, and laugh
At gilded butterflies, and hear poor rogues
Talk of court news; and we'll talk with them too,
Who loses and who wins; who's in, who's out;
And take upon 's the mystery of things,
As if we were Gods' spies: and we'll wear out,
In a wall'd prison, packs and sects of great ones
That ebb and flow by th' moon.

[5.3.8–19]

Lear, like Edgar, hopes that humility and renunciation will
take them finally out of Fortune's way, leaving them the
deeper values associated with birds, butterflies, prayers, songs,
old tales, and "the mystery of things." One last awful reversal
follows, grimly emphasized by Albany's plea, "The Gods de-

fend her!", just as Lear enters with the dead Cordelia in his
arms. Kent's horrified question, "Is this the promis'd end?",
is not only a reference to the Last Judgment; it is a final reminder of shattered expectations, of the lost consolations of
fiction. It refers us inevitably to the story that has unfolded
so jarringly on the stage and its relation to the stories we tell
ourselves about the universe, the gods, the nature of Nature
and the face of Fortune. The point is driven home with a
finality that makes our sense of the difference between wish
and fact, fiction and reality, unforgettable. The story is open-
ended, unresolvable. Albany makes a gallant attempt at the
characteristic pick-up-the-pieces closing speech of tragedy, but
again the reality before him interrupts:

> *Albany.* . . . you, to your rights,
> With boot and such addition as your honours
> Have more than merited. All friends shall taste
> The wages of their virtue, and all foes
> The cup of their deservings. O! see, see!
> *Lear.* And my poor fool is hang'd! No, no, no life!
> [5.3.300–05] [19]

Some critics have professed to find in this final scene, and
in the play as a whole, an assertion of orthodox Christian
consolation, but I do not see how they manage this. Shakespeare is attacking the pastoral values and the guarantees of
convention, but he supplies nothing in their place. To do so,
indeed, would vitiate the quality of his achievement, trading
one set of consolations for another. The difference between
Lear and such schematized dramas of ideas as morality plays
ought surely to be obvious. In a morality play the odds are
fixed, the outcome certain; the clash of ideas can produce
only one result, and the play exists to demonstrate a known
and accepted doctrine. The strength and terror of *King Lear*
lies in its doing just the opposite: keeping us uncertain, destroying guarantees, exposing assumptions, reversing our
hopes and expectations. In that sense it is closer to the mys-

19. Cf. John Shaw, *"King Lear*: The Final Lines," *Essays in Criticism*
16 (July 1966):261–67.

terious, unpredictable world of the romance, but with even
the romance's escape clause, the assurance of ultimate resolution, removed.

❧

When we have recognized that *King Lear* employs the pastoral pattern in order to negate it, that it denies its characters and audience the consolations supposed to accompany
poverty, isolation, and humiliation, that it suggests that renunciation is no insurance against suffering, we are a long
way toward identifying its central vision. Having disrupted
and challenged the conventions of pastoral, *Lear* drives on
to challenge its basic assumption about the essential harmony
of man and nature. Critics agree that the play is in large
measure about the nature of Nature, but what Nature finally
is remains a matter of considerable controversy. Perhaps it
is more profitable to ask what it is *not,* a question that the
play's relation to pastoral makes easier to pose and, I think, to
answer.

Nature in *King Lear* is not, first of all, what most of the
characters hope and believe it to be, a material and metaphysical backing for their own needs and desires. Both the
good and evil characters share an illusion of partnership with
nature that is exposed as unfounded. Lear and Gloucester see
Nature as origin and guardian of the social system which has
given them their power and authority, and they accordingly
expect it to punish "unnatural" and "unkind" behavior in
their children. Subsequent events do little to justify their
view. In fact, since both discover that they have been harbor-
ing illusions about their children, they are forced to abandon
their confidence in vengeance and natural justice in the
process of questioning themselves and their disastrous assumptions.

Edmund, spokesman for the evil characters, sees through
the illusions held by his father and the King, and consequently rests his hopes on the view that Nature will justify
and further his villainy, his "aspiring mind" and unfettered
Machiavellianism. But while his understanding of nature

seems keener and less illusion-ridden than his father's, the
events of the play do no more, other than temporarily, to
vindicate his sense of partnership, and he abandons it in
defeat. Direct appeals to Nature, in whatever form, do not
work for anyone in *King Lear*. Lear's thunderous curses are
answered simply by thunder, and when Edmund admits that
"The wheel has come full circle," he seems to recognize that
the goddess Nature he prayed to was Fortune in disguise, she
who "reigns in gifts of the world, not in the lineaments of
Nature" (*AYLI*, 1.2.45).

But when these views have been abandoned, there is a
second, and subtler, line of defense for the belief that man
has an essential harmony with Nature, and that is provided
through the experience of Lear's pastoral sojourn. As he
moves away from society to the isolation of the heath and the
buffeting of the storm, Lear learns that sometimes "man's life
is cheap as beast's," that "unaccommodated man is no more
but such a poor, bare, forked animal." A more profound kinship with Nature is thus suggested, one that takes into account Edmund's view as soon as Lear is willing to ask "Is
there any cause in nature that makes these hard hearts?"

The insights produced in the course of Lear's sojourn are
powerful and attractive, not least because Lear comes to have
strong symbolic associations with Nature in his own person.
"Nature in you," Regan tells him, "stands on the very verge /
Of her confine." This takes on new meaning when Gloucester
echoes it in the fields near Dover:

> O ruin'd piece of Nature! This great world
> Shall so wear out to naught.
>
> [4.6.136–37]

The decay of Lear is somehow the decay of Nature. He has
moved beyond the "safer sense" into a role of greater propor-
tions than his former kingship. Shakespeare draws upon myth
and folklore to strengthen the association. Dressed in his
weeds and wildflowers Lear is a kind of Summer King, center
of a ceremony for expressing the bond of human life to the

natural rhythms.[20] As an outcast king he is, in the Fool's image, a great wheel rolling downhill, as in the Midsummer ritual, where the burning wheel was both sun-symbol and instrument of purification.[21] Shakespeare had already used the image in *Hamlet,* where "majesty" is seen as:

> a massy wheel
> Fixed on the summit of the highest mount,
> To whose huge spokes ten thousand lesser things
> Are mortised and adjoined; which when it falls
> Each small annexment, petty consequence,
> Attends the boist'rous ruin.

[2.3.17–22]

At Dover, Lear's talk about authority makes him a kind of Lord of Misrule; in his Quibbling and inverting he adopts the function of his own Fool. When his pursuers arrive he says, "I am even / The natural fool of Fortune," Fortune's victim but nonetheless possessing, without dignity or rights, a deep-seated kinship with Nature.

20. Cf. John Holloway, *The Story of the Night* (London, 1961). Dressed in wildflowers and weeds, Lear is "a Jack-a-Green, at once hero and victim of a popular ceremony" (p. 97).

21. To my knowledge, the connection between the Fool's image ("Let go thy hold when a great wheel runs down a hill, lest it break thy neck with following" [2.4.71]) and the Midsummer custom has never been cited. That it was common in Shakespeare's England and that its implications were at least partly understood, is indicated by Barnabe Googe's translation (from Latin) of Thomas Kirchmayer's *The Popish Kingdome* (1570):

> Some others get a rotten wheele, all worne and cast aside,
> Which covered round about with strawe, and tow, they closely hide:
> And caryed to some mountaines top, being all with fire light,
> They hurle it down with violence, when darke appears the night:
> Resembling much the Sunne, that from the heaven downe should fal,
> A straunge and monstrous sight it seemes, and fearful to them all:
> But they suppose their mischiefes all are like wise throwne to hell,
> And that from harmes and daungers now, in safetie here they dwell.

See Frazer, *The Golden Bough,* vol. 10, *Balder the Beautiful,* pp. 16–219, and E. O. James, *Seasonal Feasts and Festivals* (London, 1961), p. 314. With the wheel of Fortune motif (and cf. *Hamlet,* 2.2.517 f.) and the Ixion image (4.7.46 f.), the wheel associations in *Lear* are extremely complex.

Lear's transformation is a moving and meaningful process, a rapid tide in which we are swept willingly along. It leads, when his sanity is restored and he is reunited with Cordelia, to his renunciation of power, his decision to remain a fool, laughing at gilded butterflies and taking upon himself "the mystery of things," as if he were a spy of the gods. If that were the end of the play we would perhaps be safe in assuming that Lear's new relation to Nature, and intimate understanding of it, is the true one. But that there is more to come should perhaps be clear to us from that touch of his old defiance as he and Cordelia are led away:

> Upon such sacrifices, my Cordelia,
> The Gods themselves throw incense. Have I caught thee?
> He that parts us shall bring a brand from heaven,
> And fire us hence like foxes. Wipe thine eyes;
> The good years shall devour them, flesh and fell,
> Ere they shall make us weep: we'll see 'em starved first.
>
> [5.3.20–25]

Nature, he implies, is finally on his side, and nothing but a divine contravention of its laws could undo their bond. In a play whose characters have suffered again and again the exposure of their false confidence about nature, such sentiments are bound to be dangerous. The death of Cordelia must force us to reassess what we have seen. In the light of it *King Lear* appears as a play in which man and nature keep coming together, only to be inexorably separated:

> Why should a dog, a horse, a rat, have life
> And thou no breath at all?
>
> [5.3.306–07]

It is a terrible question, more terrible than its complement, "Is this the promis'd end?" The death of someone like Cordelia ought to crack the vault of heaven; we feel Lear is right to say so. But we also know, from our spectator's perspective, that it will not, nor will the thunder peace at our bidding. "Nature's above art in that respect."

The fact that the play ends, after all of Lear's searching and

learning and redefinition, with a failure to identify man and
nature, with a vision of human isolation, surely gives a full
and final meaning to the notion of pastoral tragedy. In this
respect one of the most astute comments on the play is that
of Edwin Muir, in his autobiography:

> The animal world is a great impersonal order, without
> pathos in its suffering. Man is bound to it by necessity
> and guilt, and by the closer bond of life, for he breathes
> the same breath. But when man is swallowed up in
> nature nature is corrupted and man is corrupted. The
> sense of corruption in *King Lear* comes from the fact that
> Goneril, Regan and Cornwall are merely animals fur-
> nished with human faculties as with weapons which they
> have stolen, not inherited . . . They are so *unnatural*
> in belonging completely to nature that Gloucester can
> explain them only by "these late eclipses in the sun and
> moon." . . . The conflict in *Lear* is a conflict between
> the sacred tradition of human nature, which is old, and
> nature, which is always new, for it has no background.[22]

This throws a new light on Lear's horrified comment to his
daughters, "Allow not nature more than nature needs, / Man's
life is cheap as beast's." The first nature, as G. K. Hunter has
pointed out, is "human nature," the second "animal nature." [23] This is exactly what happens in *King Lear*. As the
fiction that the "sacred tradition of human nature" extends to
the natural world becomes insupportable, an identification of
man with the animal world is pressed, one that is something
like the opposite of conventional pastoral idealization. But it
cannot be sustained, as Edmund's career, for example, proves.
Edmund penetrates the fiction that human nature and the
universe it inhabits are not at harmony, but he overlooks the
fact that he cannot change his allegiance because that would
involve changing his own nature. The "plague of custom"
and "the curiosity of nations" are man-made, but Edmund,

22. Edwin Muir, *An Autobiography* (London, 1954), p. 53.
23. Cited by Kenneth Muir in the Arden edition ("Additional Notes,"
p. 258, 1962). He gives no source.

after all, is a man. He too must turn eventually to human relationship for comfort—"Yet Edmund was belov'd"—and
there is a terrible irony in the way he clings to his earlier
belief—"Some good I mean to do / Despite of mine own nature"—in his final decision.

Even the evil characters thus help to show that human
nature and animal nature are not the same. Man's life is not
as cheap as beast's unless he makes it so, and there is a difference, after all, between a dog, a horse, a rat, and Cordelia.
But this recognition does not return the play to orthodoxy.
There is no suggestion that the "tradition" of human nature
has outside support. The comments about the gods jostle and
contradict, canceling each other out. Lear's last appeal is not
to the heavens but to those about him:

> Howl, howl, howl! O! you are men of stones:
> Had I your tongues and eyes, I'd use them so
> That heaven's vault should crack.
>
> [5.3.257–59]

There is no more conversation with the elements, no further
speculation about divine justice and natural law. The last
scene shows only a few men, struggling to communicate
among themselves, alone with the weight of "this sad time."

❧

No careful reader of this great play will find it totally
pessimistic, all "dark and cheerless." But the last scene poses
a hard question: what is left to man when he finds himself
alone in a universe that differs radically from his own nature?
How does he deal with the fact that there is no check on his
capacity for evil, no outside encouragement to his capacity
for good? If answers exist at all in *King Lear* they are oblique
and tentative, and it is in that spirit that they must be
presented. All can be said to fall, I think, under Muir's
category of "the sacred tradition of human nature."

There is first our common condition. *King Lear* sweeps
aside the differences between king and beggar, justice and
thief, beadle and whore, to expose the conditions of existence

which they share. All are poor, bare, forked creatures, all
can say:

> we came crying hither:
> Thou know'st the first time that we smell the air
> We wawl and cry.
>
> [4.6.180–82]

All share the fact of birth and the burden of death, all must
endure their going hence, even as their coming hither. The
word *man* echoes again and again in the later scenes of the
play, emphasizing this context of the "little world of man":

> Why this would make a man a man of salt. . . .
> A most poor man, made tame to Fortune's blows. . . .
> I am a very foolish fond old man. . . .
> For, as I am a man, I think this lady
> To be my child Cordelia. . . .
> What! in ill thoughts again? Men must endure. . . .

Sometimes it has an irony that makes us wince:

> O! the difference of man and man. . . .
> I cannot draw a cart nor eat dried oats;
> If it be man's work I'll do it. . . .

There is no idealizing of "man" in *King Lear,* as its central
character clearly demonstrates. Lear is hero of this tragedy,
finally, not because he is a king but because he is a man, with
an imperfect sense of the human condition, perhaps, but with
an enormous power to represent it. "Man's nature cannot
carry," says Kent in the storm, "Th'affliction nor the fear."
In Lear it can and does, and it is his striving "in his little
world of man to out-storm / The to-and-fro-conflicting wind
and rain" that makes him such an expressive emblem of
humanity.

If man has little kinship with the elements, his kinship
with other men is the more important. From the general
sense of the shared features of the human condition grows a
particular regard for the value of human relationships, the
bonds and ties with which men express their interdependence

and sympathy. *Lear,* as several critics have noted, is an extremely complex study of the nature and value of these bonds of family and service "as the ultimate reality for human beings." [24] Important as they may be, they are precarious and, at times, equivocal; in this area, too, no easy answers are forthcoming. Service, in the person of Kent, is unquestionably a good, but in Oswald it is a part of evil, and in the case of Cornwall's servant it must be abandoned unilaterally for the sake of a more fundamental human bond. Lear, anxious to go to prison with Cordelia and unwilling to see "these daughters and these sisters," envisions the maintenance of one perfect relationship with his daughter. It would not be right to say that Shakespeare punishes him for "dropping out" in this way, but the play certainly shows us what Cordelia knew from the beginning, that the idealizing of isolated ties is no key to human happiness. The difficulties and ambiguities of human relatedness do not, however, obscure its importance and value; they merely emphasize that we dare not refer it for its continuity and meaning to natural or supernatural sources, and that we cannot excuse its lapses as eclipses of the sun and moon.

Finally, to separate himself from the beasts and to sustain his sacred tradition, man has his imagination. Much good it does him, might be our first reaction, in light of the proliferating and destructive illusions in *King Lear.* Most of the characters use their imaginations to deceive themselves or to practice on others. They resort to comforts and fictions about themselves and their world that are time and again exposed as false. Lear dies happy, but only because he has managed to convince himself momentarily that his daughter is not dead. It is the last effort of a powerful imagination that has resorted to almost every conceivable means—theology, philosophy, madness, idealizations of love, nature, and justice—to protect itself from the truth.

But to admit this much is not to close the subject of the value of imagination in *King Lear.* I referred earlier to the way Kent's question, "Is this the promis'd end?" suggests an

24. Mack, p. 102.

analogy between the story on the stage and the stories we tell ourselves about the nature of Nature. The point, perhaps, is not that they are valueless or meaningless, but that they *are* ours and they *are* stories. The failure to recognize them on these terms is demonstrably dangerous. Acknowledged as such, they begin to take on value. The process can be demonstrated by reference to one of the most puzzling scenes of the play, Edgar's elaborate charade at the scene of his blind father's "suicide." It has struck some readers as a kind of tasteless practical joke, others as an emblem of purgatorial suffering. Clearly, Edgar intends it as a demonstration that "the clearest Gods, who make them honours / Of men's impossibilities, have preserv'd thee," and indeed the incident succeeds in persuading Gloucester to "bear / Affliction till it do cry out itself / 'Enough, enough,' and die." Edgar achieves his end, in other words, by an enormous effort of imagination and a deliberate use of illusion. Before we object to the deception, we would do well to remember that, in the absence of "the clearest Gods," Edgar has little else to resort to to make his father's suffering bearable or comprehensible. The Olympian perspective we enjoyed in *As You Like It* is not so comfortable here. We are not Gloucester, who thinks the gods have saved him, but Edgar, who knows it is a fiction. Whether or not we prefer such a vantage point, Shakespeare provides it. And he also allows us to differentiate between Edgar's deception of his father and Edmund's. The imagination is a powerful instrument and a necessary component in human existence. Its value depends on the user. Throughout the play the good characters resort to it for disguises, deceptions, for desperate responses to experience. If Lear's tortured imagination is in part employed to protect him from the truth, it is also the means by which the play becomes comprehensive, the source of its insights into man, society, and nature. Imagination in *Lear* is not salvation; there remains about it something fundamentally ambiguous and disturbing. But there are moments when it seems to emerge as one of the play's chief values.

Such considerations lead us inevitably to the subject of art

and to the play itself as value. If we say that the characters
in *Lear* must deceive themselves in order to survive or bear
their suffering, that is the same as saying that, for the moment, at least, we do not. We are not Gloucester but Edgar,
and more than Edgar, for he too is bewildered and deceived.
It is the play, the fact that it is a play, that makes our knowledge possible. I am not urging that this makes all the difference. I have already warned against trading one set of consolations for another, and *Lear* no more pins all our hopes
on the aesthetic than it does on the theological. But our
response to it inevitably mingles our terror and pity, our
sense of lost illusions, with our pleasure at its courage, depth,
and intensity, in short, at its artistic excellence. It makes
possible an experience and a set of insights that would otherwise be too costly to welcome or want. And that fact, if it
does not sweep away what we find in the play to call tragic,
belongs to those few things we can balance against the darkness when we face the "promised end" or consider what it is
that makes a man more than a dog, a horse, or a rat. Something like this is implied, I think, in Keats's famous sonnet
about *King Lear,* a poem so perceptive about the play and its
issues that I wish to quote it in full:

> O Golden-tongued Romance, with serene Lute!
>   Fair plumed Syren, Queen of far-away!
>   Leave melodizing on this wintry day
> Shut up thine olden pages and be mute.
> Adieu! for, once again, the fierce dispute
>   Betwixt Damnation and impassion'd clay
>   Must I burn through; once more humbly assay
> The bitter-sweet of this Shakespearean fruit.
> Chief Poet! and ye Clouds of Albion,
>   Begetters of our deep eternal theme!
> When through the old oak forest I am gone,
>   Let me not wander in a barren dream:
> But when I am consumed in the fire,
>   Give me new Phoenix Wings to fly at my desire.[25]

25. As written in his *Shakespeare* facing the first page of *Lear.* See
D. G. James, "Keats and *King Lear,*" *Shakespeare Survey* 13 (1960):58–68.

There is a strong sense here, as in the "Ode to a Nightingale," of the separate "traditions" of animal and human nature. Lear cannot escape the destruction of time and fortune, but the play, as a work of art, offers the miracle of recurrent experience ("once again, the fierce dispute") stripped of its destructive character. Yet each encounter, each assay, can be hazardous. The old oak forest is a fearsome place. So the sestet moves into the subjunctive, with a wishful prayer that the cycle of destruction and renewal made possible by great art be repeated, in turn strengthening Keats's own creativity, his "Phoenix Wings" and poetic ambition. Like the nightingale's song, *Lear* is timeless and timely, outside of human time but in this case of human creation (unlike the nightingale) and available to human experience.[26] The emphasis on art and artifice in the late plays, and their primitivism, their use of old, durable motifs, is surely related to this insight of Keats about the true value and meaning of *King Lear*. The path through the oak forest leads on toward *The Winter's Tale* and *The Tempest*.[27]

26. Francis Berry, *Poets' Grammar* (London, 1958), contrasting the Indicative ("the Mood of facts, of actuality, of what has been, is, and will be") and the Subjunctive ("comes to signify that which is NOT . . . the mood of the possible . . . of hope . . . of despair . . . of frustrate desire . . . of morality. It is the Mood of that which lies outside time"), p. 7, suggests, in his analysis of the "Ode to a Nightingale" the existence of a third Mood "wherein desire and possession are both real" (p. 139). He believes that the late plays "are a testimony of a revived belief in the Subjunctive" (p. 69). See below, chapter 4, note 23.

27. Since writing this chapter, I have come across Alvin Kernan's "Formalism and Realism in Elizabethan Drama: The Miracles in *King Lear*," *Renaissance Drama* (1966):59–66. In this very perceptive account of "the tension between formalism and realism" Kernan uses the Dover Cliff scene (5.6.) to show how Shakespeare "openly dramatizes" the divisive tendencies of his art. Noting the difficulty of staging the scene, he remarks "I would suppose that the awkwardness, i.e. the stylization, would be part of the point" (note, p. 62). My agreement with this view, and my sense of its importance not only to *Lear* but to all the plays discussed in this study and the trend of development that leads from *As You Like It* to *The Tempest*, will be discussed more fully in the following chapter.

4

The Argument of Time: *The Winter's Tale*

I saw a show once, at the marriage of Magnificero's daughter, presented by Time, which Time was an old bald thing, a servant.

Marston, *The Insatiate Countess*

Art, the antidote against fortune

On rolling ball doth fickle fortune stande;
on firm and settled square sitts *Mercurie*,
The god of Arts. with wisdomes rodd in hande:
which covertlie to us doth signifie,
that fortunes power, unconstant and still frayle,
against wisdome and art cannot prevaile.

Francis Thynne, *Emblems and Epigrames,* 1600

To criticize the last plays in terms of the formal requirements of romance and the emotional response of the audience seems to me a very strenuous task considering the temptations we are exposed to of taking short cuts to Shakespeare's vision. But it is probably the only way of not falsifying those moments in these fantastic plays when Shakespeare's verse rarefies the air and we know perfectly well that something important is being said.

Philip Edwards

Because *The Winter's Tale* belongs to the group of late plays known as the Romances, in which it has long been acknowledged that Shakespeare was employing the materials of popular romance, including those of the pastoral romance, it is necessary to say something about the group as a whole before moving on to particulars about one or more of its members. This task is much simplified by the efforts of recent criticism. The long-standing opinion that Shakespeare resorted to narrative romance from some weakness—exhaustion, boredom, the constraint of fashion, or a sort of relentless optimism born of old age—has largely vanished, replaced in this century by increasing respect and enthusiasm. Efforts to reclaim the Romances as major works have sometimes been singularly misguided, but most have shared the prerequisite of adequate criticism, a willingness to examine the plays in their own right rather than berate them for not resembling, say, the Tragedies.[1]

At the same time that the Romances have been granted their right to uniqueness, however, it has been recognized that they do not differ as radically from Shakespeare's earlier works as had often been supposed. Shakespeare's interest in romance was lifelong, and the kinship among such plays as *The Two Gentlemen of Verona, The Merchant of Venice, King Lear, All's Well That Ends Well,* and *Cymbeline* is its result. The deep well of folklore and fairy tale that supplied the romance tradition was not something Shakespeare came late to; it served him throughout his career.

What does distinguish the late Romances from the rest of the canon, is the prominence given to the patterns and conventions of narrative romance. A kind of primitivism envelops these plays. Folktale motifs, episodic construction, wild improbabilities, patterns of action which rob characters of individuality and dimension, imposed and arbitrary symbolism: all these archaic features, transcended or neatly absorbed in Shakespeare's earlier use of romance, are brought to the foreground. No wonder that commentators argued for a falling-off of skill and interest. Some such reaction may have been current among Shakespeare's contemporaries. There is something almost bewildered in Ben Jonson's gibe that Shakespeare was willing to "make nature afraid" with "tales, tempests, and such like drolleries, to mix his head with other men's heels." [2] The verisimilitude and adherence to classical unities which Jonson preached were rapidly becoming the theoretical order of the day, and Shakespeare is perhaps more accurately seen

1. A useful survey of critical viewpoints can be found in Philip Edwards, "Shakespeare's Romances: 1900–1957," *Shakespeare Survey* 11 (1958):1–18.
2. In the Induction to *Bartholomew Fair.*

as bucking the fashion than succumbing to it—the intellectual fashion, at any rate. The question of popular fashion is less easily answered. But no one, it seems, is any longer content to think of the late plays simply as potboilers.

The primitivism of these plays is surely deliberate. It seeks our attention and invites our participation. The archaic elements are not meant to be ignored but to be studied and pondered. An atmosphere of double consciousness is thus evoked. On the one hand we share the wonder, delight, and mystery of these old stories and fabulous moments; and on the other, simultaneously, we see them from a sophisticated perspective, aware of their peculiarities and limitations.[3] The note is struck in the opening lines of *Pericles,* when Gower, poet of an earlier age, steps before us as presenter:

> To sing a song that old was sung,
> From ashes ancient Gower is come,
> Assuming man's infirmities,
> To glad your ears and please your eyes.
> It hath been sung at festivals,
> On ember-eves and holy-ales;
> And lords and ladies in their lives
> Have read it for restoratives.
> The purchase is to make men glorious;
> Et bonum quo antiquius, eo melius.
> If you, born in these latter times,
> When wit's more ripe, accept my rhymes,
> And that to hear an old man sing
> May to your wishes pleasure bring,
> I life would wish, and that I might
> Waste it for you, like taper-light.
>
> [Induction, 1–16]

3. A number of commentators have noted this quality, among them Frank Kermode, *Shakespeare: The Final Plays,* Writers and Their Work, no. 155 (London, 1963)—"There is an element of play in the Romances, as of a master examining his medium in an unusually detached, experimental way" (p. 8)—and E. C. Pettet, *Shakespeare and the Romance Tradition*—"There is remoteness; what we are listening to is, after all, only a play" (p. 178).

The device is old, the verse archaic; within it is expressed a clear interest in the deepest motives of art and the history of their expression. It is in part the durability of Gower's material that is to be investigated and demonstrated. What gives such old stories their lasting popularity? What value can they be said to contain? How are they related to social rituals and ceremonies—festivals, ember-eves, holy-ales—which have survived from the distant past? Can they be retold so as to maintain their appeal for riper wits and latter times? Shakespeare's interest in such questions ought not to baffle a century which has seen such a widespread revival of interest in the primitive, in the fundamental resources and motives of man's artistic activity.

Gower's lines serve to remind us of earlier moments in Shakespeare's work: of the clumsy old play performed at the heart of *Hamlet*; of Richard II's "For God's sake let us sit upon the ground / And tell sad stories of the death of kings"; of Lear's late desire to "Pray, and sing, and tell old tales, and laugh / At gilded butterflies"; of the wonderfully tender lines in *Twelfth Night*:

> O fellow, come, the song we had last night.
> Mark it, Cesario; it is old and plain;
> The spinsters and the knitters in the sun
> And the free maids that weave their threads with bones,
> Do use to chant it; it is silly sooth
> And dallies with the innocence of love,
> Like the old age.
>
> [2.4.41–47]

But the difference is that in the late Romances this interest has become a major preoccupation, one that remains in force from the opening lines of *Pericles* to the closing speech of *The Tempest*. Hence the emphatic and open use of artifice; hence the resort to archaic devices and conventions which a playwright as sophisticated and ingenious as Shakespeare need never have turned to for convenience or from laziness; hence the storms, the theophanies, the lost princess, the dances, ma-

gicians, choruses, flowers, and music; hence those stage direc-
tions which still astonish readers and baffle producers:

> *Diana appears to Pericles as in a vision.*

> *Exit, pursued by a bear.*

*Jupiter descends in thunder and lightning, sitting upon an
eagle.*

*A noise of hunters heard. Enter divers Spirits in shape of dogs
and hounds, hunting them about; Prospero and Ariel setting them on.*

The late plays are experiments in the fabulatory, investiga-
tions of the fictive, and, lest they begin to sound too studious,
celebrations of the human imagination.

In stressing Shakespeare's conscious use of the archaic in
these plays, I have not meant to suggest that they are in any
sense attempts at pure and faithful re-creation of the worlds
of Greek or Medieval or Renaissance romance. On the contrary, the double consciousness is possible only because of
their extraordinary sophistication. The highly conventional
patterns of romance coexist with moments of remarkable psychological and social verisimilitude. The notorious difficulty
of the verse is a reflection of a complexity and thoughtfulness
which are far from typical of the romance tradition.[4] A chia-
roscuro of old and new, primitive and sophisticated, artificial
and realistic, prevails. It is useful in this connection to consider Maynard Mack's suggestion that "engagement and detachment" and the tension created between them are typical
of Shakespeare's art. The poles of Shakespeare's style, in his
view, are the "emblematic" and the "psychological." Noting
that the former is "an instrument of detachment," he adds:

> Insisting on artifice, it increases our "distance" from the
> stage and makes us reflect on meaning, as Brecht desires.
> Conversely, the psychological style serves the end of en-

4. Although by no means foreign to it, as the examples of Sidney and
Spenser indicate. Cf. Kermode, p. 10.

gagement, tends to draw us in and make us share the experiences we watch, become the person we behold.[5]

In the late plays engagement and detachment in both structure and style are more pronounced, more taut and stretched. We are hurled more suddenly from one to the other. No wonder that commentators have resisted, have tried to cling to one pole (the late plays are profound religious allegories) or the other (Shakespeare was bored, senile, a slave to fashion). We cannot do justice to these plays unless we are ready to admit their scope, to understand the engagement *and* the detachment, to admit their coexistence and tension, and to avoid mistaking either one for the other.

What is the relation of pastoral to these late Romances? While it becomes, as I hope to show, extremely crucial to them, it is not present from the beginning. *Pericles* makes no use of it, but confines itself to an exploration of the pattern of Greek romance, the oldest and perhaps simplest representative of the tradition. Pericles' buffetings and reversals send him all over the Adriatic, but they do not include any interludes that could be described as pastoral sojourns. And Marina's dislocation takes her not to a wilderness or an Arcadia but to a city brothel. *Pericles* seems to be an experiment in transferring the older narrative romance, with its string of fantastic episodes, to the stage with a minimum of alteration. Whatever its problems of text and authorship, it is absurd to suppose that Shakespeare, once his hand was in it, could not have made it more like a conventional play if such had been his intention. And the power of its final scenes, along with the

---

5. "Engagement and Detachment in Shakespeare's Plays," in *Essays on Shakespeare and Elizabethan Drama in Honor of Hardin Craig*, ed. Hosley (Columbia, Mo., 1963), pp. 275–96. Passages cited are from p. 295. A somewhat similar point is made by S. L. Bethell, "Shakespeare's Actors," *Review of English Studies*, 1 n.s. 3 (July 1950):193–205: "The essential difference between naturalistic and conventional drama is that the latter demands of the audience a 'multi-conscious' response. . . . Fundamental to all multi-consciousness is the dual consciousness of real world and play world. 'Dramatic illusion' must not be complete—or virtually complete—as in naturalism, or the multi-conscious response would be impossible" (p. 202).

indications of its contemporary popularity, bespeak at least
partial success.[6] *Pericles* is the simplest and most primitive of
the late Romances, and as such, a crucial piece of groundwork.

The combination of pastoral with narrative romance opened
up new formal and intellectual opportunities for both genres,
so it was natural that as Shakespeare pursued his exploration
of the possibilities of re-creating romance more directly for the
stage, pastoral should begin to make its appearance. This is
the case in *Cymbeline,* where he casts a wide net that pulls in
the legendary history so closely allied to romance, the folk
motif of Leonatus' wager, and the pastoral figurations of
Imogen's exile and sojourn and Belarius' long spell as a
hermit, raising the lost sons of the king. Pastoral sentiments
begin to make themselves felt quite early in the play:

> Would I were
> A neat-herd's daughter, and my Leonatus
> Our neighbor-shepherd's son!
>
> [1.2.79–81]

> Had I been thief-stolen,
> As my two brothers, happy; but most miserable
> Is my desire that's glorious. Bless'd be those,
> How mean so'er, that have their honest wills,
> Which seasons comfort.
>
> [1.7.5–9]

Such responses come naturally to Imogen as her difficulties
mount, but the chief spokesman for pastoral values is Belarius,
who seldom misses an opportunity to draw our attention to
his moral and intellectual position:

6. "Even if we suppose that it is only with the third act that Shakespeare's work begins, we may still see that what now follows exploits what
has gone before, and for all the burst of dramatic intensity in this scene,
there is afterwards, and to the end, a continual return to the original
narrative manner" (John Arthos, "*Pericles, Prince of Tyre:* A Study in the
Dramatic Use of Romantic Narrative," *Shakespeare Quarterly* 4 [1953]:257–
70, esp. p. 263). A similar view is held by Howard Felperin, "Shakespeare's
Miracle Play," *Shakespeare Quarterly* 18 (1967):363–74, but Felperin assumes, I think wrongly, that the "deliberate archaism" invites an allegorical
reading.

> O, this life
> Is nobler than attending for a check;
> Richer than doing nothing for a robe,
> Prouder than rustling in unpaid-for silk.
>
> [3.3.21–24]

Two factors incline us to respond with detachment to such utterances: their sententious quality and the fact that they seldom go unchallenged:

> Haply this life is best
> (If quiet life be best) sweeter to you
> That have a sharper known, well corresponding
> With your stiff age; but unto us it is
> A cell of ignorance, travelling a-bed,
> A prison, or a debtor that not dares
> To stride a limit.
>
> [29–35]

Thus the relativity inherent in the pastoral, so succesfully cultivated in *As You Like It* and *Lear,* blooms again. And its presence is quite in keeping with the general mood of *Cymbeline,* where a spirit of detachment seems to prevail, a spirit most evident, perhaps, in the scenes where a strong emotional potential is checked by the audience's superior knowledge of circumstances. The scene of mourning for Imogen is tender and very touching (Arviragus' entrance bearing her in his arms seems a deliberate echo of *Lear*), but it is colored and distanced by our knowledge that Imogen is not dead. The same effect is achieved in the following sequence, where Imogen's grieving for Posthumus is directed at the headless corpse of Cloten.[7] Such moments send us skidding between sorrow and amusement, and substantiate the claim that Shakespeare's 'art of multiplicity' reached a culmination in the late plays. The difference between *Pericles* and *Cymbeline* is significant in this

7. J. P. Brockbank, "History and Histrionics in *Cymbeline,*" *Shakespeare Survey* 11 (1959):42–49, notes: "The prevailing transparency of artifice makes me suspect that the 'clotpole' stage head was deliberately displayed as a hollow property to give bizarre point to the lines introducing it, 'an empty purse, . . . There was no money in't' " (p. 47).

respect. *Pericles* has a kind of fixed relativity, asking us to commit ourselves to Gower's old tale while keeping us strongly aware of its artifice and simplicity; *Cymbeline* introduces a more fluid set of circumstances, in which we range freely among several traditions and styles, with rapidly fluctuating reactions. More is demanded of us—some would say too much —and more is given.

The use of pastoral motifs in *Cymbeline* seems to have re-awakened its author's interest in the difficult questions involving the nature of Nature that were vital to *As You Like It* and *King Lear*. It is Nature as creator that is given special attention in this play, and she is often compared and contrasted with man as creator, who is sometimes seen as her rival:

> The chimney
> Is south the chamber, and the chimney-piece,
> Chaste Dian bathing: never saw I figures
> So likely to report themselves; the cutter
> Was as another Nature, dumb; outwent her,
> Motion and breath left out.
>
> [2.4.80–85]

In the last act, Iachimo, rather elaborately recalling the wager, says that the Italians were praising their women's beauty as "beyond brief Nature" (5.5.165). Man's desire to rival Nature and to have no partners in creation and procreation is reflected in Posthumus' disgust when he believes Imogen to be false:

> Is there no way for men to be, but women
> Must be half-workers? We are all bastards,
> And that most venerable man, which I
> did call my father, was I know not where
> When I was stamp'd. Some coiner with his tools
> Made me a counterfeit.
>
> [2.4.152–58]

A counterfeiter is of course engaged in artifice in a double and especially negative way. For Posthumus, however, as for the other characters in the play, Nature as creator and partner is

gradually vindicated. Much of the attention given to this vin-
dication is centered on the two boys, Guiderius and Arviragus.
Imogen sees them as exemplars of the pastoral ideal:

> Great men,
> That had a court no bigger than this cave,
> That did attend themselves, and had the virtue
> Which their own conscience seal'd them, laying by
> The nothing-gift of differing multitudes
> Could not out-peer these twain. Pardon me, gods!
> I'ld change my sex to be companion with them,
> Since Leonatus false.
>
> [3.7.54–61]
>
> These are kind creatures. Gods, what lies I have heard!
> Our courtiers say all's savage but at court;
> Experience, O, thou disprov'st report!
> Th'emperious seas breed monsters; for the dish
> Poor tributary rivers as sweet fish.
>
> [4.2.32–36]

But Imogen's claims have ironic qualification; unwittingly,
she is talking about her royal brothers. We cannot take her
sentiments at face value. It is Belarius who, knowing the secret
of their birth, is in a position to be more convincing:

> How hard it is to hide the sparks of Nature!
> These boys know little they are sons to the king,
> Nor Cymbeline dreams that they are alive.
> They think they are mine, and though train'd up thus
>   meanly,
> I'th' cave wherein they bow, their thoughts do hit
> The roofs of palaces, and Nature prompts them
> In simple and low things to prince it, much
> Beyond the trick of others.
>
> [3.3.79–86]
>
> O thou goddess,
> Thou divine Nature; thou thyself thou blazon'st
> In these two princely boys; they are as gentle
> As zephyrs blowing below the violet,
> Not wagging his sweet head; and yet, as rough,

> (Their royal blood enchaf'd) as the rud'st wind
> That by the top doth take the mountain pine
> And make him stoop to th' vale. 'Tis wonder
> That an invisible instinct should frame them
> To royalty unlearn'd, honor untaught,
> Civility not seen from other, valour
> That wildly grows in them, but yields a crop
> As if it had been sow'd.
>
> [4.2.169–81]

These speeches have an impressive emphasis, but again there are factors that qualify our acquiescence. Belarius, as noted earlier, is a figure of gentle fun, and indeed the cave scenes have in general an air of grotesque comedy.[8] The boys are not totally convincing as representatives of perfect royalty. There is, moreover, as I noted in the first chapter of this study, an ambiguity in claiming good breeding as solely a natural virtue, since it partakes of nurture (inherited, in this case) as well. Finally, when Belarius returns the boys to Cymbeline, he speaks not of sparks of Nature or invisible instincts, but of his own tutelage:

> These gentle princes
> (For such and so they are) these twenty years
> Have I train'd up; those arts they have; as I
> Could put into them.
>
> [5.5.337–40]

Nature receives her full pastoral measure in *Cymbeline*, but our awareness of the artificiality of means by which she gets it, kept constantly before us by the playwright, makes it a questionable victory. As Guiderius is being identified by the time-worn romance device of the birthmark, Belarius proudly says: "This is he, / Who hath upon him still that natural stamp; / It was wise Nature's end, in the donation / To be his evidence now" (5.5.366 f.). This picture of wise Nature, doling out birthmarks to resolve the complicated plots of romances, is

8. Kermode, in *The Final Plays*, calls the cave scenes "suspiciously simple and open, as if Shakespeare were covertly parodying Fletcher" (p. 28).

surely too playful to be taken seriously. It directs our attention not so much to Nature as to the artist, man the creator,
calling Nature to his aid. Life resolves itself into art. Such an
approach aids greatly in understanding something like Posthumus' Vision. It is not, as some have argued, necessary to
straighten out the plot.[9] Things are already posed for a more
natural resolution (by the assembling of all the characters in
one place) when Jupiter makes his appearance. It is more to
the point to say that such an obtrusive use of *deus ex machina,*
cast in an antiquated style and reminiscent of the masque, in
which artifice is always well in the foreground, serves to remind us not so much of supernatural intervention as of au-
thorial manipulation. "Such disorder," says Nosworthy, "can
be remedied only by a god, a magician or, as in *The Winter's
Tale,* by an extraordinary series of coincidences."[10] But we
can add, comprehending all these possibilities: *or by an artist,
who set the disorder in motion in the first place.* The late
plays see pastoral restored, along with much else from the romance tradition, but restored in such a way that we are left
unmistakably aware of its fictitious and ideal character.

❦

The pastoral romance heritage of *The Winter's Tale* is well
known. The play is closely based on *Pandosto,* one of Greene's
pastoral novels. In many respects it resembles *The Thracian
Wonder,* an earlier dramatization of Greene's other pastoral
romance, *Menaphon.* To standard features of the tradition
drawn from Greene—the oracle, the lost child raised by shepherds, the prince disguised as a swain—Shakespeare adds a few
from other sources: the bear who disposes of Antigonus,
equally familiar to readers of the *Arcadia* and to spectators of
Mucedorus; the court-country witticisms of Autolycus; and the
famous sheep-shearing feast of the fourth act. The elements of
pastoral romance stand forth in *The Winter's Tale,* especially
in its second half, with a distinctness that is unique in Shake-

9. E.g., J. M. Nosworthy, in the Introduction to the Arden edition
(1955), p. xxxvii.
10. Ibid.

speare. The transforming and complicating urge which often
pushed past the external features of pastoral in *As You Like
It* and *Lear* to get to the center of its vision, here gives way
to an interest in preserving and examining the surface features
and plot design that is quite consistent with Shakespeare's preoccupation in the late plays with the archaic and the outmoded in literature and drama.[11]

At the same time it must be said that the relation of *The
Winter's Tale* to its basic source and to the pastoral tradition
is not nearly so simple as it appears at first glance. Nor is its
relation to concurrent examples of staged pastoral romance
such as John Day's *Humour Out of Breath* or *The Thracian
Wonder* so close as we might suppose. Like *Pericles* and
Cymbeline, The Winter's Tale was long suspected of being
a clumsy example of a clumsy tradition; it is, rather, again
like them, a radically experimental play, quite unlike anything Shakespeare or anyone else had hitherto attempted.

It is the structure of the play that is noticeable first. Shake-
peare has allowed his story to break into two distinct and unlike halves, denying it even the basic unity it had in Greene's
narrative. Moreover, instead of attempting to conceal this bi-
furcation, he has emphatically exposed it by the use of an
archaic chorus who announces the transition between the two
parts and in effect invites us to consider the peculiar and un-
orthodox structure.[12] It is scarcely surprising that this deliberate simplification, this exaggeration of outline, has dismayed

11. Jerry H. Bryant, "*The Winter's Tale* and the Pastoral Tradition,"
Shakespeare Quarterly 14 (1963):387–98, surveys those aspects of the play
that can be described as traditional to pastoral, noting Shakespeare's
"transformation of hackneyed conventions into living situations" (p. 396).

12. Cf. S. L. Bethell, *The Winter's Tale: A Study* (London, 1947):
"[Shakespeare] draws attention to the play as play by obtruding matters
of technique upon the audience, and I believe that in the previous
romances the function of the old-fashioned technique is precisely the
same" (p. 52); Northrop Frye, "Recognition in *The Winter's Tale*,"
Essays on Shakespeare and Elizabethan Drama in Honor of Hardin Craig,
pp. 235–46: "We notice that Shakespeare seems to be calling our attention
to the incredibility of his story and to its ridiculous and outmoded devices"
(p. 240).

commentators. The author seems like an astonishingly literal-minded man who, attempting to write tragicomedy, assumes that it must mean a tragedy joined to a comedy. Knowing that pastoral was by this time thought to be proper to the stage only in the form of tragicomedy, and realizing that the structure of the play is a deliberate rehandling of the more unified source, there is good reason to suspect that the deliberately naive structure of *The Winter's Tale* was Shakespeare's joke on those who took their categories too seriously and who would not or could not question the rules.

But the radically simplified and divided structure, if it is a joke, is not simply that. It has justifications that go to the heart of the play's vision. For the moment, let us note two major effects. The juxtaposition of tragic and comic sections, firmly differentiated and exposed to our consideration, serves to stress their opposition, and, ultimately, to emphasize the arbitrary aspects of genre. Coming to *The Winter's Tale* by way of *As You Like It* and *Lear* makes it easier to see this as a natural development in Shakespeare's consideration of the pastoral. In all three plays there is an examination of the peculiar and intricate relation of art to nature that includes a special interest in the relation of literature to the reality or realities it tries to express. Genre plays a significant part in both the comic and tragic handlings of the pastoral design in the two earlier plays in so far as it is seen as protective and artificial in the comic world of *As You Like It* and as insistent on certain consequences and realities in the tragic world of *Lear*. The juxtaposition of these worlds is a natural step for *The Winter's Tale* to take, and the dual consideration of the genres gives their artificiality and relativity an unprecedented stress. The total effect is a sense of widened scope through the inclusion of separate genres and of artistic retrenchment through the abandoning of either genre's implicit claim to tell the whole truth about any given set of circumstances.

The second effect is closely related. The stucture of *The Winter's Tale* serves to polarize its elements—good and evil, life and death, loss and restoration, creation and destruction, winter and spring, youth and age—and to throw the traditional pastoral oppositions—court and country, fortune and nature, sophistication and innocence, complexity and simplicity—into vivid relief. Again the effect is dual: a widening of the meaning of pastoral by bringing its antinomies into line with a number of other clearly defined opposites, and a stress on the arbitrary and artificial character of all such distinctions in light of their relation to the play's exaggerated outlines. Both of these effects are very much in keeping with the strong interest in artifice that pervades Shakespeare's late work, and with the consciousness of relativity that he seems always to have brought to such "theories" as that of the pastoral, a consciousness he embodied in this play in the person of Time.

The experience of reading or watching the play is a remarkable one. The opening scenes are a curious combination of the mannered and the naturalistic. Leontes' sudden onslaught of jealousy is bound to be puzzling, but its consequences are engrossing, and the rapid unfolding of his tragedy is deeply engaging. While there are some effects of distancing—the use of the oracles, the ironies arising from the many references to illusion and acting, the seriocomic exchanges with Paulina— they are scarcely greater than those of, say, *Hamlet*. It therefore comes as a considerable shock, when the destruction has reached its swift climax, that archaic patterns should begin to reassert themselves so strongly. The abandoned baby, the bear, the shipwreck, Antigonus' emblematic dream: these are conventional features used unconventionally, and their effect is to create an unexpected sense of detachment. We scarcely know how to react, and the tension generated between the fictive and the real is considerable:

> O, the most piteous cry of the poor souls! sometimes to see 'em and not to see 'em: now the ship boring the moon with her main-mast, and anon swallowed with yest and froth, as you'd thrust a cork into a hogs-head. And then for the land-service, to see how the bear tore out his shoulder-bone, how he cried to me for help and said his name was Antigonus, a nobleman. But to make an end of the ship, to see how the sea flap-dragoned it: but first,

> how the poor souls roared, and the sea mocked them: and
> how the poor gentleman roared, and the bear mocked him,
> both roaring louder than the sea or weather. [3.3.90–101]

The roaring and the mockery, along with the comically inept
rhetoric, express the division of our own feelings, and we
should recognize in the old shepherd's reaction to all this—
"Heavy matters! heavy matters! But look thee here, boy. Now
bless thyself: thou met'st with things dying, I with things new-
born"—not only the emergence of the dual structure and a
natural eloquence, but the spectrum of reactions called forth
from us.

The appearance of Time the chorus takes us further. Here
suddenly is a Presenter like Gower, somewhat after the fact,
to guide our reaction and place us in a new perspective. The
vantage point he offers stresses relativity and artifice. The
story has an arbitrary shape, and the power to reverse direction. The conventional side of Leontes' history re-emerges; it
is not a tragedy but an old tale, and a stale one at that. But
what is staleness? In the perspective of eternity anything is
stale, or nothing, and sixteen years in the turning of a glass:

> I witness to
> The times that brought them in; so shall I do
> To th' freshest things now reigning, and make stale
> The glistering of this present, as my tale
> Now seems to it.
>
> [4.1.11–15]

Our engagement with the past is altered to a detachment
which we will now carry with us into the future, the second
and comic half of the play. Tragedy and comedy, things dying
and things new born, have an unsuspected similarity, like the
twin halves of an hourglass. May not the same be true of reality and the imagination? The lines between art and life have
begun to shift and blur, a necessary preparation to our full
enjoyment of the great sheep-shearing scene that is to follow,
and to the remarkable moments of reconciliation and restoration that will conclude the play.

The experience I have outlined suggests that the stylistic extremes of engagement and detachment, stretched to a new intensity in the late plays, have in *The Winter's Tale* become a matter of structure as well. The outlines of pastoral romance, with its extravagant events, its sharp contrasts, its reversals of fortune, its shepherds and courtiers, and its improbably harmonious conclusion, had been playfully subverted and complicated in *As You Like It*; in *Lear* they had been grimly put to the service of unpleasant fact. But *The Winter's Tale* treats them as if for their own sake, heightening them (Shakespeare's conclusion, for example, is both happier and more improbable than Greene's), exploring their potential, insisting on a union of the emblematic and the psychological rather than on the existence of one at the expense of the other. The result is not so much a drastic change in Shakespeare's practice as a further refinement of it, and a play whose basic design, naive and clumsy though it may seem, serves its author's deepest purposes. Just how this is the case can be further demonstrated by a close examination of two of *The Winter's Tale*'s leading themes, that of art and nature and that of Time, in relation to the play's unique form.

❧

That the interrelation of art and nature forms a leading theme of *The Winter's Tale* has long been recognized; the famous argument between Polixenes and Perdita on the subject in act 4, scene 3, is unmistakably a moment of thematic significance.[13] This famous topic, so intimately connected with the pastoral and capable of so many permutations in Renaissance thought, is in *The Winter's Tale* particularly

13. Among those who have discussed the theme: Bethell and Frye, cited above; F. D. Hoeniger, "The Meaning of *The Winter's Tale*," *University of Toronto Quarterly* 20 (1950):11–26; M. M. Mahood, *Shakespeare's Wordplay* (London, 1956), pp. 146–63; John Lawlor, "*Pandosto* and the Nature of Dramatic Romance," *Philological Quarterly* 41 (1962):96–113; L. G. Salingar, "Time and Art in Shakespeare's Romances," *Renaissance Drama IX* (1966), pp. 3–35.

focused on the real and the unreal, the substantial and the insubstantial. The topic is first realized in the design of the play itself. The stylized and exaggerated structure, with its swing from one genre to another, along with many of the most archaic and conventional features of the romance tradition, provides a framework in which the playwright can set up an extremely complex interplay between the fictive and the real, imagination and reality. The effect is sometimes like that of the surrealist paintings of Magritte, in which a painting of the sky on an easel merges completely with the "real" sky of the window beyond, the whole composition presented in a fashion that makes the viewer highly aware of the witty manipulations of the artist. Just how completely this interplay permeates the play has not, I think, been recognized. Little has been said, for example, about it in the first half, but that is where it begins, in the characterization of Leontes and the nature of his dilemma.

Leontes' behavior, famous for its lack of motivation, is typical of the pastoral romance tradition of violent and inexplicable passions. He shares with Lear, with Duke Frederick, and with a host of rulers in the novels of writers like Greene and Sidney, a kind of helpless impulse to tyranny, a combination, perhaps, of the pastoral criticism of court life and the romance tradition of arbitrary fortune. But if Leontes exists within a convention that accounts for his extravagant irrationality, it is just at that point—where a Greene or a Lodge, having set him up in the pattern of abrupt and arbitrary character change, would turn to something else—that Shakespeare picks him up and begins to interest us in him. What emerges is a surprise, as if the dramatist were saying: "You think this merely artifice and convention. Just see what potential it contains." The natural resources of an apparently outmoded style are given new life.

There arises, then, a remarkable tension in the character of Leontes between his place in a conventional pattern and the psychological verisimilitude that bursts out in his speech. As a romance figure he is a standard tyrant; as a man he is almost too real, with a tortured and obsessed mind that

stands fully revealed to us. Shakespeare even gives his first
symptoms a kind of medical basis:

> I have *tremor cordis* on me; my heart dances,
> But not for joy—not joy.
>
> [1.2.110–11]

This recalls Lear's, "O, how this mother swells up toward my
heart! / *Hysterica passio*—down, thou climbing sorrow" (2.4.
55–57), and the pain that disfigures Leontes' speech as he
tries to amuse himself with his little boy is as real and moving
as anything in *King Lear*:

> Why, that's my bawcock. What! Hast smutch'd thy nose?
> They say it is a copy out of mine. Come, captain,
> We must be neat; not neat, but cleanly, captain:
> And yet the steer, the heifer and the calf
> Are all call'd neat. —Still virginalling
> Upon his palm!—How now, you wanton calf!
> Art thou my calf?
>   *Mamillius.* Yes, if you will, my lord.
>   *Leontes.* Thou want'st a rough pash and the shoots that
>   I have
> To be full like me: yet they say we are
> Almost as like as eggs; women say so,
> (That will say any thing): but were they false
> As o'er-dy'd blacks, as wind, as waters; false
> As dice are to be wish'd by one that fixes
> No bourn 'twixt his and mine, yet were it true
> To say this boy were like me.
>
> [1.2.121–35]

We are moved, inevitably, by such skillful creation, from the
detachment of recognizing the implausible circumstances surrounding this passion to the engagement of sharing its intensity. Such movement is to be characteristic of *The Winter's
Tale,* though it is as often in the opposite direction, as when
the first scene of the play, cast in a realistic and contemporary
idiom of polite court conversation, suddenly gives way to the
artificial style of Polixenes at his entrance:

> Nine changes of the watery star hath been
> The shepherd's note since we have left our throne
> Without a burden.
>
> [1.2.1–3] [14]

In the case of Leontes, moreover, it is not only his character-ization which contributes to the interplay of art and life in *The Winter's Tale*. The same strange texture is created by the situation in which he finds himself. No sooner has he dis-covered his jealousy than he is raising questions about its reality:

> Affection! thy intention stabs the centre:
> Thou dost make possible things not so held,
> Communicat'st with dreams;—how can this be?—
> With what's unreal thou coactive art,
> And fellow'st nothing: then 'tis very credent
> Thou may'st co-join with something; and thou dost,
> (And that beyond commission) and I find it,
> (And that to the infection of my brains
> And hard'ning of my brows).
>
> [1.2.138–46]

The passage is famous for its difficulty. It deliberately confuses Leontes' speculation about how Hermione progressed from lustful imaginings to lustful acts with his own attempt to make what he has imagined into a correct guess about reality. As the sense of "affection" shifts from "lust" to "imagination," from lover to lunatic and poet, Leontes' words are infused with irony: the creation of something out of nothing, going "beyond commission" and suffering an "infection" in his brains, these phrases have an application that escapes his notice.[15] In his subsequent actions he resembles at least two

14. "After the naturalistic prose dialogue with which the play began, this orotund phrase achieves one of those swift changes in the pressure of realism—here from contemporary Court life to the world of the Player King—which is typical of the dramatic climate of these late plays" (Mahood, pp. 146–47). See also Kermode, *The Final Plays*, p. 32.

15. For discussions of this passage and particularly of the term "affec-tion," see J. H. P. Pafford's Arden edition (1963), Appendix I, pp. 165–67;

of Shakespeare's tragic heroes, Othello and Macbeth, who
desperately try to remake their worlds to fit their horrible
imaginings. The difference with Leontes lies in the way he
unconsciously and insistently reminds us of his plunge into
illusion, his acting out of a fiction within a fiction:

> Go, play, boy, play: thy mother plays, and I
> Play too; but so disgrac'd a part, whose issue
> Will hiss me to my grave. . . . There have been
> (Or I am much deceiv'd) cuckolds ere now. . . .
>
> [1.2.187–91]
>
> [Camillo, unsuspecting, is like] a fool,
> That seest a game play'd home, the rich stake drawn,
> And tak'st it all for jest.
>
> [247–49]
>
> There is a plot against my life, my crown;
> All's true that is mistrusted.
>
> [2.1.47–48]
>
>   No: if I mistake
> In those foundations which I build upon,
> The centre is not big enough to bear
> A school-boy's top.
>
> [100–04]

The word "play" and the accompanying images neatly sum
up the ambiguity of action.[16] What one "performs" may be
real or illusory. The sense in which Leontes is playing is one
he can never recognize; he is an actor who has forgotten that
he stands on a stage, part of a play. "What is this?" asks
Hermione when he brings her first into his mad world,
"Sport?" Later, at the trial, she sums up her situation with
chilling accuracy:

> You speak a language that I understand not:
> My life stands in the level of your dreams,
> Which I'll lay down.
>
> [3.2.80–82]

H. H. Furness' New Variorum edition (rep. 1964), pp. 27–31; and Hallett
Smith, "Leontes' *Affectio*," *Shakespeare Quarterly* 14 (Spring 1963):163–66.
   16. Cf. Mahood, p. 150.

Leontes' answer is, "Your actions are my dreams." For him there can be no multiple meanings; for us they are everywhere. It takes a death and an oracle to deflect him from his attempt to realize his delusions. He has moved from the standard romance pattern of a man ruled by Fortune to the position of a mad artist, creating to destroy. The imaginings of a king, we are reminded, can be especially costly. And as there is an ambiguity of action, so there is one of creation. The sense in which the "issue" of the part Leontes played would hiss him to his grave is one he did not suspect. The tragic hero's failure to recognize the degree to which his dilemma is of his own making is a characteristic weakness; this facet of tragedy is emphasized in Leontes' case by the absence of an Iago, a Lady Macbeth, indeed of any outside agency or evidence for his delusion. Greene's Pandosto had some grounds for jealousy and suspicion; Shakespeare gives Leontes none, and he proves able to make this feature serve both the psychological and the emblematic at once.

As Leontes' tragedy completes itself and the play begins to turn on its gigantic hinge, we are thrust more and more toward the emblematic. The insistence on fiction *as fiction* is notable in the shipwreck scene and is intensified by the appearance of Time, a figure drawn from the standard iconography of the emblematic imagination. A new sense of what is real subsumes the verisimilitude of Leontes' characterization, and a vast perspective is opened in which not only old tales but all human events are seen as illusory because relative to their immediate circumstances. The hourglass which represents Time's superior understanding (and the very shape of the play)[17] is turned, and we will not be asked again to engage ourselves in the same way to the dramatic action. Instead, as from a height which "takes survey of all the world," we will witness the rest of the play and the other half of the truth.

This process continues with the introductory matter of the two short scenes between Camillo and Polixenes, and Auto-

17. Noted by Ernest Schanzer, "The Structural Pattern of *The Winter's Tale*," *Review of English Literature* 5 (April 1964):72–82, esp. p. 79.

lycus and the Clown (4.2, 3), and then moves into the long
scene of the sheep-shearing feast (4.4), perhaps the most remarkable mixture of realism and artifice ever managed by
Shakespeare. The narrow and mannered pastoral design suddenly seems capable of containing everything, from the Jacobean underworld practices of Autolycus, fleecing the silly
shepherds, who are in turn real Cotswold figures, to the great
seasonal myths of Flora and Persephone. Through it all there
runs an exquisite sense of *play,* and that word takes on a different character than it had in Leontes' mouth.[18] Florizel,
strewn with flowers, would be for Perdita "like a bank, for
love to lie and play on . . . quick, and in mine arms" (130–
32). Perdita hesitates, confused by her boldness, and adds:

> Come, take your flowers:
> Methinks I play as I have seen them do
> In Whitsun pastorals: sure this robe of mine
> Does change my disposition.
>
> [132–35]

The playing here, where a boy actor plays a princess who
thinks she is a shepherdess playing a May Queen ("most god-
dess-like prank'd up") is more complicated than Perdita can
imagine or express; the audience has all it can do to keep
up.[19] And "Whitsun pastoral," a country celebration of man's
kinship with nature, an "art that nature makes," is a delightful emblem for what we are seeing. Nature and art are becoming indistinguishable, and reality and imagination seem
to be intertwining and merging within a benevolent framework of artifice. The dances act out these partnerships and
harmonies, and Autolycus with his ballads gives us a wonderfully grotesque reflection of them:

> *Mopsa.* Pray now, buy some: I love a ballad in print,
> a life, for them we are sure they are true.
> *Autolycus.* Here's one, to a very doleful tune, how a

18. Cf. Mahood, p. 154.
19. Cf. Bethell, *The Winter's Tale,* p. 57.

usurer's wife was brought to bed of twenty money-bags at a burden, and how she longed to eat adders' heads and toads carbonadoed.

Mopsa. Is it true, think you?

Autolycus. Very true, and but a month old.

Dorcas. Bless me from marrying a usurer!

Autolycus. Here's the midwife's name to 't, one Mistress Taleporter, and five or six honest wives that were present. Why should I carry lies abroad? . . . Here's another ballad of a fish that appeared upon the coast on Wednesday the fourscore of April, forty thousand fathom above water, and sung this ballad against the hard hearts of maids: it was thought she was a woman, and was turned into a cold fish for she would not exchange flesh with one that loved her. The ballad is very pitiful, and as true.

Dorcas. Is it true too, think you?

Autolycus. Five justices' hands at it, and witnesses more than my pack will hold.

[4.4.261–85]

Here are our own needs and anxieties, mirrored at a level we can all laugh at. We must have fictions, we all delight in marvels and myths, but we want the reassurance that comes from confounding them with reality, with measurable and testifiable fact. Or at least we did until we came this far into *The Winter's Tale* and began to feel that such distinctions are arbitrary. What is the artist, peddler, and magician to say to us? "Why should I carry lies abroad?" It is in the late plays that Shakespeare deals with his most open hand, lays bare the fable and hopes we will join him in pondering it as it is, with no illusions intervening.

The sense of the fictive is kept strongly before us throughout this part of the play. Many of the references, like Perdita's allusion to playing in Whitsun pastorals, remind us that we are watching a staged performance:

> *Camillo.* . . . it shall be so my care
> To have you royally appointed, as if

The scene you play were mine.

[4.4.592–94]

    Perdita. . . . I see the play so lies
That I must bear a part.

[655–66]

Leontes. . . . No more such wives; therefore, no wife:
one worse,
    And better us'd, would make her sainted spirit
    Again possess her corpse, and on this stage
    (Were we offenders now) appear soul-vex'd,
    And begin, "Why to me?"

[5.1.56–60]

First Gentleman. The dignity of this act was worth the
audience of kings and princes; for by such was it acted.

[5.2.79–80]

Others, like the earlier mentions of old tales and ballads, refer
us to the legendary and incredible nature of the events we are
witnessing:

    Paulina. . . . Is't not the tenor of his Oracle,
    That King Leontes shall not have an heir,
    Till his lost child be found? which, that it shall,
    Is all as monstrous to our human reason
    As my Antigonus to break his grave
    And come again to me.

[5.1.38–43]

Second Gentleman. . . . Such a deal of wonder is
broken out within this hour, that ballad-makers cannot
be able to express it.

[5.2.23–25]

. . . This news, which is called true, is so like an old
tale that the verity of it is in strong suspicion.

[27–29]

Third Gentleman. Like an old tale still, which will
have matter to rehearse, though credit be asleep and not
an ear open.

[62–64]

> *Paulina.* . . .That she is living
> Were it but told you, should be hooted at
> Like an old tale: but it appears she lives,
> Though yet she speak not.
>
> [5.3.115–18]

The last of these comes from the statue scene, and it should be noted that the many allusions to the plastic arts that accompany the discussion and unveiling of Hermione's "statue" form another means by which Shakespeare keeps the subject of fiction and artifice in the foreground of attention.

Curiously, however, all these references do not really act to sharpen our sense of the gap between reality and artifice. At the same time that Shakespeare has been insisting on fiction as fiction, he has found ways of steadily closing the distance between art and nature. There is, in the first place, the greater reliance on nature in this part of the play. Paulina's "great nature" (2.2.60) and "good goddess Nature" (2.3.103) becomes a preoccupation of most of the characters. Perdita and Polixenes may differ in their views about gillyvors, but both speak from what they consider an adherence to "great creating nature." And Florizel, in his love of Perdita, feels he has so committed himself to nature that he literally swears by it and in relation to it:

> It cannot fail, but by
> The violation of my faith; and then
> Let nature crush the sides o' th' earth together,
> And mar the seeds within!
>
> [4.4.477–80]
>
> Not for Bohemia, nor the pomp that may
> Be thereat glean'd: for all the sun sees, or
> The close earth wombs, or the profound seas hides
> In unknown fathoms, will I break my oath
> To this my fair belov'd.
>
> [489–93]

Picking up the familiar pastoral dichotomy, he sees himself as opposed to Fortune:

> . . . let myself and fortune
> Tug for the time to come.
>
>   ❦   [497–98]
>
>   Dear, look up:
> Though Fortune, visible an enemy,
> Should chase us, with my father, power no jot
> Hath she to change our loves.
>
>   [5.1.215–17]

Concurrent with these pronouncements of allegiance to nature, there are increasing allusions, reminiscent of *Cymbeline*, to nature as artist-creator. Leontes, considering Mamillius' face as "a copy out of mine" in act 1, was, like Posthumus, obsessed with man's necessary involvement in natural processes which aroused his disgust and suspicion of women. In act 5 he sounds very different:

> Your mother was most true to wedlock, prince;
> For she did print your royal father off,
> Conceiving you. Were I but twenty-one,
> Your father's image is so hit in you,
> His very air, that I should call you brother,
> As I did him, and speak of something wildly
> By us perform'd before. Most dearly welcome!
> And your fair princess,—goddess!—O, alas!
>
>   [5.1.123–30]

Nature's masterpiece is Perdita, and the value of the work lies in fidelity to the original and the quality of workmanship:

> The majesty of the creature in resemblance of the mother, the affection of nobleness which nature shows above her breeding, and many other evidences proclaim her, with all certainty, to be the king's daughter.
>
>   [5.2.36–40]

She is Hermione's living likeness, as the statue is supposed to be her "dead likeness" (5.3.15). These images of nature producing perfect copies and images of nobility are distanced by their grotesque reflections among the comic characters, as in Autolycus' "Yet nature might have made me as these are; / Therefore I will not disdain" (4.4.747–48), and in his later exchange with the shepherds "in the blossoms of their fortune":

> *Autolycus.* I know you are now, sir, a gentleman born.
> *Clown.* Ay, and have been so any time these four hours.
> *Shepherd.* And so have I, boy.
> *Clown.* So you have: but I was a gentleman born before my father; for the king's son took me by the hand, and called me brother; and then the two kings called my father brother; and then the prince, my brother, and the princess, my sister, called my father father; and so we wept; and there was the first gentleman-like tears that ever we shed.
>
> [5.2.135–45]

A healthy perspective is maintained, through the last half of the play, against the notion of either art or nature as supreme creative agents, as when Polixenes is given the stronger case in his argument with Perdita, but ironically made to contradict his position by his attitude toward Florizel's alliance:

> You see, sweet maid, we marry
> A gentler scion to the wildest stock,
> And make conceive a bark of baser kind
> By bud of nobler race.
>
> [4.4.92–95]

> Thou art too base
> To be acknowledg'd: thou a sceptre's heir,
> That thus affects a sheep-hook!
>
> [419–21]

The final scene draws art and nature together through the magnificent image of the living statue, the dead likeness joining the living, mother and daughter reunited.[20] While there

20. ". . . because Nature is at the mercy of Time, Leontes' renewal through Perdita's return is only a token rejuvenation; the life of the next

have been hints of this moment—e.g., Paulina's "Unless another, / As like Hermione as is her picture, / Affront his eye."
(5.1.73–75)—the audience is little more prepared for it than
the characters, and is led toward it with what seems once
again to be a separation of art and nature, even a rivalry:

> A piece many years in doing and now newly performed
> by that rare Italian master, Julio Romano, who, had he
> himself eternity and could put breath into his work,
> would beguile Nature of her custom, so perfectly is he her
> ape. [5.2.94–99]

There is fun here, as in the ballad scene, at simplistic responses to art, in this case the assumption that perfect imitation is the highest reach of skill the artist can attain. The
artist as nature's ape was not an image likely to appeal to
the dramatist who had so emphatically violated the unities of
time, place, and action here and elsewhere. As the statue is
unveiled we begin to hear the word "mocked," which figures
prominently in the shipwreck scene, in its dual sense of copy-
ing and of making fun:

> But here it is: prepare
> To see the life as lively mock'd as ever
> Still sleep mock'd death.
>
> [5.3.18–20]
>
> The fixture of her eye has motion in 't,
> As we are mock'd with art.
>
> [67–68]
>
> Still methinks
> There is an air comes from her. What fine chisel
> Could ever yet cut breath? Let no man mock me,
> For I will kiss her.
>
> [77–80]

There is a wonderful sense of play, a gaiety, throughout this
scene, which has perhaps been observed by solemn allegorical

---

generation is their own, not ours. . . . The past, however, is restored to
Leontes in the person of Hermione, whose revival is Shakespeare's second
statement of drama's power to reconcile art and nature" (Mahood, p. 187).

interpretations. Paulina's enjoyment, as she watches the dichotomies of nature and art, life and death, past and present break down, gradually becomes our own, as we realize the extent of the trick being played on us. A boy actor is impersonating a woman who is impersonating a statue of herself, and this woman-statue-actor figure provides the climax of a fiction that might well be "hooted at / Like an old tale." The interpenetrating levels of art and nature are too much for us to sort out. We must simply acquiesce, with Leontes, in what we are witnessing:

> O, she's warm!
> If this be magic, let it be an art
> Lawful as eating.

[109–11]

Perhaps Polixenes' formula comes back to us too:

> Yet nature is made better by no mean
> But nature makes that mean: so, over that art,
> Which you say adds to nature, is an art
> That nature makes.

[4.4.89–92]

Art should be lawful as eating because it is as natural as eating, the imagination as real as the "reality" against which it plays. And *The Winter's Tale*? Do questions of its artificiality, staleness, and improbabilities any longer matter? Are we not more likely to accept it as Polixenes has the gardener's art?

> This is an art
> Which does mend nature—change it rather—but
> The art itself is nature.

❦

"Time," Rosalind tells Orlando in *As You Like It*, "travels in divers paces with divers persons." This insight, as we have seen, is developed in Arden through characterization which stresses the subjectivity of temporal experience, and through verbal play which explores the relativity of many concepts, time among them. In *The Winter's Tale* the issue is raised again, and this time, as with the art-nature theme, the playwright moves beyond the playful stylistic gestures by which opposites are mingled and relativity stressed, to a play whose very structure proposes the relativity of time and examines its relation both to nature and to art.[21] The two halves of the play present us with two distinct kinds of time: the first, linear, impetuous, irrevocable, enemy to human aspirations; the second, cyclic, leisurely, restorative, in harmony with man's hopes. Between them stands the personified figure of Time, as chorus, to reveal his multiple nature and to point out that the play as a whole, both halves taken together, constitutes a pattern of his own devising, "the argument of Time." It is from this initial and crucial design that the play proceeds to its very complex awareness of the meaning and nature of Time.

That the two basic kinds of time manifested in the two halves of the play are closely related to the contrasting genres seems unmistakable. Indeed, the sense of time and the sense of genre, in both cases, work to support each other. Our assurance that Leontes' part of the tale is tragic comes in great part from his and our experience of Time as a surrounding element. Polixenes' nine-month visit, combined with Hermione's success in persuading him to stay an extra week, feeds Leontes' suspicion. Once embarked on his disastrous course, he is all haste and hurry. Polixenes must be dispatched, and, when he and Camillo have fled, Hermione must be speedily brought to trial and executed, and her child killed or abandoned. The other characters, too, are enveloped in this headlong movement. Polixenes and Camillo must "take the urgent hour" and leave Sicily instantly, Hermione is "something before her time, deliver'd," Cleomenes and Dion, whose "speed" in going to the Delphic Oracle and returning "Hath been

21. Useful discussions of the theme of Time and the use of Time as chorus include Bethell, pp. 35–44; Inga-Stina Ewbank, "The Triumph of Time in *The Winter's Tale,*" *Review of English Literature* 5 (April 1964): 83–100; and Salingar, pp. 3–6.

beyond account," are worried about the "violent carriage" of Leontes' justice and aware that on the unsealing of the Oracle, "something rare / Even then will rush to knowledge." It is scarcely surprising to discover, at the climax of the trial scene, that Leontes' haste and impetuosity have led him into irrevocable error, that his poor "timing" has intensified the devastating consequences of his decisions. The swiftness with which retribution ensues, in the destruction of his family, strikes us as appropriate to the "time-scheme" of this part of the play, and Paulina speaks for our sense of events as she makes Leontes face his irrecoverable loss and shows him a temporal prospect of the bleakest sort:

> Do not repent these things, for they are heavier
> Than all thy woes can stir: therefore betake thee
> To nothing but despair. A thousand knees
> Ten thousand years together, naked, fasting,
> Upon a barren mountain, and still winter
> In storm perpetual, could not move the gods
> To look that way thou wert.
>
> [3.2.208–14]

Leontes, who was all haste, is now strangely arrested in a "shame perpetual," condemned to a repetitious, fruitless cycle:

> Once a day I'll visit
> The chapel where they lie, and tears shed there
> Shall be my recreation. So long as nature
> Will bear up with this exercise, so long
> I daily vow to use it.
>
> [238–42]

For sixteen years both he and Hermione will be, in effect, outside time, suspended beyond the tragic, linear movement which brought them to this fate, and not yet part of the comic, cyclic phase which will restore them to Perdita and to each other. Time and tragedy are so closely associated by this point that we tend to take their interpenetration for granted; were it not for the second half of the play, we would see no alterna-

tives to this set of circumstances, either in their tragic outcome
or their hurried, irreversible pace.

The intervention of a sixteen-year gap in the action at this
point has a curious double effect. In one sense it represents an
astonishingly swift passage of time, a wild acceleration of the
hectic pace of the first three acts; in another and more important sense, however, it introduces a new temporal framework of larger and more extended rhythms: the minutes,
hours, days, and months of Leontes' fevered world are suddenly replaced by the more spacious and deliberate movement of the seasons of the year and the succession of human
generations.[22] The first three acts now represent a small frac-
tion of the total time scheme of the play, and the accompanying shift in perspective makes possible our acceptance of the
comic, cyclic time of the second part; we realize that it belongs to a different, and larger, scale.

The fourth act, then, provides a markedly different time
sense. The dramatic movement itself is much more leisurely,
almost dangerously so. After two short preparatory scenes, in
which first, two old men discuss a lengthy period of time ("It
is fifteen years since I saw my country") and a younger genera-

22. Cf. Frye, p. 236. Modern biological studies have an interesting
relevance here. John Bleibtreu writes: ". . . seen purely as a biological
phenomenon—that is taking time *out* of the environment, not making it
extrinsic to the organism, but including it as part of the stuff of life itself
—the linear aspect of time is its most frivolous aspect. In biological systems
time represents the metabolic process, the absorption and utilization of
energy. And seen from this point of view, time is rhythmic—the heart
beats, the respiration goes in and out; time is cyclical.

"This is the aspect of time most important to all animals and humans
except those of us tightly caught in the coils of a technological society.
. . . we don't live our lives in accordance with the knowledge of the
importance of cycles on our physiological and psychological well-being. We
know that flowers bloom in the spring, and that the swallows *return* to
Capistrano, but as regards the conduct and apprehension of ourselves
inside the phenomenon of time, we are still entranced by the fallacy of
Western causal logic. The fallacy involves the idea of closed systems.
There are no closed systems in nature; everything involves everything else"
(*The Parable of the Beast* [New York, 1968], chapter 2, "Cyclical Time,"
pp. 32–33).

tion ("when sawest thou the Prince Florizel, my son?"), and second, a Falstaffian rogue who tells time by the seasons, lives for the present, and affirms the sustaining power of comedy over tragedy ("A merry heart goes all the day, / Your sad tires in a mile-a"), Shakespeare moves into one of the longest single scenes he ever wrote (843 lines; the corresponding scene in the first half, 1.2, is 465 lines). The sheep-shearing feast is in itself a means of marking or telling time, one that goes by seasonal event (the harvesting of wool) and is an affirmation of man's relation to natural rhythms and seasonal cycles. It is in many ways a standard pastoral interlude, taking its meaning through the perspective it provides on juxtaposed and neighboring worlds by positing a natural environment where the experience of time is an identification with processes of natural growth and decay, and a celebration of human and natural interrelatedness. The time sense it offers is complex and by no means escapist. There is, for example, the aching awareness of and regard for ephemeral beauty expressed in the talk about flowers:

> O Proserpina,
> For the flowers now that, frighted, thou let'st fall
> From Dis's waggon! daffodils,
> That come before the swallow dares, and take
> The winds of March with beauty; violets, dim,
> But sweeter than the lids of Juno's eyes
> Or Cytherea's breath; pale primroses,
> That die unmarried, ere they can behold
> Bright Phoebus in his strength (a malady
> Most incident to maids); bold oxlips and
> The crown imperial; lilies of all kinds,
> The flower-de-luce being one. O, these I lack,
> To make you garlands of; and my sweet friend,
> To strew him o'er and o'er!
>
> [4.4.116–29]

And there is Florizel's transfer of these qualities to Perdita's own beauty, in his ardent response to her dancing:

What you do
Still betters what is done. When you speak, sweet,
I'd have you do it ever: when you sing,
I'd have you buy and sell so, so give alms,
Pray so, and, for the ord'ring your affairs,
To sing them too: when you do dance, I wish you
A wave o' th' sea, that you might ever do
Nothing but that, move still, still so,
And own no other function.

[135–43]

If we compare this image to Paulina's picture of Leontes'
arrest in time in the play's first half ("A thousand knees /
Ten thousand years together, naked, fasting, / Upon a barren
mountain, and still winter / In storm perpetual"), we can pin-
point the basic features of tragic and comic time in this play.
Paulina envisions the tragic moment as infinitely prolonged
and incessantly re-enacted, perpetual suffering with nature as
a hostile agent; time is a series of fruitless repetitions stretching ahead forever. Florizel relates Perdita's beauty and his
happiness to cyclic patterns, her dance to the natural movement of the wave, "still" only by virtue of endless movement;
it is perfectly clear that her dance cannot be perpetual, any
more than the flowers can last beyond their season, but the
knowledge is acceptable, even pleasurable, against a background of unceasing reproduction and recurrent natural
rhythms. Florizel's wish links art and nature; he has the
artist's urge to capture changing beauty in more permanent
form (to be realized shortly in the statue scene) and the lover's
desire to find some means to perpetuate the beloved through
procreation. His reaction is the opposite of Leontes' revulsion
from women and sex, his bond with time a harmonious and
fruitful one.

The last act completes the traditional pastoral romance
pattern of extrusion and return by reassembling all the characters in Sicily for a series of reunions and revelations. The
pace is brisker ("Such a deal of wonder is broken out within
this hour," "Every wink of an eye, some new grace will be

born"), and the unfolding events are seen both as natural ("Welcome hither, / As is the spring to th' earth" [5.1.150–51] and incredibly artificial ("This news, which is called true, is so like an old tale that the verity of it is in strong suspicion." [5.2.27–29]). The extensive use of the subjunctive mood throughout this section of the play makes its relation to temporal actuality doubtful and complex, but our overall sense of the matter is surely that we are witnessing the attempt, through an extremely artificial and arbitrary mode, to express the restorative value of Time at the extreme of possibility—or, indeed, beyond that extreme, in a realm of wish or ideality where the artist can and must venture.[23] The coming to life of Hermione's statue is an exquisite summary of the temporal complexity we have reached: in terms of the story she is moving back into Time from her suspension outside of it; in terms of our sense of the deliberate and open fiction that is *The Winter's Tale,* she is doing something like the opposite. She is really no less an artifact when she has resumed her place in the story, but in being less obviously so she is really more artificial. Paulina's sleight-of-hand is nothing compared to Shakespeare's, and the deliberate drawing out of suspense in this scene, Paulina's command " 'Tis time," and the statue's slowness to move, all contribute remarkably to the intensification of the Time theme. It is not possible by this point to say with any certainty that the time sense of one genre is superior to another. The larger temporal appeals of comedy and pastoral have in effect subsumed tragedy's vision of time as crisis, but they have accomplished this in a way so markedly artificial as to leave them sharply qualified. To speak of a final understanding of time in *The Winter's Tale,* it is necessary to go beyond genre; and in order

23. Francis Berry, *Poets' Grammar,* contains some interesting speculation on the implications of the subjunctive mood in *The Winter's Tale.* He notes that the handling of verbs in act 5, scene 3 reenacts sixteen years, and says of the lines "Chide me (deire Stone) that I *may say* indeed / Thou *art* Hermione" that "the play achieves its end as the Subjunctive Verb in the first line of the quotation becomes the Indicative Verb of the second" (pp. 73–74).

to do that to turn, not to the play's concluding moments, but to its center, to the peak and vantage point where stands Time himself, the tale's remarkable chorus.

Time's speech has been much impugned by commentators. Its difficulties, even for the reader in sympathy with the style and manner of the play, are real enough that the temptation is strong to pass over the moment as a charming and deliberately archaic device for accomplishing some necessary plot information while intentionally flaunting the play's disregard for classical unity of time, place, and action. While there is much that is right in this response, it is not, as I shall try to show, adequate to the situation or to the speech itself.

Certainly the archaism is undeniable. Father Time had long been a familiar figure in masks and pageants, and he derived from the long-standing catalogue of emblematic figures which were still popular in illustration and moralistic literature.[24] The style and content of his speech are reminiscent of the choric appearance of Fortune in *The Rare Triumphs of Love and Fortune,* the old play which Shakespeare had apparently re-examined in the writing of *Cymbeline*:

Lo, such I am that overthrows the highest-reared Tower,
That changeth and supplanteth realms in twinkling of an
     hour,
And send them hasty smart whom I devise to spoil,
Not threat'ning or forewarning them, but at a smile.
Where joy doth most abound, there do I sorrow place,
And them I chiefly persecute that pleasure did embrace.[25]

Time had indeed already made a choric appearance in another staged pastoral romance, *The Thracian Wonder,* based on Greene's *Menaphon*:

   Chorus. This storm is o'er:
   But now, a greater storm is to be fear'd,

24. See Appendix III, "Time, the Chorus," in Pafford's Arden edition, pp. 167–69, and Samuel C. Chew, "Time and Fortune," *English Literary History* 6 (1939):83–113.
25. *Dodsley's Old English Plays,* ed. Hazlitt, vol. 6, pp. 152–53.

That is, your censures of this history.
From cruel shipwreck you have here beheld
The preservation of these banish'd princes:
Who being put to sea in mastless boats,
With several winds and tides, were driven back
To the same coast that they were banish'd from:
Which understanding, lest they should be known,
They change their names, and habits, and persuade
The silly shepherds they are foreigners:
In several cottages remote from court
These lovers live, thinking each other dead.
The sighs, the tears, the passions that were spent
On either side, we could describe to you;

Enter Time, with an hourglass, sets it down, and exit.

But Time hath barr'd us. This is all you see
That he hath lent us for our history:
I doubt we hardly shall conclude so soon:
But if you please to like our author's pen,
We'll beguile Time, and turn his glass again. *Exit.*[26]

The conventional and archaic aspects of this figure, however, as with the character of Leontes and so much else in the play, merely mark the beginning of Shakespeare's interest. Time has not been brought on, moreover, simply to take care of a problem in the exposition of the plot; all the information he gives us, as Coghill points out, is provided elsewhere in a more natural and acceptable fashion.[27] It behooves us to examine in some detail just what it is that Time has to say to us.

He begins by identifying himself in terms of his multiple functions, using antinomies that reflect the sharp stylistic and structural divisions of the play:

I that please some, try all: both joy and terror
Of good and bad, that makes and unfolds error,

26. Webster, *Dramatic Works,* ed. Hazlitt, vol. 4, p. 136.
27. Nevill Coghill, "Six Points of Stage-craft in *The Winter's Tale,*" *Shakespeare Survey* 11:31–41; esp. p. 35.

> Now take upon me, in the name of Time,
> To use my wings.

Time's omnipotence is established in these lines, but a question lurks around the matter of his identity. The speaker is making his gesture "in the name of Time," so that he is an emblem of Time and someone who assumes that guise, not so much the actor taking the role as the artist who also "makes and unfolds error" and who has a similar power over his material and a similar privilege to use his wings. The Time-artificer identification is pressed in the lines that follow:

> Impute it not a crime
> To me, or my swift passage, that I slide
> O'er sixteen years, and leave the growth untried
> Of that wide gap, since it is in my power
> To o'erthrow law, and in one self-born hour
> To plant and o'erwhelm custom.

The putative crime is an artistic one, the violation of a supposed natural unity in the relation of a story. But unity of time, in light of the relativity of temporal experience and the shaping power of the artistic imagination, is a false criterion. The natural metaphors in these lines—the sixteen years gap is a "growth," custom can be planted and overwhelmed as quickly as a flower is removed by a gardener who has changed his mind—prefigure the vision of time as incessant, fertile change that will pervade the sheep-shearing scene. They also emphasize the relativity of "rules" like unity of time, as perishable as law in a long perspective and likely to be manifestations of the more ephemeral "custom."

The next lines stress the enduring authority of time with particular firmness; but the dual meaning of the speech is by now established in such a way that they seem also to be conferring a similar magnitude and perspective on the imagination, which has after all created the figure of Time and the vista he spreads before us:

> Let me pass
> The same I am, ere ancient'st order was,

> Or what is now receiv'd. I witness to
> The times that brought them in; so shall I do
> To th' freshest things now reigning, and make stale
> The glistering of this present, as my tale
> Now seems to it.

Time subsumes, among other things, the varying notions about art's relation to nature. The staleness of a tale, which will make it seem irrelevant to reality, is something that can overtake the freshest things, presumably including works of art which exhibit great verisimilitude; given this, staleness begins to seem illusory and ephemeral, and old tales take on a new interest; the insight here is not difficult to relate to the attitude which seems to have governed the writings of all the late plays and not a few of the earlier ones.

Time's next statement begins with the phrase, "Your patience this allowing." Patience is the virtue most closely associated with time, the one which informs the actions of Paulina and Hermione in particular, and the one which Shakespeare had earlier associated with art in the images of "Patience on a monument, / Smiling at grief" in *Twelfth Night* (2.4.112–13) and "Patience gazing on kings' graves and smiling / Extremity out of act" in *Pericles* (5.1.139–40). Patience, as Hermione's statuelike time-suspension suggests, is an almost superhuman virtue, oppugnant to time and therefore artificial or unnatural, but it has its rewards in making human suffering bearable and comprehensible. A small measure of it is the condition to the audience for continuing with *The Winter's Tale* and discovering what freshness its stale exterior conceals:

> Your patience this allowing,
> I turn my glass, and give my scene such growing
> As you had slept between: Leontes leaving,
> Th' effects of his fond jealousies so grieving
> That he shuts up himself, imagine me,
> Gentle spectators, that I now may be
> In fair Bohemia, and remember well
> I mentioned a son o' th' kings, which Florizel
> I now name to you; and with speed so pace

> To speak of Perdita, now grown in grace
> Equal with wond'ring.

The only sense in which Time can be said to have "mentioned" Florizel is in his role as maker of the story. In suggesting that he is "leaving" Leontes and going to Bohemia, he identifies himself with the plot, the story line itself. *The Winter's Tale* is Time's tale; Time is the essence of the tale. His role as artificer-presenter is further emphasized in the lines that follow:

> What of her ensues
> I list not prophesy; but let Time's news
> Be known when 'tis brought forth. A shepherd's daughter,
> And what to her ensues, which follows after,
> Is th' argument of Time.

The final conventional flourish of the speech has an air of paradox about it:

> Of this allow,
> If ever you have spent time worse ere now;
> If never, yet that Time himself doth say,
> He wishes earnestly you never may.

To be told by Time himself that it is up to you to decide whether listening to him and a story which is his "argument" is a profitable way to spend *time* is to be left a little bewildered and more than a little disarmed.

Time's speech, as I have tried to suggest, offers the reader or spectator a unique perspective, one which partakes of the artist's attitude toward his materials (a peculiar mixture of engagement and detachment) and of a strong sense of relativity—the relativity of genres, laws, fashions, and categories. It spreads a world before us in which anything is possible, but everything is subject to change, including the meaning of experience in nature and in art. The effect of the speech is to add to the peculiar bilateral symmetry of the play a kind of radial symmetry as well, since every possibility of human life and human art exists as a result of Time's sway, his centrality to existence. It is one of the most remarkable and revealing moments in all of Shakespeare's art. And surely too it is significant that so much of *The Winter's Tale*'s complex vision —a vision of human life and of human attempts to arrive at expression and understanding of that life—should come to us through the most obviously outmoded dramatic device in the whole melange of archaic and primitive materials that go to make up this play. Time's overview refers us once more to the uniqueness that arises from the very structure of *The Winter's Tale*: its striking rehandling, through juxtaposed genres, of the pattern of extrusion and restoration, the dual worlds so characteristic of pastoral romance. The roots of the story are the same ones that gave rise to *As You Like It* and *King Lear*; yet it is at least as different from them as they are from each other. Apparently not satisfied to have produced these three great branches from the trunk of pastoral romance, Shakespeare turned in his next play to yet a fourth, and it is to that last effort, *The Tempest,* that we turn our attention now.

5

Rough Magic: *The Tempest*

> We have seen that the act of imagination is a magical one. It is an incantation destined to produce the object of one's thought, the thing one desires, in a manner that one can take possession of it. In that act there is always something of the imperious and the infantile, a refusal to take distance or difficulties into account.
>
> Jean-Paul Sartre, *The Psychology of Imagination*

> *Ferdinand.* This is a most majestic vision and
> Harmonious charmingly. May I be bold
> To think these spirits?
> *Prospero.*   Spirits, which by mine Art
> I have from their confines call'd to enact
> My present fancies.
>
> *The Tempest*

The story of castaways on a desert island is such a familiar and popular narrative design that we are more apt to think of it in terms of its "modern" manifestations (from *Robinson Crusoe* to *The Admirable Crichton* to *The Lord of the Flies,* not to mention innumerable cartoons, films, and jokes) than to trace its literary ancestry back to the *Odyssey* or to consider its longstanding relation to the pastoral mode. Yet its pastoral character is undeniable. It embodies the same ambivalence between a desire to escape to a simpler form of existence and a fear of being cut off from society, civilization, indeed all human company. It raises the same questions about man's essential goodness or savagery, nature versus nurture. And despite its emphasis on an alien and alternative setting, it often serves mainly as a mirror of society, tracing the formation of a readjusted social microcosm and testing familiar values and customs.[1]

An island may differ very slightly from the more traditional pastoral landscapes, the Arcadias, Ardens, and Bohemias, but it differs in interesting ways. It is apt to be more alien and strange, harder to reach and harder, of course, to escape from. It has a self-contained, consistent quality that makes it easy to present as a utopia, untouched by outside influences, or as a society in miniature, the model of a commonwealth or kingdom. If it is a "desert" island, that is, deserted or nearly so, then it raises the questions of self-sufficiency and survival: how does the castaway procure enough food, shelter, and protection from animals or savages? Many of these features were of course associated with pastoral settings other than islands, but taken together they suggest why a writer of pastoral might choose such a setting and what he might do with it.

It would have been remarkable indeed if Renaissance pastoral, in an age of discovery and exploration, had not resorted to the island setting as a response to popular interest and to the imaginative horizons that were being opened by the tales of mariners and rescued castaways. The pastoral concern with alternatives to urban society and the courts of monarchs expanded easily to a consideration of the distant and unfamiliar places that explorers were finding and colonizers were venturing toward.

But that is not the whole story of the desert island branch of the pastoral. If it were, *The Tempest* might well be set in the Caribbean or the Pacific.[2] That it is not, is an indication of the continuing strength of the tradition of classical epic and

1. Other discussions of *The Tempest* and the pastoral mode include Carol Gesner, "*The Tempest* as Pastoral Romance," *Shakespeare Quarterly* 10 (Autumn 1959):531–39, which argues for *Daphnis and Chloe* as a direct influence on the play; Leo Marx, "Shakespeare's American Fable," chap. 2 in *The Machine in the Garden: Technology and the Pastoral Ideal in America* (New York, 1964), pp. 34–72; and Frank Kermode, "Introduction," *The Tempest*, Arden edition (rev. 1958).

2. As Fletcher's *The Island Princess*, though scarcely a pastoral, is set in the East Indies.

romance. If Shakespeare draws upon the pamphlets of the voyagers for some of the details of his island and refers us to the "still-vex'd Bermoothes," he nevertheless sets Prospero's island in the Mediterranean, amid the currents of older civilizations and literary traditions. The isle is full of noises, and some of them seem to echo Virgil, Ovid, Homer, and the romance tradition stretching back to Longus and Heliodorus.[3] The old and the new, ancient myth and legend on the one hand, and the True Declarations and True Repertories of the pamphlets on the other, are simultaneously invoked.

The islands of the older tradition were as often as not enchanted, the realm of a Circe or a hermetic sorcerer. Perhaps that is why the Bermuda pamphlets had to contradict the rumors that spirits and devils inhabited the islands. The assumption, given the literary tradition, was not unwarranted, and recalling that the islands of epic and romance were sometimes realms of enchantment gives us another way of stressing the fact that the island setting in pastoral was more self-contained, more marvelous, and, often, more terrifying. If one's pastoral sojourn was spent combatting or submitting to the power of a ruler who was also a necromancer, the results were apt to be more spectacular and less peaceful.

Once again, then, Shakespeare has founded a play on the characteristic pattern of pastoral romance, with its story of exile, sojourn, and reunion, and its emphatic use of setting. This time he has ventured into a notable variation, where the setting is an island, and the accelerated sojourn is dreamlike and amazing because it is entirely the product of an enchanter's art—an enchanter who is himself a long sojourner. The result is a play that differs markedly from any of the other pastorals in structure, texture, and tone, a play at once disarmingly simple and bafflingly complex.

While my remarks have thus far suggested that the combination of an enchanted island, ruled by a magician, with the standard pastoral story of extrusion, sojourn, and return was readily available to Shakespeare, given the romance tradition

3. J. M. Nosworthy, "The Narrative Sources of *The Tempest*," *Review of English Studies* 24 (1948):281–94, puts particular stress on *The Aeneid*.

and the natural coincidence of interests and possibilities such materials shared, it is nevertheless necessary to consider carefully whether the combination already existed in some form which may have influenced the character and construction of *The Tempest.* The answer, which can be confidently put in terms of existence and more cautiously advanced as regards influence, is somewhat surprising. This time we are not concerned with the pastoral novels by writers like Greene, Lodge, and Sidney that were so strong an influence on English stage pastoral in general and Shakespeare in particular. This time the influence, if that is what may be claimed for such a surprisingly close analogue, or group of them, is dramatic and continental: the *Commedia dell'Arte.* These plays survive only in their rough outlines, the *scenari* from which the players improvised their performances, using a stock of tried and tested comic bits called *lazzi.* What the collections of *scenari* clearly show is that the Italian comedians, combining literary fashions with their sense of what could be made effective for a diverse audience on the stage, worked up their own special genre of pastoral, a combination of horseplay, music, spectacular magic, love interest, and mistaken identity. The enchanted island was a standard setting for such plays, and the action was often initiated by a shipwreck.[4]

These "shipwreck pastorals" had in common with *The Tempest* the following more or less standard features: characters cast ashore and dispersed to wander on an enchanted island, the domain of a magician who was generally both mischievous—so he could play tricks on the castaways—and benign—so that he could straighten out misunderstandings, prevent tragedy, and neatly resolve complications at the finish; humor based on fearful recognition by survivors who

4. The best account of such plays and their possible relation to *The Tempest* is to be found in K. M. Lea's two volume study *Italian Popular Comedy* (Oxford, 1934). She describes the pastorals (1:201–12), considers *The Tempest* in light of its relationship to them (2:442–53), and in an appendix includes nine examples of pastoral scenari. An imaginative recreation and discussion of the performance of one of these, *Arcadia incantata,* may be found in Allardyce Nicoll, *World Drama from Aeschylus to Anouilh* (New York, 1950), pp. 191–95.

think each other ghosts of drowned comrades; natives so awed
by the visitors that they worship them as gods; spirits who
make use of invisibility to echo, mislead, and confuse their
victims; such standard pieces of stage magic as charmed
swords, disappearing food, and spirits in grotesque and fright-
ening guises; and a generous proportion of singing and dancing. None of these features are found all together in one existing scenario, an *Ur-Tempest,* but they are common enough
to the genre that if, as Lea suggests, a scenario of *The Tempest*
were inserted in one of the existing collections of *commedia
scenari,* the resemblance would be remarkable.[5] However we
are to account for it, there seems to be something more than
coincidence at work.

The obstacles to declaring the pastoral tragicomedies of the
commedia players an important source for *The Tempest* have,
however, proved manifold, and the relationship has yet to
win wide acceptance. There is, in the first place, the traditional preference of Shakespearean source hunters for nondramatic as opposed to dramatic sources, and for textual as
opposed to nontextual influences. We have traditionally been
willing to assume that if a book was in print or even available
in manuscript, then Shakespeare had it to hand and read it;
textual parallels have always had a comfortable solidity and
certainty. We know far less about stage practices and styles,
however, both in England and on the Continent. As a result,
source studies have shied away from these areas, and what
may be a somewhat lopsided picture of Shakespeare as a working dramatist has inevitably emerged. In the case of the *commedia* shipwreck pastorals, textual evidence is of course un-
available. What remains? The fact that Italian players had
visited England from the 1570's onward, and possibly as close
to the writing of *The Tempest* as 1610.[6] The additional fact
that Englishmen regularly travelled to Italy and brought back
detailed accounts of what they had seen, including theatrical

5. Lea, 2:434.

6. For a general account see Chambers, 2:261–65. For the 1610 date see
Chambers, "The Integrity of *The Tempest*," *Review of English Studies* 1
(April 1925):133.

performances. And, finally, what seems to me the common sense view that Shakespeare, as a man of the theater as well as the study, had every reason to inform himself, in as much detail as possible and by whatever means, about the resources available to him through theatrical styles and modes in other countries. Judging by its wide influence and great popularity, both in Italy and elsewhere, the *commedia dell'arte* is scarcely something Shakespeare could have ignored or overlooked. There is evidence in plays as early as *The Comedy of Errors* and *Love's Labour's Lost* to suggest his familiarity with it.

Another obstacle to acceptance of the *commedia* influence on *The Tempest* has been the peculiarly sacrosanct status of the play itself. There is a question, apparently, of dignity. A lesser play, *The Merry Wives of Windsor*, for instance, might readily be admitted to have such roots. But *The Tempest* has a special status—it is the last play, a final statement, a summary and farewell. Commentators have delighted to conclude that, indebted to no source for its story, it shows Shakespeare at his most inventive and ingenious. And those who have found in the play autobiography, profound religious allegory, Neo-Platonic mysteries, and immense erudition, have scarcely wished to connect it with the debased literary values and low improvised theater of the Italian comedians. It would seem rather like saying that Henry James found his inspiration for *The Ambassadors* by attending the Folies Bérgère. Even Frank Kermode, the play's best modern editor and one of its most astute commentators, succumbs to this attitude. Concluding a discussion of the possibility of the *commedia* as a source, he suggests that "Shakespeare had other and more suggestive materials for speculation. He did not need a jocose pantomime to teach him how to think about it." [7]

We need only recall Shakespeare's deep and fully demonstrated interest in the rudimentary, popular, and supposedly obsolete materials of his art, especially in the late plays, to find this unfair and misleading. Indeed, Kermode himself is on much firmer ground when he remarks, earlier on, that "The presence of primitive elements in the deeply considered

7. Arden edition, p. lxviii.

structure of *The Tempest* need not surprise us; they are a normal Shakespearean phenomenon. . . ." [8] It seems a short step from an interest in crude romances, folk tales, and archetypal characters and situations, to an intensely vigorous and highly stylized popular theater using masks and "jocose pantomime." Given Shakespeare's interest in clumsy old plays and crude forms of popular entertainment (e.g., the Whitsun pastoral), there is little that can be called new in the suggestion of the *commedia* influence but the Continental flavoring, and even that, as I have suggested, was not finding its way into Shakespeare's dramatic repertoire for the first time.

I have put this stress on the question of source materials for *The Tempest* because I believe, with E. E. Stoll, that the play "stands like a tub on its own bottom," [9] and that it is important to recognize that bottom for what it is. Once again Shakespeare is revealing rather than concealing the artifice on which his theater is inevitably based; once again he is inviting the audience to join him in considering the nature of art, fiction, fable, tale, and to be conscious of the way in which he is transforming and sophisticating crude and unlikely materials. Such claims could be made for *The Tempest* even without the recognition of the *commedia* influence. The magician, the wild man, perhaps even the shipwrecked clowns and courtiers, were scarcely foreign to the English stage. But once one has begun to consider the play in this light, once the psychological barrier to crude theatrical sources has dropped away, the *commedia* parallels are simply too strong to ignore or make light of. My suggestion, then—and it must remain that in the absence of firmer evidence than is likely to turn up—is that in *The Tempest* Shakespeare was deliberately resorting to the organization and manner of the pastoral tragicomedies of the *commedia dell'arte*. Far from attempting to conceal this fact

8. Ibid., p. lxiii.

9. *Shakespeare and Other Masters* (1940), p. 281. I would also stress Northrop Frye's comment: "*The Tempest* is not an allegory, or a religious drama: if it were, Prospero's great 'revels' speech would say, not merely that all earthly things will vanish, but that an eternal world will take their place" (*The Complete Pelican Shakespeare*, ed. Alfred Harbage [Baltimore, 1969], p. 1370).

from his audience, he expected from them some measure of recognition, the kind he had relied on, in varying degrees, concerning the antecedents of *Pericles, Cymbeline,* and *The Winter's Tale.* Much of the recognition would have come, of course, in extra-textual areas, in the style of playing and general tone. In addition, we need not exclude the possibility of an earlier English play, fairly well-known and closely based on *commedia* pastoral tragicomedy. Once again there is evidence, but it is too slender to allow us to speak with certainty.[10]

One benefit of this approach to *The Tempest,* through the "back door" of dramatic resources, is that it allows us to differentiate sharply between this play and the other late romances in the matter of structure. If the other plays were self-conscious attempts to transfer narrative materials to the stage with a minimum of alteration, *The Tempest* emphatically is not. That, indeed, is what suggests it is built on a dramatic model rather than on a pastoral novel. If Shakespeare knew of the shipwreck pastorals of the *commedia,* he would immediately have understood how the players had solved the problem of finding dramatic form for the lyric and narrative elements of pastoral. The enchanted island gave a single, highly flexible setting; the shipwreck provided a fortuitous assembling of characters who were to discover their identities and relationships; and the magician's omnipotence excused wild improbabilities of time scheme and resolution. The resulting plots were highly unlikely, but admitted both tight organization and great variety of incident. The comedians had resolved the problem of achieving the neoclassical unities by simply imposing them from the outside, without regard to the ques-

10. The New Cambridge editors found traces of rhymed couplets and doggerel in the text, which they took to indicate that Shakespeare was working from an old manuscript. Examples:

> I did not give the lie. Out of your wits, and hearing too?
> A pox of your bottle! this can sack and drinking do.

> [3.2.76–78]

> If you'll sit down, I'll bear the logs the while:
> Pray give me that; I'll carry it to the pile.

> [3.1.23–25]

tion of improbability. Shakespeare's pleasure in duplicating this design, with the same double-consciousness provided for the audience that was present in *The Winter's Tale*'s treatment of genre, seems a likely explanation for the unusually tight structure of *The Tempest*. Adhering to the unities becomes a kind of game, with so many references to the exact timing of the action scattered through the play that the spectator begins to feel he can almost set his watch by it.

This point raises the larger question of theatricality and open artifice in *The Tempest*, a subject generally neglected by interpreters anxious not to detract from the foundations of what they see as an allegorical structure. For if the play, like the other late romances and like the other pastorals, is concerned to point up the fictive and wishful characters of the ideals it advances and explores, then it is markedly different in tone from the play that is so reverently served up to us in most commentaries and stage productions. This is not to deny the ultimate seriousness of *The Tempest* or, indeed, its complexity of vision; it is rather to suggest that these are accomplished by the playful double-consciousness about the materials being used, in particular their distance from reality, that we found to be so pervasive in *The Winter's Tale*.

Consider the opening scene. Without questioning its effectiveness in relation to the play as a whole, we can readily admit that it was impossible to stage such a scene realistically in a Jacobean theater—whether the Globe or the Blackfriars. *The Tempest* opens, then, by putting a strain on the capacities of its medium. Its audience is unlikely to be transported from the theater; they are rather kept highly conscious of it. Within the scene are strongly realistic elements in the behavior and speech of the characters; but the storm itself, and the shipwreck, must remain, as Coleridge suggested, "poetical, though not in strictness natural." [11]

The appropriateness of the artifice is quickly revealed in the following scene, where we discover that the storm was in fact illusory, the product of a magician's art. We now meet the man who is to be not only the principal actor in the events

11. *Shakespearean Criticism*, ed. T. M. Raysor (London, 1960), 1:118.

that follow, but their author, director, and stage manager as well. Sharing Prospero's consciousness will in effect keep us "backstage" throughout, with a special knowledge of events, their appearance and their reality, their origins and consequences. Prospero's control of the action, the dramatizing properties of his magic, and his vision of life itself as a gigantic theater of illusion, all contribute greatly to the theatrical atmosphere of *The Tempest*.[12]

This second scene takes us through the exposition. The one drawback to observing the neoclassical unities, especially in dealing with the time span involved in a romance story like *The Tempest*, is the necessity for a detailed exposition early in the play. Character X must tell character Y, at some length, what character Y would probably, under normal circumstances, know already. This cumbersome bit of artifice, then, was the necessary prelude to the supposed verisimilitude that the unities were intended to secure. Is it not possible to suppose that Shakespeare is emphasizing this point, in a spirit of playfulness, rather than concealing it? Miranda says Prospero's tale "would cure deafness," but it is in fact a dangerously tedious device to spring on an audience at this point. It has been suggested that Prospero's interruptions to make sure Miranda is paying attention are a clever method for breaking up his long monologue and giving it dramatic interest; I think rather they call attention, not to his state of mind or to Miranda's behavior, but to the strain on the medium that Shakespeare's choice of subject and structure has entailed. The game of observing the unities, as I have called it, really begins here.

As the play moves forward, the theatricality of the opening scenes is carefully sustained. The fact that Prospero's magicianship is a *role* he plays is emphasized by the special garment it requires, a costume which he dons and doffs, and by special props, his book and staff. With Ferdinand and Miranda he must play a calculated part, that of the jealous ruler and gruff father, and he keeps the audience informed of the fact that he is *acting*. We are less sure whether the attitudes

12. Cf. Anne Righter, *Shakespeare and the Idea of the Play* (London, 1962), p. 201.

he assumes with Ariel and Caliban are spontaneous or calculated; some mixture of the two seems most likely. In the last
scene we watch him assume his pre-play identity, the one by
which most of the characters, with their limited awareness,
must know him:

> Not one of them
> That yet looks on me, or would know me: Ariel,
> Fetch me the hat and rapier in my cell:
> I will discase me, and myself present
> As I was sometime Milan.
>
> [5.1.82–86]

Then, for the audience, who have been privy to all the details
of his "project" (see 2.1.294 and 5.1.1 for his use of that
term), he makes one last appearance, adopts one final role: in
the Epilogue he speaks to us in his identity as actor, an enter-
tainer revealing the special purpose of his "project . . . which
was to please." Which is the real Prospero? The last of these
roles only, or the sum of all of them?

Prospero's "art" consists mainly of shows and spectacles.
Their purposes are varied—to entertain, to punish, to en-
lighten, to instruct—and our sense of their reality fluctuates,
even as we learn that they have an illusory content in common.
Was there, for example, a storm? Ariel "Perform'd" a tempest,
"flam'd amazement," simulated lightning and made a storm
"Seem to besiege" the sea. But Miranda, an uninformed witness, is convinc'd that she saw "a brave vessel . . . Dashed all
to pieces." Prospero's last show, the tableau of Ferdinand and
Miranda playing chess, is quite real, although Alonso is justified in questioning it:

> If this prove
> A vision of the island, one dear son
> Shall I lose twice.
>
> [5.1.175–77]

Between these events are a number of "performances" which
are, we understand, illusory, since we are told that they consist of "spirits" playing "strange Shapes," mythological figures,
and "dogs and hounds." Yet at the interruption of one of these

shows Prospero tells Ferdinand that the evanescent character of such "revels," performed by spirits to "enact" the "present fancies" of a magician, reflects the very substance of the world and of human life. Our certainty is once more undermined.

It is ironic, in these circumstances, that theatrical metaphors should be associated with the behavior of the villains. Prospero tells Miranda that his brother was not content to be the acting Duke:

> To have no screen between this part he play'd
> And him he play'd it for, he needs will be
> Absolute Milan.
>
> [1.2.107–09]

Antonio himself, inciting Sebastian to the murder of his brother, argues that they were cast ashore on the island,

> . . . by destiny, to perform an act
> Whereof what's past is prologue; what to come,
> In yours and my discharge.
>
> [2.1.247–49]

Even Stephano, parodying these illusory conspiracies, tries to sound like a villain out of an old tragedy, and mistakes costume for the reality it is meant to clothe:

> *Stephano.* Give me thy hand. I do begin to have bloody thoughts.
> *Trinculo.* O King Stephano! O peer! O worthy Stephano! Look what a wardrobe here is for thee!
>
> [4.1.220–23]

Most of the events of *The Tempest* acquire a theatrical quality by virtue of the fact that they consist of actors and audience. Miranda witnesses the storm, and she and Prospero discuss the bewildered Ferdinand before he is aware of their presence. Prospero oversees the young couple's courtship as a concealed, appreciative spectator:

> Fair encounter
> Of two most rare affections! Heavens rain grace
> On that which breeds between 'em!
>
> [3.1.74–75]

He later makes them the audience to a betrothal masque in their honor. Prospero also watches from "on the top" the scene of the disappearing banquet, at which the courtly party first think themselves audience ("A living drollery," exclaims Sebastian), then find themselves actors, so that they become a sort of show within a show. In the last scene, nearly everyone is audience to the revelation of Ferdinand and Miranda, where once again, as Ferdinand steps forth to embrace his father, the line between witnesses and performers dissolves.

We may observe, finally, in the very neatness and wholeness of the design of the play an artificial quality that I do not think we are meant to overlook. Everything occurs on schedule, with a clockwork precision that allows Gonzalo to marvel, in the final moments of the play, at the mechanism that has just been revealed to him:

> Was Milan thrust from Milan, that his issue
> Should become Kings of Naples? O, rejoice
> Beyond a common joy! and set it down
> With gold on lasting pillars: in one voyage
> Did Claribel her husband find at Tunis,
> And Ferdinand, her brother, found a wife
> Where he himself was lost, Prospero his dukedom
> In a poor isle, and all of us ourselves
> When no man was his own.
>
> [5.1.205–13]

This is very tidy indeed, perhaps a little too tidy. We have had no concern for Claribel finding a husband, and what Gonzalo seems to see as the operation of destiny we have come to recognize as largely the result of Prospero's theatrical magic. We appreciate the conciseness of it all, but we do not believe in it quite the way that Gonzalo appears to believe in it ("Look down, you gods . . . For it is you that have chalk'd forth the way / Which brought us hither."). Our sense of its total artifice is very much stronger.

The qualities of artifice and theatricality seem to be the best basis for further exploration of the characters, themes, and atmosphere of *The Tempest*. I referred earlier to the observation of the unities as a kind of game shared by the playwright with his audience. I have been describing another kind of game as well: that of taking slightly shabby and popularized materials, long associated with the stage and especially with the stock plots of the *commedia dell'arte,* and restoring their serious artistic purpose, creating from them a fresh new fable with a peculiarly self-contained quality and a profundity and mystery all its own. In a sense, this had been Shakespeare's practice throughout his career as a dramatist. But in *The Tempest,* as with the other pastorals and the late plays in general, the success of the enterprise depends on the openness with which the materials are employed and the degree to which the fable is seen as fable throughout. As we shall see, Shakespeare's handling of the magician and his magic, the dreamlike and unstable world that is built up, and the treatment of the great pastoral themes of art and nature, are all related intimately to the deliberately unrealistic materials from which the play is shaped.

❧

No one would contest, on the evidence of plays as diverse as *Henry VI* (parts 1 and 2), *A Midsummer Night's Dream,* and *Macbeth,* Shakespeare's interest in magic; but it is just as evident that the presence of magic and the centrality of the magician is one of the features that most clearly distinguishes *The Tempest* from the other late romances. We have only Cerimon's brief appearance in *Pericles* and the quasi-magical powers of the Queen in *Cymbeline* and Paulina in *The Winter's Tale* as points of comparison. Just why Shakespeare centered this play on the figure of the magician and gave it his point of view, then, is a subject of considerable interest, and an investigation of it should help to understand the uniqueness of Prospero as a dramatic character and his relation to the play as a whole.

I have already suggested that there hung about the familiar figure of the stage magician a certain ambivalence. On the one hand his power made him a fearful figure, not least because he tended to be whimsical and irritable, easily moved to practice his art on helpless victims; on the other hand he was inclined to benevolence, fulfilling the desires of others and helping them out of difficulties. These qualities can be seen in Bacon, the famous conjurer of Greene's comedy, *Friar Bacon and Friar Bungay*, who alternates between discomfiting those who cross him, and aiding those who seek him out for help. In Anthony Munday's *John a Kent and John a Cumber*, each of the rival magicians belongs to an opposing faction, to which he remains loyal. But before the contest is fully under way, we see a mischievous urge to complicate things for his own faction overtake John a Kent. He has no sooner succeeded in uniting the lovers, as instructed, than he is thinking of ways to delay and complicate the resolution:

> Heers loove and loove: Good Lord! was nere the lyke!
> But must these joys so quickly be concluded?
> Must the first Scene make absolute a Play?
> No crosse, no chaunge? What! no varietie?
> One brunt is past. Alas! what's that, in loove?
> Where firme affection is most truly knit,
> The loove is sweetest that moste tryes the wit.
> And, by my troth, to sport my selfe awhyle,
> The disappoynted brydegroomes, these possest,
> The fathers, freendes, and other more besyde,
> That may be usde to furnishe up conceite,
> Ile set on woorke in such an amorous warre,
> As they shall wunder whence ensues this jarre.[13]

Similar qualities can be found in the tragic figure of Marlowe's Faustus: while a greater proportion of his drama is concerned with the psychology of the magician, personal fulfillment turning to self-gratification, a number of scenes are devoted mainly to his relations with others; once again there is a mixture of punishing and rewarding, most of it in the form of vigorous and farcical horseplay. These scenes have seemed so much at variance with the tragic portions of the play that commentators have questioned both their relevance

13. Munday, *John a Kent and John a Cumber,* Shakespeare Society Reprints (London, 1851), p. 22.

and authenticity. Yet they do reflect in a crude form the duality of magic, its potential for good and evil, self-realization and self-indulgence, a duality that accounts in part for Faustus' inner struggle. Part of his magicianship is noble: a search for knowledge and truth. Part is ignoble: the desire for superiority and complete power over others. The scenes of practical joking and flashy conjuring dramatize the ignoble side effectively; they are also, whether or not they are Marlowe's, clearly the stuff of rousing popular theater.

If the magician was ambivalent, his art was not less so. Bacon's magic causes inadvertent destruction, and he consequently decides to renounce it, the comic equivalent, roughly, of Faustus' damnation. Prospero is of course a "white" magician, who does not traffic with devils or endanger his soul, but there is a sense in which he can be seen as a kind of cross between Friar Bacon or John a Kent on the one hand, and Doctor Faustus on the other. Like the former he is set in a comic context, where he can practice and ultimately renounce his art with relative impunity. Like the latter he is a serious and complex figure, whose point of view the audience is allowed to share in full. Many of his qualities and characteristics are perfectly familiar in terms of the tradition that Faustus, Bacon, and John a Kent share. His control of his spirits is uneasy (Ariel's restiveness is quite within the tradition). He has a comic, grumbling servant whom he sometimes uses his spirits to torment. He discovers plots against himself and others through an omniscience partly based on his own power of invisibility. He protects himself by charming the swords of potential enemies. And his role disturbs him enough that he is inclined to give it up; Bacon renounces magic and Faustus' last desperate offer is to burn his books, while Prospero promises to drown his book and break his staff. There is much about Prospero, in other words, which Shakespeare's audience would have found recognizable and familiar.

One way of understanding the magician's role is to consider it as an expression of power, and we can accomplish that by comparing Prospero to a king. Shakespeare's audience was well versed in the implications of kingship—its potential for

self-indulgence and concomitant need for self-control, its isolating tendencies, and the responsibility for the welfare of
others it entailed. A concentration of power in the hands of
an individual, they knew, involved unusual psychological
stress. And they were often reminded that, in metaphysical
terms, the worldly authority of the monarch was an illusion.
Pastoral could be used to make such a point, and one of the
effects of the storm that opens *The Tempest* is to assert the
relativity and fragility of political power in the face of ungov-
ernable elements:

> *Boatswain.* . . . What cares these roarers for the name
> of King? To cabin: silence! Trouble us not.
> *Gonzalo.* Good, yet remember whom thou hast aboard.
> *Boatswain.* None that I love more than myself. You are
> a counsellor; if you can command these elements to si-
> lence, and work the peace of the presence, we will not
> hand a rope more; use your authority: if you cannot, give
> thanks you have lived so long, and make yourself ready
> in your cabin for the mischance of the hour, if it so hap.
> [1.1.16–26]

The reader will recall similar expressions in *As You Like It*
and *Lear*: the difference here, as we discover in the following
scene, is that there does exist someone whose name "these
roarers" care for, who can command the elements to silence.
As the illusion of political power is stripped away, Prospero
steps in to fill the vacancy, not only as ruler of the island, or,
ultimately, restored Duke of Milan, but as a kind of meta-
king whose power, based on knowledge, extends to nature and
is, paradoxically, more real because it is grounded in illusion.

Shakespeare's interest in the character of this magician-king
is considerable, and Prospero's speeches and actions are rich
in psychological implication. It is important to recognize,
however, that Prospero is not a character study in the sense
that Lear and Macbeth and Othello are. He is the inhabitant
of a fable, a dream vision, a tale which is acknowledged to be
a kind of giant hypothesis, combining the ideals of pastoral
and magic: what if you had an island all your own, where

you were not only lord and master, but had an absolute power, even over the elements, that gave you an astonishing harmony with your environment and complete control over others, including your enemies? *The Tempest* is the complicated answer to that question, and much of its complexity comes from Prospero. Least surprising, perhaps, is the great satisfaction he takes in the successful exercise of his power:

> Now does my project gather to a head:
> My charms crack not; my spirits obey; and time
> Goes upright with his carriage.
>
> > [5.1.1–3]

That this is an unnatural power over others, with selfish implications, does not go unnoticed:

> Go charge my goblins that they grind their joints
> With dry convulsions; shorten up their sinews
> With aged cramps; and more pinch-spotted make them
> Than pard or cat o' the mountain.
> > . . . At this hour
> Lies at my mercy all mine enemies!
>
> > [4.1.258–63]

Prospero, as many commentators have noted, experiences some struggle between the urge to be merciful, playing the role of Destiny rightly and well, and the urge to carry out his unimpeded revenge:

> Though with their high wrongs I am struck to th' quick,
> Yet with my nobler reason 'gainst my fury
> Do I take part: the rarer action is
> In virtue than in vengeance: they being penitent,
> The sole drift of my purpose doth extend
> Not a frown further.
>
> > [5.1.25–30]

The immediate result of this decision is Prospero's renunciation of his "so potent Art," a renunciation accompanied by a magnificent catalogue of the wonders he has been able to accomplish. To forego his power to revenge himself is, in a sense, to forego his "rough magic" altogether.

It has also been recognized that the play involves Prospero,
and us, in the discovery that his magic, absolute as it seems
at the outset, has limitations. It cannot, apparently, alter Antonio's evil nature. It achieves Ariel's cooperation only by a
combination of threats and promises. And it has been distinctly unsuccessful with Caliban, a fact that seems to affect
Prospero deeply:

> *Prospero.* [*Aside.*] I had forgot that foul conspiracy
> Of the beast Caliban and his confederates
> Against my life. . . .
> *Ferdinand.* This is strange: your father's in some passion
> That works him strongly.
> *Miranda.* Never till this day
> Saw I him touch'd with anger, so distemper'd.
>
> [4.1.139–45]
>
> *Prospero.* A devil, a born devil, on whose nature
> Nurture can never stick; on whom my pains,
> Humanely taken, all, all lost, quite lost;
> And as with age his body uglier grows,
> So his mind cankers. I will plague them all,
> Even to roaring.
>
> [188–93]

While these touches quicken our interest in Prospero and give
him a measure of psychological truth, it would be a mistake
to overemphasize them. Little suspense, in light of the overriding hypothesis of the play, can attach to them. To think of
The Tempest as in the main devoted to Prospero's discovery
of the limitations of his magic and the need for mercy and forgiveness, is to seriously distort it and its central character.
Prospero's complexity, ultimately, is based on the fact that
Shakespeare has concentrated in him a number of possibilities and themes; if he is a man learning about power and forgiveness, he is also a kind of god, a hypothetically extended
consciousness. Shakespeare has brought together in his character the old bald thing, the Time of *The Winter's Tale* who
authors the story and can thus offer us the largest perspective
(and a degree of choric detachment), the wronged duke of

pastoral romance (here, as in *Lear,* upstaging the lovers of the next generation), and the mage or sorcerer whose power is such that he can guide events to a succesful, if artificial, conclusion.

To these observations about the magician, it is necessary to add some consideration of his magic. What are its characteristics, and how does it operate? We can begin by noting the natural tendency of stage magic to acquire a theatrical character, introducing spectacle, coups de théâtre, and pageantry. Bacon, Faustus, and the two Johns of Kent and Cumber illustrate this nicely. Bacon's magic mirror, the "glass prospective," becomes the means for presenting dramatic vignettes, little plays within the play, while the conjuring contest involving Bungay, Vandermast, and Bacon gives opportunity to present that familiar Elizabethan stage prop, the magic tree with golden apples, accompanied by a fire-breathing dragon. In *Doctor Faustus* the tendency toward spectacular theatrical display is especially evident in the pageant of the seven deadly sins, the conjuring of Alexander and his paramour, and the raising of Helen to the accompaniment of music. The rivalry between John a Kent and John a Cumber involves their abilities as conjurers and showmen. John a Cumber, posing as John a Kent, introduces a pageant of supposed "Antiques" who are in fact his faction of lovers, using the device to take over the castle. John a Kent's revenge comes in similar terms; he so confuses shadow and substance during a "show" that John a Cumber is trying to present, that the latter becomes the butt of everyone's humor, and is made to wear the fool's costume in a morris dance. The *commedia* pastorals are full of similar tricks, pageants, conjurings, and spectacles, and their property lists regularly call for the necessary equipment: "Chains, earthquakes, flames, and a hell to open for Pluto"; "Temple of Bacchus to open, fountain, grotto, fiery gulf to open, meat and drink"; "Tree, rock to explode, whale, fountain, temple"; "a tree with fruit which will disappear into the air." [14]

Shakespeare has, if anything, intensified the theatricality of

14. Lea, 2:636–37, 648, 663, 674.

stage magic in *The Tempest*. Both the unity and diversity of
the play depend in great part on this element, since it provides a variety of events which nevertheless have in common
their source in Prospero's art. One way of describing the structure of *The Tempest* is as a series of magic tricks engineered
by Prospero. He begins with the storm, involving all of the
visitors to the island, with his daughter as audience and himself and Ariel as producer and chief actor. He then divides the
shipwrecked characters into three parties (Ferdinand being a
party of one) and disperses them around the island. Ariel figures in the separate adventures of each party—leading Ferdinand to Miranda with music, interrupting Antonio's conspiracy, and tricking the clowns, first into the beating of Trinculo,
then into the horsepond near Prospero's cell—and in each case
these adventures are climaxed with a show, a phantasmagoric
pageant performed by Prospero's spirits.[15] The courtly party
are treated to the disappearing banquet and Ariel as a harpy;
Ferdinand and Miranda are shown the betrothal masque with
the descent of Juno, the appearance of Ceres, and the dance
of nymphs and reapers; and the clowns are beguiled by the
frippery and set upon by the hunt. In the first and last of these
cases, the audience becomes unwilling participants in the
show, while Ferdinand and Miranda enjoy a security that allows them to become involved in their pageant only as recipi-
ents of the goddesses' blessing. These three shows climax their
respective plots, and the play ends with a grand reunion and
a final piece of theater: the revelation-tableau of Ferdinand
and Miranda at chess.

A great part of Prospero's magic, then, seems to be based
on visual deception and display, an art that is plainly analogous to the world of the theater in which it all takes place. The
difference, of course, lies in the victimization of the magician's
audiences, which can seldom pierce the appearance to discover
what lies behind, a difference that is underlined by the open
artifice of *The Tempest*. Even when Ferdinand is allowed to
speculate on the true nature of what he is seeing, he does not

15. Cf. Frye: "Each goes through a pursuit of illusions, an ordeal, and
a symbolic vision" (*The Complete Pelican Shakespeare*, p. 1369).

get very far. "May I be bold," he asks Prospero, "To think these spirits?" Prospero admits that they are, and adds that he has called them from their confines, by means of his art, to enact his "present fancies" (5.1.118–22). This will suffice for Ferdinand, but for us, the audience, it is scarcely so simple, as Tillyard's comment suggests:

> When we examine the masque, we find that, though its function may be simple, the means by which it is presented are complicated in a manner we associate rather with Pirandello than with the Elizabethan drama. On the actual stage, the masque is executed by players pretending to be spirits, pretending to be real actors, pretending to be supposed goddesses and rustics.[16]

The parallels and contrasts between Prospero's magic and the world of dramatic illusion he inhabits, greatly enlarge the interest of the play.

Another important aspect of Prospero's magic seems to lie in its ability to weaken, to cramp, confine, and imprison its subjects. Prospero's own freedom, which is closely linked to Ariel's ability to be everywhere and to continually change shape and character, exists at the expense of similar abilities in others. In this he is contrasted to Sycorax, "who with age and envy / Was grown into a hoop" (1.2.258–59). She "did confine" Ariel in "a cloven pine" that was his prison for a dozen years. She could not undo her act, but Prospero could. Yet Prospero's service is not enough for Ariel; he seeks complete freedom, a freedom Prospero promises at the same time that he threatens to punish Ariel's disobedience:

> If thou more murmur'st, I will rend an oak,
> And peg thee in his knotty entrails, till
> Thou hast howl'd away twelve winters.

[294–96]

Ariel's previous suffering, spirit though he is, is strangely like Caliban's, who, after his attempt on Miranda, was "Deservedly confin'd into this rock, / Who hadst deserv'd more

16. E. M. Tillyard, *Shakespeare's Last Plays* (London, 1938), p. 80.

than a prison" (363–64). Prospero's domination over him is
asserted by the kind of pain Ariel felt:

> For this, be sure, to-night thou shalt have cramps,
> Side-stitches that shall pen thy breath up; urchins
> Shall, for that vast of night that they may work,
> All exercise on thee; thou shalt be pinch'd
> As thick as honeycomb, each pinch more stinging
> Than bees that made 'em.
>
> [327–32]

> . . . I'll rack thee with old cramps,
> Fill all thy bones with aches, make thee roar,
> That beasts shall tremble at thy din.
>
> [371–73]

Prospero visits exactly this punishment (as Caliban—"he'll
fill our skins with pinches"—has predicted) on the clowns, in
a speech quoted earlier. And he threatens Ferdinand with
servitude ("I'll manacle thy neck and feet together") although
Ferdinand, once Prospero's charm has weakened him, becomes
a willing prisoner, "Might I but through my prison once a
day / Behold this maid" (493–94).

If this pinching, cramping, and imprisoning is a traditional
aspect of magic, especially fairy magic, Shakespeare gives it a
psychological dimension as well. Ferdinand, whose arms were
"in this sad knot" from grief for his father, suffers from near
paralysis and physical weakness at the hands of Prospero's enchantment, but can also admit "My spirits, as in a dream, are
all bound up." And while the clowns are beaten, sinew-short-
ened, and pinch-spotted for their conspiracy, their courtly
counterparts suffer parallel inward tortures:

> All three of them are desperate; their great guilt,
> Like poison given to work a great time after,
> Now 'gins to bite the spirits.
>
> [3.3.104–06]

> Thy brother was a furtherer in the act.
> Thou art pinch'd for 't now, Sebastian. Flesh and blood,
> You, brother mine, that entertain'd ambition,

Expell'd remorse and nature; whom, with Sebastian,—
Whose inward pinches therefor are most strong,—
Would here have kill'd your King. . . .

[5.1.75–78]

Since even good characters like Miranda, Ferdinand, and
Gonzalo, are, if not pinched or confined, at least subjected to
the weakness, heaviness, and sleepiness that Prospero's magic
sometimes visits on others, and since Ariel, that protean spirit,
has been imprisoned in a tree and can be again, Prospero
seems the one person in the play who is invulnerable to the
effects of the magic he eventually renounces. It is the more
surprising, then, when he appears in the Epilogue, claiming
the same symptoms as his victims:

> Now my charms are all o'erthrown,
> And what strength I have's mine own,
> Which is most faint: now, tis true,
> I must be here confin'd by you,
> Or sent to Naples. . . .

Several ideas arise from this passage. One is the reminder that
Prospero's renunciation of his magic has made him human
and vulnerable; he is not master of illusion now, but its potential victim if his audience is not willing to use its imagination to send him home and applaud his efforts. But we are
not listening to Prospero, really, but rather the actor who
played him. And he has put us in the place he vacated, where
it was necessary to exercise good judgment and mercy if he
was not to abuse his power over others or make them suffer
unduly. At the same time he has managed to suggest the existence of a curious process whereby confinement, rightly borne,
can lead to freedom. We recall that once, while Prospero's
brother was allowing his ambition to grow out of all bound,
for Prospero "my library / Was dukedom large enough," and
that Prospero served a twelve-year confinement on the island.
We are reminded that Ferdinand accepted his servitude
("space enough / Have I in such a prison") and thus escaped
it, that Ariel too found willing servitude the best means to

the absolute freedom he desired. And we compare Caliban, dancing and singing to celebrate an unearned freedom which in fact is taking him into worse bondage. We are in the presence of paradox here, and there is no need to impose allegorical meanings on the play to discover that it suggests, finally, that confinement and freedom, mastery and servitude, are not so much unalterable opposites as they are mutually complementary, aspects of the same thing. The magician who cannot recognize this will be a Faustus, clinging to the illusion of mastery which is in fact his bondage to greater powers; he who can will be a Prospero, setting his servants free and returning to the status of "sometime Milan," whose every third thought, given his age, "shall be my grave." Both Prospero and Faustus embody, in very different ways, a familiar Renaissance insight about men of extraordinary talents and position, an insight expressed in Shakespeare's 94th sonnet:

> They that have pow'r to hurt and will do none,
> That do not do the thing they most do show,
> Who, moving others, are themselves as stone,
> Unmoved, cold, and to temptation slow;
> They rightly do inherit heaven's graces
> And husband nature's riches from expense;
> They are the lords and owners of their faces,
> Others but stewards of their excellence.
> The summer's flow'r is to the summer sweet,
> Though to itself it only live and die;
> But if that flow'r with base infection meet,
> The basest weed outbraves his dignity:
>   For sweetest things turn sourest by their deeds;
>   Lilies that fester smell far worse than weeds.

❧

I have already described *The Tempest* as a kind of giant hypothesis, one that gives free reign to the wishes and fancies of its central character while it subjects the subsidiary characters, through a set of fantastic experiences, to his will. The fictive and abnormal state of affairs is, as I have suggested, reflected in the self-conscious theatricality of *The Tempest* and in the dominance of Prospero's magic. But it is also greatly reinforced by Shakespeare's handling of the setting. An Arcadia may be a fairly rational daydream; but Prospero's island is an Arcadia *incantata,* a realm more purely composed of imagination and nightmare, of nature at its most unstable and inscrutable. So dense and pervasive is the dreamlike atmosphere of the play that it scarcely needs pointing out.[17] Key words—"dream," "wonder," "strange," "amazement"— recur constantly. At the very outset, a delirium descends on Prospero's victims:

> Not a soul
> But felt a fever of the mad, and play'd
> Some tricks of desperation.
>
> [1.2.208–10]

And it persists to the end of the play:

> All torment, trouble, wonder and amazement
> Inhabits here: some heavenly power guide us
> Out of this fearful country!
>
> [5.1.104–06]
> These are not natural events; they strengthen
> From strange to stranger.
>
> [227–28]

One image of the play is that of the maze, a bewildering artifice imposed on nature:

> My old bones ache: here's a maze trod, indeed,
> Through forth-rights and meanders!
>
> [3.3.2–3]
> This is as strange a maze as e'er men trod;
> And there is in this business more than nature
> Was ever conduct of.
>
> [5.1.242–44]

17. An illuminating study of the play's atmospheric effects and their relation to its "metaphorical design" may be found in Reuben Brower, *The Fields of Light* (New York, 1951), chapter 6.

An exploration of the setting of *The Tempest* in terms of its
effects on the characters and on the audience should help to
clarify our sense of the play and lead us toward some of its
major insights.

One characteristic of the island—and it reflects a familiar
aspect of dreams—is its tendency to dissolve the normal barriers between the physical and the mental, exterior and interior events. We have already noted that Prospero's magic has
psychological equivalents, "inward pinches," to the torment
he visits on the clowns. This is but part of a pattern whereby
mental experience takes on physical characteristics, and vice
versa. Ferdinand's spirits are all "bound up," as the entire
court party "are all knit up / In their distractions," their brains
"Now useless, boil'd within thy skull!", guilt biting their spirits. Gonzalo's prattle, earlier, has a palpable effect on Alonso:

> You cram these words into mine ears against
> The stomach of my sense.
>
> [2.1.102–03]

Caliban will not take "any print of goodness," because nurture "can never stick" on his devilish nature. The cry of those
in the shipwreck, says Miranda, "did knock / Against my very
heart!" One of the characteristic verbs in the play is "beat."
It is used in familiar physical senses—Ferdinand beats the
surges, the clowns beat each other, Ariel beats his tabor—but
it is also attached to inward experience, not the physical activity of the heart, but the obsessive tendencies of the mind:

> And now, I pray you, sir,
> For still 'tis beating in my mind, your reason
> For raising this sea-storm?
>
> [1.2.175–77]
>
> . . . a turn or two I'll walk,
> To still my beating mind.
>
> [4.1.162–63]
>
> Sir, my liege,
> Do not infest your mind with beating on
> The strangeness of this business.
>
> [5.1.245–47]

The effect of these transfers of physical activity to mental experience is to give such experience an especially vivid character. There is likewise a tendency in the language of the play to give external experience a dreamlike and illusory quality. One form this takes is a confusion between dreaming and waking. People in *The Tempest* sleep and wake with alacrity and frequency, and they tend to lose track of which is which. The world of dream invades everywhere. For Miranda, her images of the past are "rather like a dream than an assurance," although they are in fact correct, while Ferdinand's subjection to Prospero calls forth the same comparison:

> *Prospero.* . . . Thy nerves are in their infancy again,
> And have no vigour in them.
> *Ferdinand.* So they are:
> My spirits, as in a dream, are all bound up.
>
> [1.2.487–89]

Antonio and Sebastian, with unconscious irony, discuss their conspiracy in the same terms:

> *Antonio.* . . . My strong imagination sees a crown
> Dropping upon they head.
> *Sebastian.* What, art thou waking?
> *Antonio.* Do you not hear me speak?
> *Sebastian.* I do; and surely
> It is a sleepy language, and thou speak'st
> Out of thy sleep. What is it thou didst say?
> This is a strange repose, to be asleep
> With eyes wide open; standing, speaking, moving,
> And yet so fast asleep.
> *Antonio.* Noble Sebastian,
> Thou let'st thy fortune sleep—die, rather; wink'st
> Whiles thou art waking.
> *Sebastian.* Thou dost snore distinctly;
> There's meaning in thy snores.
>
> [2.1.203–13]

Antonio's "sleepy language" is a language of desire and gratification, of the self feeding upon illusions, and Caliban knows it well:

Sometimes a thousand twangling instruments
Will hum about mine ears; and sometimes voices,
That, if I then had wak'd after long sleep,
Will make me sleep again: and then, in dreaming,
The clouds methought would open, and show riches
Ready to drop upon me; that, when I wak'd,
I cried to dream again.

[3.2.135-41]

If Prospero, the most wakeful of the characters, escapes such confusion, then the mariners are his opposite. They sleep out the play under the hatches of their ship, and the Boatswain, whisked to Prospero's cell by Ariel in the last scene, is understandably baffled:

Alonso. . . . Say, how came you hither?
Boatswain. If I did think, sir, I were well awake,
I'ld strive to tell you. We were dead of sleep,
And—how we know not—all clapp'd under hatches,
. . . .
We were awak'd . . .
                     . . . on a trice, so please you,
Even in a dream, were we divided from them,
And were brought moping hither.

[5. 1. 228-40]

These moments recall Shakespeare's playful confusing of dreaming and waking in an earlier magic play, *A Midsummer Night's Dream,* and they point toward their culminating expression in Prospero's famous speech, his contention that "We are such stuff / As dreams are made on; and our little life / Is rounded with a sleep." To say that there is a "stuff" of which dreams are made is to give them a certain palpability and substance; to say that all of life is no more than the same substance and character is to radically alter basic notions of shadow and substance, illusion and reality.[18] I shall return to this speech and its astonishing claim in a moment.

18. "Prospero's 'Our revels now are ended' suddenly distance all these worlds into a common unreality" (Tillyard, p. 80). "Always before in Shakespeare, the play metaphor had served as a bridge between the

As the enchanted island blurs the boundaries of the physical and the mental and confuses the waking and sleeping states, it also besets its visitors with problems of identity and belief. Identity in this case involves both the recognition of others and knowledge of oneself. Miranda first thinks Ferdinand a spirit and "a thing divine"; he in turn takes her for a goddess. Trinculo does not know whether Caliban is a man or a fish, dead or alive:

> I do now let loose my opinion, hold it no longer: this is no fish, but an islander, that hath lately suffered by a thunderbolt.
>
> [2.2.35–37]

Stephano, in turn, runs through a number of possibilities for Caliban-Trinculo—devils, salvages, men of Ind, and "some monster of the isle with four legs"—while Caliban first takes Trinculo for one of Prospero's spirits, then considers Stephano "a brave god" and is easily convinced that he was the man in the moon. When Ariel plays his music to this crew, he is "the picture of Nobody" and a man or a devil. Gonzalo is sure that Prospero's spirits are "people of the island," while Sebastian, after Ariel's speech, takes them to be fiends. The same kind of confusion about natural and supernatural, substantial and insubstantial, persists in the last scene, as all the characters are gradually reassembled. It is of course closely allied to the problems of self-knowledge that originally afflicted Antonio ("he did believe / He was indeed the duke"), that are visited upon the innocent Ferdinand ("myself am Naples"), that lead to the two conspiracies, and that are indeed widespread enough that Gonzalo can conclude his summary of resolutions by reference to them:

---

audience and the domain of the stage. It guided that relationship of actors and audience upon which Elizabethan drama relied, reminding the latter that life contains elements of illusions, that the two worlds are not as separate as might be supposed. Now, the barriers have been swept away altogether; the play metaphor, like the distinction upon which it was based, no longer exists. . . . Life has been engulfed by illusion" (Righter, p. 203).

> . . . Ferdinand . . . found a wife
> Where he himself was lost, Prospero his dukedom
> In a poor isle, and all of us ourselves
> When no man was his own.
>
> [5.1.210–14]

Belief poses similar problems for the characters. Its extremes
are illustrated in Antonio and Sebastian, who at first, aside
from their conviction that Ferdinand is drowned, pride themselves on their skepticism, scoffing at Gonzalo's wondering ap-
praisal of the island. The appearance of the strange shapes
and the banquet reverse this dramatically; they begin to vie
with each other for the greatest credulity:

> *Sebastian.*   Now I will believe
> That there are unicorns; that in Arabia
> There is one tree, the phoenix' throne; one phoenix
> At this hour reigning there.
> *Antonio.*   I'll believe both;
> And what does else want credit, come to me,
> And I'll be sworn 'tis true: travellers ne'er did lie,
> Thou fools at home condemn 'em.
>
> [3.3.21–27]

Gonzalo joins them—"When we were boys, / Who would believe that there were mountaineers / Dew-lapp'd like bulls,
whose throats had hanging at 'em / Wallets of flesh?"—but he
also joins Alonso in the last scene in being unable to persuade
himself that he is facing Prospero:

> *Alonso.*   Whether thou be'st he or no,
> Or some enchanted trifle to abuse me,
> As late I have been, I not know. . . .
>   . . . this must crave—
> An if this be at all—a most strange story.
>   . . . But how should Prospero
> Be living and be here?
> *Prospero.*   First, noble friend,
> Let me embrace thine age, whose honour cannot
> Be measur'd or confin'd.

> *Gonzalo.*   Whether this be
> Or be not, I'll not swear.
>   *Prospero.*   You do yet taste
> Some subtleties o' the isle, that will not let you
> Believe things certain.
>
> [5.1.111–25]

Caliban is more certain, by the end, that he has misdirected his belief:

> What a thrice-double ass
> Was I, to take this drunkard for a god,
> And worship this dull fool!
>
> [295–97]

The ending contains affirmations of belief as well as doubts. Ferdinand's "Though the seas threaten, they are merciful" when he sees his father, has a calm assurance that is juxtaposed to the greater excitement of Sebastian—"A most high miracle!"—and Gonzalo's "Look down, you gods, / And on this couple drop a blessed crown! / For it is you that have chalk'd forth the way / Which brought us hither." Since our perspective here is that of Prospero, it must be more skeptical about such claims, and it finds expression after Miranda's exclamation—"O brave new world, / That has such people in 't!"—in the curt reply, "Tis new to thee." Our special knowledge and our sense of the artifice of the entire enterprise places us above the fluctuations of belief and disbelief that swirl around the characters. We know there was an auspicious star and a lot of hard work on the part of Prospero and Ariel; and we know it is mostly "rough magic" and an "insubstantial pageant" based on a special knowledge of the insubstantial character of the world.

The problems of identity and belief that the atmosphere of the island seems to produce are closely linked with problems of reality, of "Whether thou be'st he or no," of "Whether this be or be not," of "If this prove a vision of the island, one dear son / Shall I lose twice." "Who am I," "Who are you?", and

"What do I believe," easily become "What, if anything, is real here?" But to make it a question of discriminating between the real and the unreal is to simplify too greatly; it is rather a matter of having continually to try to determine levels and kinds of reality. One method Shakespeare uses is to juxtapose two states in order to undermine an accepted notion about the greater reality of one over the other.[19] Thus the play begins with a storm which we subsequently discover was a "spectacle" created by Prospero and Ariel. We have been pulled away from the "reality" of weather and the elements to the "illusory" realms of magic and theater, realms which thereby assert their own greater reality. The storm likewise, as we have noted, subverts the reality of worldly power and authority, the "name of king," and thus sets up Prospero's subsequent account of how he and his brother elected different realities— knowledge, "neglecting worldly ends," versus "th' outward face of royalty" and the chance to be "Absolute Milan." Within that account is the ironic recognition that Antonio's apparent achievement, "so dry he was for sway," was illusory from the start. To achieve the worldly power he coveted, he had to "subject his coronet" to the King of Naples, "and bend / The dukedom, yet unbow'd . . . To most ignoble stooping," an irony neatly reflected in Caliban's illusion that he has freed himself by adopting a new form of bondage.

Thus is established a pattern whereby realities are not merely juxtaposed, but tend to give way to one another, creating a world in which we are pulled further and further into an overwhelming sense of the basically illusory character of experience and of firm categories, a reality so shifting and impermanent that only a man who has penetrated and accepted its protean nature, a man like Prospero, can have any mastery of it. This sense of things is greatly supported and intensified by the images of water—fluid states, ebb and flow, melting, dissolving, sea-change, shifting elements, drift of purpose, clouds and mist—which are so ubiquitous and so familiar an

19. E.g. "What seems at first illusory, the magic and the music becomes real, and the *Realpolitik* of Antonio and Sebastian becomes illusion" (Frye, p. 1370).

aspect of the play. They give a marvelous particularity to what would otherwise remain rather theoretical.

We are now in a position to understand how effectively Prospero's climactic speech unites and summarizes the various qualities that make up the world and atmosphere of *The Tempest*. The beautiful and highly mannered reality of the masque has had suddenly to give way to the reality of time, as Prospero remembers the clown-conspirators and realizes that "the minute of their plot / Is almost come." His loss of self-control is apparent to Ferdinand and Miranda, and sensing their distress he offers an explanation, one that begins by acknowledging how one thing must give way to another and then, imperceptibly, soars up and out to become a panorama of the experience and language of the play, touching on dreams and fantasies, on the world of theatrical illusion, on inner and outer distinctions, on problems of belief, identity, and reality, on an existence that is fluid, metamorphic, insubstantial:

> You do look, my son, in a mov'd sort,
> As if you were dismay'd: be cheerful, sir.
> Our revels now are ended. These our actors,
> As I foretold you, were all spirits, and
> Are melted into air, into thin air:
> And, like the baseless fabric of this vision,
> The cloud-capp'd towers, the gorgeous palaces,
> The solemn temples, the great globe itself,
> Yea, all which it inherit, shall dissolve,
> And, like this insubstantial pageant faded,
> Leave not a rack behind. We are such stuff
> As dreams are made on; and our little life
> Is rounded with a sleep. Sir, I am vex'd;
> Bear with my weakness; my old brain is troubled:
> Be not disturb'd with my infirmity:
> If you be pleas'd, retire into my cell,
> And there repose: a turn or two I'll walk
> To still my beating mind.

[4.1.146–63]

In its very movement—from Ferdinand's dismay and Prospero's revels, out to a sweeping vision of the entire play and
to statements that characterize the nature of all existence, back
down to Prospero's troubled brain, an old man taking a stroll
to calm himself—and in its fluid, continually revelatory language and imagery, the speech acts out its vision of existence.
It is the central vision of the play, akin to Time's speech in
The Winter's Tale, and its claim that existence is unstable
and life illusory is remarkable and moving. Prospero hurries
on from the insight, as if it were too much to ask Ferdinand
and Miranda to ponder it. But we have been prepared for it
by the whole world of the play, and if we begin to assent to
it, then we are apt to realize with a start that the dreamlike
atmosphere and events of *The Tempest* give a more realistic
image of life than the pungent, faithfully detailed comedies of
Ben Jonson. Within this speech, this microcosm of the world
of *The Tempest,* lies the justification for the play's style, tone,
and structure, the answer to Jonson's charge that Shakespeare
was making nature afraid "with tales, tempests, and such like
drolleries." It is perhaps the most spacious and visionary moment in all of Shakespeare.

※

There is scarcely anything in *The Tempest* that is unrelated
to the characteristics and concerns of the pastoral. The open
theatricality of the play keeps in view the fictive and theoretical nature of pastoral. Its exploration of the magician and his
art presents the pastoral ideal of harmony between man and
nature in an extreme and spectacular form. And its dreamlike
atmosphere and events provide the familiar pastoral romance
experience of dislocation and juxtaposed opposites—emotional
states, ideas, environments—again in an especially emphatic
fashion. But it is in its treatment of the perennial topics of art
and nature that the play reveals most clearly its membership
in the literature of pastoral, and it is thus appropriate that
we close our consideration of *The Tempest* by examining its
treatment of these twin themes.

We can begin by using *The Winter's Tale* as a point of

comparison. We noted that in the course of that play there grows on the reader or spectator a complex sense of the essential unity, even identity, of nature and art. We noted too that this was not accomplished by mingling the two through such devices as dramatic verisimilitude, but rather by sharply differentiating them, so that we begin with a strong sense of their immediate opposition and end with a stronger sense of their ultimate congruity. No such process is to be traced in *The Tempest*. The union of art and nature, no less complex and subtle, is present from the beginning, and their similarities and differences hold constant until the end, when the partnership is dissolved, as if to suggest that such ideal conjunction is temporary at best.

The basis for the harmony of art and nature in *The Tempest* lies of course in the fact of Prospero's magic. It is, we are reminded again and again, an art. To the other characters, its workings can scarcely seem natural:

> These are not natural events; they strengthen
> From strange to stranger. . . .
> . . . there is in this business more than nature
> Was ever conduct of. . . .
>
> [5.1.227–28, 243–44]

But to Prospero and to us, his privileged spectators, the magic is not contrary to nature but very much a part of it: a penetration of natural mysteries, an unusual harmony between a human will and natural processes and forces. The storm that opens the play is not a supernatural event, but an all-too-familiar state of nature; Ariel and his cohorts are neither demons nor angels, but spirits of wind, water, earth and fire. They continually express their kinship with the natural world; even when they perform as goddesses in the masque, it is to celebrate the fertility and regularity of cyclic nature.

In more than one sense, then, the maze is an excellent figure for *The Tempest*: bewildering to those who must pass through; artful and coherent from the point of view of its designer; and completely natural in its substance, a playful trope for the world from which it is formed and of which it forms a part.

When Alonso succumbs to terror and despair, the image, as
Kermode points out, "is of the whole harmony of nature en-
forcing upon Alonso the consciousness of his guilt":[20]

> Methought the billows spoke, and told me of it;
> The winds did sing it to me; and the thunder,
> That deep and dreadful organ-pipe, pronounc'd
> The name of Prosper: it did bass my trespass.
> Therefor my son i' th' ooze is bedded; and
> I'll seek him deeper than e'er plummet sounded,
> And with him there lie bedded.
>
> [3.3.96–102]

This is nature sounding like a consort of musicians, and for
us it is juxtaposed to Prospero's backstage congratulations, the
director complimenting his actor:

> Bravely the figure of the Harpy hast thou
> Perform'd, my Ariel; a grace it had devouring:
> Of my instruction hast thou nothing bated
> In what thou hadst to say: so, with good life
> And observation strange, my meaner ministers
> Their several kinds have done. My high charms work.
>
> [83–88]

That so much art was the basis of Alonso's experience does
not subvert it as nature; Ariel and the meaner ministers are
indeed the billows, winds, and thunder that Alonso recognized. The authority and strength of the "high charms"
reside in their natural basis; they seem to be "an art that
nature makes." We note that their proper working is intimately associated with natural processes:

> The charm dissolves apace;
> And as the morning steals upon the night,
> Melting the darkness, so their rising senses
> Begin to chase the ignorant fumes that mantle
> Their clearer reason.
>
> [5.1.64–68]

---

20. Arden, p. 92.

Two of the verbs in this passage—"dissolve" and "melting"
—are used in Prospero's "Our revels now are ended" speech.
They emphasize the intimacy between the natural world of
The Tempest—fluid, mysterious, metamorphic—and Prospero's magic, an intimacy that finds full and frequent expression, and that is surveyed and summarized in his final
invocation:

> Ye elves of hills, brooks, standing lakes, and groves;
> And ye that on the sands with printless foot
> Do chase the ebbing Neptune and do fly him
> When he comes back; you demi-puppets that
> By moonshine do the green sour ringlets make,
> Whereof the ewe not bites; and you whose pastime
> Is to make midnight mushrooms, that rejoice
> To hear the solemn curfew; by whose aid—
> Weak masters though ye be—I have bedimm'd
> The noontide sun, call'd forth the mutinous winds,
> And 'twixt the green sea and the azur'd vault
> Set roaring war: to the dread rattling thunder
> Have I given fire, and rifted Jove's stout oak
> With his own bolt; the strong-bas'd promontory
> Have I made shake, and by the spurs pluck'd up
> The pine and cedar: graves at my command
> Have wak'd their sleepers, op'd, and let 'em forth
> By my so potent Art.
>
> [5.1.33–50]

The speech has two sections: the invocation of spirits, listing
them, and the recital of the accomplishments they have made
possible. In each case the list moves from the familiar to the
mysterious, from hills, brooks, and lakes to midnight mush-
rooms and solemn curfew, and from the sun and winds to
the raising of the dead. This last achievement might seem to
be the one really "unnatural" act of Prospero's magic; but
it is surely meant to sound like a rehearsal of the Day of
Judgment, an event that for Shakespeare's audience was to
be the last chapter in the story of the natural world as they

knew it. Prospero concludes by promising to return the instruments of his magic to the infinite and mysterious nature
from which they derive their power:

> . . . I'll break my staff,
> Bury it certain fadoms in the earth,
> And deeper than did ever plummet sound
> I'll drown my book.

[54–57]

Drowning and burial are two kinds of death (cf. Alonso's
"I'll seek him deeper than e'er plummet sounded, / And with
him there lie bedded."), images of the human return to nature. When he has retired to Milan, Prospero says, "Every
third thought shall be my grave." His partnership with nature
is to take a different form, his life to be "rounded with a
sleep."

This, then, is the framework for nature and art in *The
Tempest*: a temporary, spectacular, successful, and fictive conjunction of opposites. Within this framework we are aware
of each as separate entities and of their astonishing variety.
Nature has many forms and many versions. The island itself
is multi-faceted, a place of deep nooks and odd angles, forth-
rights and meanders. It can seem fertile and hospitable, with
berries, fresh springs, crabs, pig nuts, clustering filberts and
young scamels from the rocks, or it can appear barren and
hostile, with brine pits, toothed briers, sharp furzes, pricking
gorse, thorns, withered roots and husks for diet, and a filthy-
mantled pool that smells of horse-piss. It is set, moreover, in
a vast universe of sea, thunder, lightning, curled clouds, frost-
baked veins of the earth, auspicious stars, the ooze of the salt
deep, the dark backward and abysm of time, a universe containing the still-vexed Bermoothes, Arabia with a phoenix
throne, unicorns, mountaineers dew-lapped like bulls and
men whose heads stand in their breasts.[21] We are continually

---

21. Wolfgang Clemen, *The Development of Shakespeare's Imagery*
(Cambridge, Mass., 1951), notes the use of images that "direct the eyes of
our imagination into that depth which, like "the veins o' the earth," is
solely accessible to Ariel . . . a deeper level of nature" (p. 185).

made aware of a nature that has vast distances and infinite possibilities.

Nature is also various because it is seen from many viewpoints. Early in the second act we begin to realize that the barrenness or fertility of the island is in the eye of the beholder:

> *Adrian.* The air breathes upon us here most sweetly.
> *Sebastian.* As if it had lungs, and rotten ones.
> *Antonio.* Or as 'twere perfum'd by a fen.
> *Gonzalo.* Here is everything advantageous to life.
> *Antonio.* True; save means to live.
> *Sebastian.* Of that there's none, or little.
> *Gonzalo.* How lush and lusty the grass looks! how green!
> *Antonio.* The ground, indeed, is tawny.
>
> [2.1.45–52]

Nature here is the same multiple mirror we have seen in *As You Like It, King Lear,* and *The Winter's Tale.* Many of the characters consider it beneficent. Gonzalo founds his imaginary commonwealth on its apparent fecundity:

> All things in common Nature should produce
> Without sweat or endeavour: treason, felony,
> Sword, pike, knife, gun, or need of any engine,
> Would I not have; but Nature should bring forth,
> Of it own kind, all foison, all abundance,
> To feed my innocent people.
>
> [2.1.155–60]

A similarly ideal view is expressed in the masque:

> Earth's increase, foison plenty,
> Barns and garners never empty;
> Vines with clust'ring bunches growing;
> Plants with goodly burthen bowing;
> Spring come to you at the farthest
> In the very end of harvest!

> Scarcity and want shall shun you;
> Ceres' blessing so is on you.
>
> [4.1.110–17]

We feel no need to choose between such idealized versions of nature and the more cynical responses of Antonio and Sebastian, who see it as a source of disease and discomfort and a neutral backdrop to their evildoing. Nature, we feel from watching the play, is all these things.[22] It is both Ariel —delicate, quicksilver, sympathetic and leaning from the amoral toward the good—and Caliban—heavy, clumsy, grotesque and deformed, given to bestiality and evil. And it is the contradictions in these characters as well: Ariel's restive servitude, Caliban's poetry and occasional good sense.

As nature is shown to be multi-faceted and changeable, we are less and less likely to accept any one view of it. What may seem to one of the characters the whole truth about nature, we are more apt to accept as one-sided and partial. We note that *The Tempest* is full of versions of nature that seem too confident in their self-projection and wish fulfillment. Caliban is the most obvious example of this tendency. His curses call on nature ("As wicked dew as e'er my mother brush'd / With raven's feather from unwholesome fen," "All the infections that the sun sucks up / From bogs, fens, flats, on Prosper fall") to act out his desires, just as he would have the world made all in his image:

> O ho, O ho! would 't had been done!
> Thou didst prevent me; I had peopled else
> This isle with Calibans.
>
> [1.2.351–53]

22. Leo Marx discusses the opposed views of nature in relation to contemporary views of the New World: "On the spectrum of Elizabethan images of America the hideous wilderness appears at one end and the garden at the other. The two views are traditionally associated with quite different ideas of man's basic relation to his environment." The garden image, he goes on to show, implies "joyous fulfillment," while the hideous wilderness calls for "the exercise of power . . . a need to mobilize energy, postpone immediate pleasures, and rehearse the perils and purposes of the community" (*The Machine in the Garden,* pp. 43 ff.).

Other characters—Gonzalo, Ferdinand, Antonio, Stephano—project their wishes as images of nature in similar but subtler ways. Even Prospero, in the masque, expresses his hope that nature's abundance will consistently serve his daughter and her husband. The difference is that he seems more conscious that it is all his "present fancies" rather than the whole image of nature; the mythic and mannered style of the masque underlines this attitude. Earlier, Prospero spoke to Miranda of the winds "whose pity, sighing back again, / Did us but loving wrong," but he likewise recognizes exactly how intractable to goodness Caliban is, how much the brother whom he describes as "unnatural" is indeed an aspect of the whole truth about nature. Nor does his view of nature as infinite, various, and in flux allow him to assign it universal characteristics with the confidence of others. He is like Lear in knowing what he would like nature to be and do, unlike him, even though he commands the elements, in thinking that his expectations will be automatically fulfilled.

Prospero's overview of the world and action of the play also faces him, as it does us, with the nature-nurture question. It is anything but simple. If we ask where evil resides, then the answer must be: several places. In Caliban, first of all, the "salvage and deformed slave," the wild man who in this play replaces the more characteristic natural men of the pastoral mode, the shepherds, hermits, and savages. Caliban's education has failed. He is "a born devil, on whose nature / Nurture can never stick." Is evil a natural thing, then, lower on the scale of being, characteristic of savages and beasts? We might like to think so. But we are confronted with Antonio and Sebastian, handsome and highly civilized Italian aristocrats, who easily match Caliban in evil tendencies. As their mockery of Gonzalo's utopian talk makes clear, they regard their civilization as perfect and themselves as perfect expressions of it. There are two sides to the coin of evil: what in Caliban is physical, natural, and open deformity recurs as spiritual, acquired, and hidden deformity in Antonio and Sebastian.

Goodness has the same kind of duality in *The Tempest*.

It can reside in Miranda, innocent, natural, unworldly, and in Ariel, presumably a manifestation of the best qualities of the natural world; but it is also present in Ferdinand and Gonzalo, who have lived in the court and tasted civilization without experiencing corruption. Such a precise balancing and distribution of good and evil seems to take us a long way from *King Lear*. But the distance would scarcely be so great if the island lacked the protection of Prospero's magic, that is, if a more *natural* state of affairs were allowed to prevail. At any rate, the nature-nurture question, like the "nature of nature" question, has no one answer in *The Tempest*, but rather a rich complexity that leaves us pondering contradictory but coexisting possibilities.

The nature-nurture question involves art as much as nature. Caliban's and Miranda's tutoring, Antonio's sophistication, Ferdinand's princeliness—these are, or appear to be, human attempts to alter, order, and improve nature. This is but one instance of what must by now be apparent—so closely are nature and art intertwined in *The Tempest* that to speak of one is to speak of the other. All that has so far been said about nature holds equally true for art. Like nature, art is many-faceted; it is variously linked to music, order, illusion, entertainment, personal wisdom, dreams, and wish fulfillment. Like nature it varies according to viewpoint and situation. And like nature it is again and again a means of self-projection and idealization.

This last point especially deserves attention. Gonzalo idealizes nature in the course of imagining his utopian commonwealth, but the imagining makes him a kind of artist, designing the "plantation" of the island. Earlier he is teased about his imaginative powers when he tells Adrian that Tunis was Carthage:

> *Antonio.* His word is more than the miraculous harp.
> *Sebastian.* He hath rais'd the wall, and houses too.
> *Antonio.* What impossible matter will he make easy next?

> *Sebastian.* I think he will carry this island home in his pocket, and give it his son for an apple.
> *Antonio.* And, sowing the kernels of it in the sea, bring forth more islands.

[2.1.83–89]

But such certainty about the real world and the realm of imagination is dangerous on an island brimming with enchantments; the conspiracy of Antonio and Sebastian will prove no less fanciful under the circumstances. And if all such attempts to manipulate the world by imposing imaginary orders upon it are to be exposed as illusory, then we will prefer the idealistic to the selfish, Gonzalo's commonwealth and Prospero's masque to the plotting of Antonio or Caliban. Moreover, we shall gain some faith in the powers of imagination and art by seeing one such attempt, Prospero's project, successfully sustained through the course of the play and brought to a graceful resolution. The efficacy and variety of art are most of all demonstrated in Prospero's magic, in its music—"Allaying both their fury and my passion / With its sweet air"; in its imposition of order where chaos threatens to reign;[23] in its spectacular devices and shows, both as learning and as sheer entertainment; in the wisdom with which it is exercised, the recognition that it is partially dream and wish fulfillment, easily abused, and that like all things in this world of illusion and flux, it must change. It is through Prospero that we learn the most about the function and value, as well as the limitations, of art.

Any drama can be described as a set of experiences in two distinct ways. On the one hand it is an account of the experience undergone by a group of fictitious characters and

---

23. For a discussion of the order-chaos themes, see Rose A. Zimbardo, "Form and Disorder in *The Tempest*," *Shakespeare Quarterly* 14 (Winter 1963):49–56. She concludes that Prospero's art, an ordering principle, "can order what is amenable to order, but it can only affect temporarily that which is fundamentally chaotic" (p. 55). The temporary quality is also stressed by Marx: "What finally enables us to take the idea of a successful 'return to nature' seriously is its temporariness" (p. 69).

held in common by them. In addition, however, as played
before an audience, it is also an experience undergone by a
group of real characters, as witnesses, and held in common by
them. Often these two senses of dramatic experience are carefully separated; in Shakespeare they are again and again con-
founded, so that their relationships become astonishingly rich
and complex. We recall how Prospero's shows tend to blur
the line between actor and spectator. So in fact do his creator's. It is possible to see *The Tempest* as a sort of huge
mirror held up to the audience, a giant metaphor for the
value of art constructed by an artist who understood very
thoroughly both the strengths and limitations of his craft.
The metaphor is worth exploring: all the characters who are
washed ashore at Prospero's bidding undergo an experience
of self-knowledge, which may or may not change them. Any
given audience is in a sense washed ashore too, to accompany
the cast on their adventures. In both cases the experience will
be illusory—the result of art, shadowy, an insubstantial pageant—but that will not make it any less valuable. On the
contrary, it will make possible events and recognitions not
otherwise attainable. Some of the people in both groups will
be there just for a good time, like Trinculo. Others may find
lasting happiness, like Ferdinand. Some will come to new
knowledge and self-recognition. Evil will not be changed or
dismissed—that is beyond art's power—but it will be located
and described for a clearer understanding, and momentarily
subdued that the good and the beautiful may shine more
clearly. Listen to Prospero:

> Here in this island we arriv'd; and here
> Have I, thy schoolmaster, made thee more profit
> Than other princess' can, that have more time
> For vainer hours, and tutors not so careful.
>
> [1.2.171–74]

Or listen to Gonzalo:

> Was Milan thrust from Milan, that his issue
> Should become Kings of Naples: Oh, rejoice

> Beyond a common joy! And set it down
> With gold on lasting pillars. In one voyage
> Did Claribel her husband find at Tunis,
> And Ferdinand, her brother, found a wife
> Where he himself was lost, Prospero his dukedom
> In a poor isle, and all of us ourselves
> Where no man was his own.
>
> [5.1.205–13]

Not *quite* accurate, but then what account of a play ever is? If gold on lasting pillars is not Shakespeare's medium, he understands Gonzalo's impulse perfectly and views it with compassion. Listen finally to Prospero's alter ego, the actor who appears before us in the epilogue:

> Now I want
> Spirits to enforce, Art to enchant;
> And my ending is despair
> Unless I be reliev'd by prayer,
> Which pierces so, that it assaults
> Mercy itself, and frees all faults.
>> As you from crimes would pardon'd be,
>> Let your indulgence set me free.

Epilogue

By swaggering I could never thrive. If I thought I could claim that I had revolutionized our understanding of Shakespeare or invented an entirely new way of approaching his plays, I would say so, with appropriate fanfare. But flourishes of that sort, even when partially justified, begin to echo ironically in the many-roomed mansion of Shakespearean studies as the years pass and that huge and endless endeavor that constitutes Shakespearean study, performance, and commentary continues. The company is numerous, honorable, eccentric. One need not demand a room of one's own.

If this Epilogue is not intended to celebrate *The Heart's Forest* then, what should its purpose be? I need not reiterate my conclusions about the individual plays, but it might be useful to cast one last look at them as a group, to ask what kinds of rewards the approach to Shakespeare I have here undertaken can be said to hold. It may further be rewarding to ask what, if anything, we have learned about Shakespeare as a working artist, and to consider one last time the general subject of pastoral in relation to his interest in it.

As a group the plays are remarkably disparate. If they share a common plot model and crucial accompanying themes—art and nature; man, nature, and society—and if certain prototypical characters and situations can be found recurring in all of them, they are also stunningly varied: a masterwork of comedy, rich in stylistic diversity and witty complication, sparkling with detached sophistication; a tragedy that has seemed to some so bleak and painful as to be unbearable, anticipating every subsequent shade of pessimism that might have seemed to rival it; and two late plays that, while close in date and manner, have astonishing disparities of structure and theatrical means.

And what does this variety reveal? The fundamental fecundity of the pastoral ideal and, more particularly, of its romance narrative embodiment? In part, no doubt; but what it more surely points to is Shakespeare's own imaginative fertility, his restless experimentation, and his ability to transform and transcend convention. He was no more limited by what people thought pastoral was or ought to be than he was by their definition of proper comedy or tragedy. He picked up what must have seemed to other playwrights an unpromising and rather predictable plot pattern that had already been overused in narrative fiction and that had produced some particularly undistinguished plays by his predecessors and contemporaries, and used it to great effect, transcending the apparent limitations of its conventions as easily as a thoroughbred race horse might outdistance a drayman's nag.

Who would apologize for trying to follow so great an artist on so dizzying a journey? When I began this project I thought to write a book that divided its interest fairly evenly between Shakespeare and the pastoral convention as his age defined and practiced it. I ended, obviously, by writing a book about Shakespeare. The problem has not been one of regret at the transformed and disappearing conventions; it has been that of keeping up with the transformations and trying to do them justice.

But this is not an admission that the idea of pastoral becomes irrelevant once Shakespeare has begun to make his own use of it. That is no more true than it is to say that we need not try to understand *Macbeth* or *Coriolanus* in terms of what we understand tragedy to mean and be because Shakespeare has begun to handle its patterns and conventions in an unusual manner. The fact is that the individuality of those plays most truly emerges when they are measured against the tragic norm, for it is then that we begin to realize that they are in part meditations on the idea of tragedy, testings of its strengths and limitations, explorations of its boundaries and sources. I suggest that the more readily and easily Shakespeare was able to transcend genre and convention, turning them to his most original uses, making them uniquely his, the greater his interest in them seems to have grown. The curve of originality that leads from *As You Like It* to *The Tempest* by way

of *Lear* and *The Winter's Tale* is also a curve in which the
conventions and origins of the materials on which these plays
are based come more and more to occupy the foreground of
our attention, and, by implication, the author's.

I think that Shakespeare's transformations and variations
on the pastoral ought to help us understand that often
maligned mode more clearly too. What one of the greatest
artists in the history of the human imagination chose to
make of any form—sonnet, chronicle play, holiday game, revenge tragedy—ought to illuminate that form for us, its best
and furthest possibilities. A specific example may be useful:
I recently had occasion to reread Andrew Marvell's exquisite
pastoral poem, "The Nymph Complaining for the Death of
her Fawn." The poem has been much subjected to allegorical
readings, religious and political, in an attempt to explain the
peculiar sense of significance that hovers around its apparent
inanities and overrefined details. But to have read and studied
Shakespeare's pastorals, especially the late plays, is to have
little difficulty in identifying the effectiveness of the poem.
Like them, it pursues excessive artifice in order to subvert and
confound the art-nature dichotomy; the natural objects and
values disappear into their stylized representations, and the
poem's drama is resolved by having nymph and fawn turn
(hypothetically) into statues, the sort you might come across
in a great man's park or garden. Meanwhile, like the Forest
of Arden, the poem becomes a limpid mirror, capable of reflecting any interest but only by virtue of being so clear and
simple. As we peer into it and see religious, political, erotic,
dramatic, historical, or aesthetic implications, we do well to
realize that it is a mirroring surface: to allegorize is to make
it a cloudy window through which only one thing can be seen.
The same principle holds for *The Tempest*. If pastoral helps
us read Shakespeare more ably, he in turn sends us back to
pastoral with a clearer notion of its best possibilities; it is
the kind of mode that mirror-makers like Marvell and Shakespeare could scarcely resist.

It may be that Shakespeare's preoccupation with form and
structure, his interest in artifice and genre, is the aspect of

his art that has most baffled his commentators. "How," they
might ask, "could an artist who saw so clearly the foolish
limitations of the pastoral, and who did not need, in his unparalleled artistic originality, the support of a mannered and
repetitive convention that could scarcely begin to support the
complexity and wisdom of his visions, return to it so readily
and so often?" One answer has been given above, in terms of
pastoral's efficacy, the complexity it afforded artists who understood that its artificial praise of nature, its complex celebration of simplicity, its sophisticated pursuit of innocence,
held marvelous possibilities. A more important answer, if the
emphases and discoveries of this study have correctly high-
lighted Shakespeare's artistic means, is that he seems to have
had a deep and abiding interest in the products, however
lowly and ridiculous they might sometimes become, of the
human imagination. We don't have to think twice to understand his interest in kingship or in mythic patterns; when
it comes to magic and folklore and popular entertainment we
are a little more stretched. Our sympathies, perhaps, are not
so wide-ranging as his. He had a way of cherishing imaginative forms, whatever their sources and however laughable
their contours; this tenderness was mixed with amusement,
with a detachment rather like that of a good anthropologist:
but a tenderness it was, a sympathy, an understanding that
the high-flown theologian, the prating player, the crackpot
astrologer, and the crafty statesman are brothers under the
skin, a quality they share with the loftiest tragedy, the
clumsiest ballad, the organ grinder and his monkey, and the
refinements of baroque architecture. His sense was the sense
of the sleight-of-hand man, who knows it is all a trick and
that the trick somehow contains the meaning and wonder of
everything. If his nature was subdued to what it worked in,
like the dyer's hand, that subduing seems to have strengthened his greatness; for the subduing of hand, heart, and head
was at the same time an exaltation, and it is to the duality
and simultaneity of that process that we may in great part
owe, finally, Shakespeare's undeniable and unfathomable
greatness.

Appendix: Producing the Pastorals

Each of the four plays discussed in the preceding study has been seen to contain strong elements of theatricality. Their concern with nature has not, we have discovered, made them "natural." On the contrary, they are self-conscious and self-referring; to a certain extent each is *about* drama, drama as literary expression and as theater. In quite different ways they seem to join the category that Lionel Abel has called *meta-theater*:

> Only certain plays tell us at once that the happenings and characters in them are of the playwright's invention, and that insofar as they were discovered—where there is invention there also has to be discovery—they were found by the playwright's imagining rather than by his observing the world. Such plays have truth in them, not because they convince us of real occurrences or existing persons, but because they show the reality of the dramatic imagination, instanced by the playwright's and also by that of his characters. Of such plays, it may indeed be said: "The play's the thing." Plays of this type, it seems to me, belong to a special genre and deserve a distinctive name.[1]

Abel's "special genre" offers a useful distinction, although it does not sufficiently acknowledge the way in which plays that are openly imaginative and self-referring can partake of and belong to the familiar genres and traditional modes. The theatricality of Shakespeare's pastorals means, for one thing, that they cultivate mixed effects: at times they are intensely realistic, in the commonplace dramatic sense of that term; at other times they deliberately swing away into nonrealistic

1. Lionel Abel, *Metatheater* (New York, 1963), p. 59.

forms of expression—the symbolic, the emblematic, the alle-gorical. The reader will recall Mack's stylistic polarities—en-gagement and detachment—Kernan's terms—formalism and realism—and the suggestion by such critics as Bethell, Frye, Nosworthy, and Brockbank that the late plays, especially, call attention to their own improbability and artifice.

The question I wish to treat here is: how is this insight to be translated into terms that will be of use in productions, and which of my particular findings about the four plays treated above may be of use in illuminating their possibilities on the stage? To the most general part of the question, there is, I believe, a general answer, and it involves a greater will-ingness to experiment with stylization, in the multitude of possibilities that term suggests. If we acknowledge that Shake-speare's texts often employ detachment, formalism, self-con-sciousness and theatricality, it follows that directors and actors must find means to control these effects of distancing as accurately as possible. This does not imply "camping." What is required is not distance from the text, but loyalty to the distances the text contains. When the plays are taken on their own terms, their effects of alienation (by analogy to Brecht) and theatricality can emerge naturally, excitingly. The problem has been, often, too great an anxiety about the unrealistic elements of the plays; our notions of theatrical realism have made us impose a rigid decorum on the plays of the past, a decorum that is not to be broken by modern dress or gimmicky surface effects, but by rethinking the whole question of theatrical illusion. A fear of subverting emotional impact may have supported this decorum, but greater styliza-tion does not necessarily destroy intensity. It may, on the contrary, enhance it. If we see a *Lear* or a *Tempest* in which the elements of artifice and theatricality are frankly acknowl-edged by stylistic expression, we have an opportunity to ex-perience these plays with a fullness and richness they seldom approach in modern productions. While I cannot hope to specify successfully all the means and possibilities by which this goal is to be achieved, I should like here to survey briefly some of the areas of theatrical production in which the plays I have been discussing might benefit from careful rethinking and experimentation with more stylized treatments.

Setting

It should be clear that this is a crucial area for the pastoral. And it ought to be evident that realistic natural settings cannot capture the flavor or meaning of Shakespeare's pastoral plays. Nothing was more misguided, in light of Shakespeare's emphasis on the literary and hypothetical qualities of his pastoral settings, than those nineteenth century productions in which real brooks babbled across the stage and live rabbits hopped among true-to-life bushes and trees. We laugh at such excesses now, but we are not completely weaned from the habit of mind that produced them.

As You Like It furnishes a useful example. A production of this play might well start by trying to find the right setting, and working out from that to staging and characterization that matched. I had the opportunity in 1967 of seeing concurrent productions of this play by England's two great repertory companies, the Royal Shakespeare and the National Theater. Each production had real merit, not least in the solid and imaginative acting for which both groups are famous. If the Royal Shakespeare's was on the whole the better of the two, steady and sane throughout, its setting was at best a compromise: two large treelike forms, that is, trunks with branches, that could be swung around to various positions. It suggested a natural setting and gave the actors something to sit or lie on, but it did not begin to characterize Arden. The National Theater production by Clifford Williams, which is unfortunately likely to be remembered for its least successful feature, an all-male cast, and which devoted itself all too exclusively to rendering the sexual ambiguity of the play, had in fact a most interesting design, by Ralph Koltai. The set was somewhat geometrical—a pale yellow grid on which cubes and triangles were variously placed—and had backdrops and hangings of unusual plastic materials. The costumes were vaguely futuristic—vinyl tunics and jumpsuits, for example. The *Times* critic saw no point in it at all:

> Ralph Koltai's plastic decor—dangling transparent tubes and dappled overhead cut-outs, and a variety of silver boots, PVC macs, and tattered regimentals—may relate to modern costume; but it is hard to see what contact they have with an Arcadia, whether sweet or bitter.[2]

But their contact with Arcadia was surprisingly effective, to my mind. They combined familiarity with otherness, reality with fantasy. One echo they produced was that of science fiction, our own most viable version of pastoral. Koltai's Arden was hypothetical, but not obtrusively so. If his settings had been used as the starting point for a production that put more faith in Shakespeare and less in Jan Kott—if they had been employed, for example, in the Royal Shakespeare production—the result might have been a truly effective *As You Like It*.

One thing a design for a pastoral need not do is belabor the obvious. We *know* that *As You Like It* is set in a forest, and we know, similarly, from their language, a great deal about the physical circumstances of the other pastorals. Prospero's island would be vivid and real to us if the play were performed in utter darkness. Keeping this in mind should help to encourage a light touch, and it should free designers to explore the metaphorical richness of pastoral settings —Arden's mirroring propensities, *Lear*'s inwardness and startling confrontations, the folktale reality and careful perspectives of *The Winter's Tale,* and the engineered mazes of *The Tempest.* A case in point is Peter Brook's recent production of *A Midsummer Night's Dream.* A sense of the play as performance was stressed, with accompanying effects that suggested a circus or carnival. The result was not to obscure significantly the forest setting of most of the play's action, but rather to release its theatrical meanings, with an accompanying freshness and exhilaration. In this respect the production

2. *London Times,* 4 October 1967.

put a greater trust in the text itself and in the audience's imagination, and the success of the enterprise was encouraging.

The Tempest, of all the pastorals, offers perhaps the most deceptive problems for the designer. So solemnly regarded is this play, and so tempting are its special effects to the resources of modern stage technology, that I think it gets shortest shrift among the pastorals. Misplaced reverence, combined with a welter of tricky lighting and spectacular staging that tends to obliterate the text, generally makes *The Tempest* a tedious business for actors and audience alike. Yet it seems to me that the play's apparent links with the Italian popular theater, *commedia dell'arte,* offer exactly the kind of opportunity to experiment that I have been urging. I offer here a hypothetical design for *The Tempest* based on this possibility.

Suppose that on the stage itself there is a small stage area, suggestive of a makeshift stage set up by a troupe of players. This "inner" area should give a pronounced "play-within-a-play" feeling to the action of *The Tempest.* It would also give emphasis to the confinement-freedom dichotomy, as Prospero, Ariel, and perhaps Miranda would be free to move in or out of it, while the shipwrecked characters and Caliban would never move out of it (with the exception of Ferdinand when he is freed and made audience to his betrothal masque) and would show no awareness that it was a confined area. The artificiality of this inner stage could be emphasized by the use of painted backcloths, as well as by our sense that the surrounding area was a kind of unconcealed backstage. Thus the first scene, the shipwreck, could take place on the inner stage, before a painted cloth depicting a stormy sea, while Prospero and Miranda watched from the sides and Ariel and his spirit-helpers (harlequins of a kind) performed the special effects, the thunder and lightning, with primitive equipment (sheets of tin, etc.) and in full view of the audience. The change of scene could then be effected by dropping a new cloth, showing the entrance to Prospero's cave, and having Prospero and Miranda move onto the inner stage for their exposition. A sense of *The Tempest* as a piece of popular entertainment,

Prospero's magic show, performed by a company of "comedians" whose means of illusion are unconcealed, would illuminate the meaning of its pastoral setting significantly. And not,
I think, at the cost of its poetry. Within the context of stylization I have suggested, both naturalness and immediacy can be
achieved. The distancing effects need not weaken the poetry;
they should rather give it point and emphasis. If the verse is
clearly and beautifully spoken, the human situations and
the intense transforming beauty of the play will engross us
more than ever.

Characterization

The problems that arise in this area are not perhaps so
peculiar to pastoral as are matters of setting, but they are
scarcely less crucial. Consider the case of *King Lear*. If *As
You Like It* needs to eschew realistic stage settings, *Lear*
seems most to need to move away from the urge to present realistic characterizations. The personages of this play
are not consistently motivated ordinary people—at least
not exclusively so. They carry much of the symbolic and
schematic meaning of the play, meaning that cannot be
stripped from them without leaving the play ridiculous and
the characters incomprehensible. Edgar does not choose to
disguise himself as Poor Tom for reasons that must be ac-
counted for by some sort of psychological verisimilitude. He
is, at that moment of the play, a symbolic character adopting
a symbolic role. If this doesn't come through in some fashion,
then Edgar is naked indeed, and the actor who is asked to
play him deserves our utmost sympathy.

It is not just directors and actors who have a tendency to
try to account psychologically for what is emblematic in *Lear*.
Audiences share the propensity, and for this reason modern
productions may need to overcompensate somewhat in order
to restore to the play aspects that Shakespeare's audience
would have been able to take for granted. Stylization in acting, costume, and makeup seems a logical area to explore if
one is interested in achieving what Maynard Mack suggests
that the play calls for:

> . . . a performing style that has absorbed both epic dis-
> engagement and psychic intimacy, renders the implaus-
> ible event plausible, moves easily from personification
> to personality, effectively marries the tragic to the ab-
> surd, and, above all, represses the urge to regularize and
> unify by twentieth-century psychological principles a play
> whose actual mode of unity is partly medieval and homi-
> letic.[3]

The opportunity to experiment with larger-than-life effects
of characterization ought to be an attractive challenge in the
current atmosphere of interest in the mythic and ritual elements of drama. Perhaps we can look forward to productions
of *Lear* that explore the symbolic and "metatheatrical" elements of the play to greater effect.

As Mack's comment suggests, the problem of achieving effective characterization in these plays is not a matter of choosing one style over another, but of balance. This can be shown
by reference to *The Winter's Tale*. Leontes and his "tragedy"
offer exactly the kind of psychological depth that modern performers of Shakespeare can understand and render; the result
has been a tendency to give too great an emphasis to this part
of the play, leaving the second half a kind of silly, romantic,
and anti-climactic idyll. But this problem of imbalance is not
to be solved by an opposite distortion. We should not have to
abandon Leontes' intensely realized characterization as long
as we do not lose sight of the artificial framework in which
that characterization is set. From the detachment that accom-
panies a recognition of the archaic and formal materials on
which the play is based comes a balanced sense of the relation
of each part to the whole; when this is accomplished, Leontes'
psychological verisimilitude can coexist with his mythic, fictive surroundings, allowing him a comfortable place in the
total design.

I have not, so far, been specific about means. To begin to
particularize is to create a need for a great deal more detail

3. Mack, pp. 77–78.

than I am prepared to offer. But let me return to my hypothetical *commedia* version of *The Tempest* for an example of the practical possibilities that the view of characterization I have been suggesting entails. Surely that play's apparent connection to the *commedia dell'arte* offers a convenient alternative to naturalistic, psychologically based modes of actings, for we know in some detail about the traditional roles, stylized movements, and standard comic business that these players developed so successfully. The idea of a *Tempest* built on a foundation of stock physical comedy and caricature may seem startling at first, but consider whether Ariel, so often a sort of fluttering, bouncing embarrassment on the stage, might not benefit by absorbing some of the characteristics of Harlequin and other styles of *zanni*. His cohort spirits could do the same. And is Gonzalo as a kind of Pantalone so inappropriate? Prospero is of course more complicated, but a Prospero whose character had something of Pantalone, something of the Magnifico, and a great deal of the *mago,* the traditional stage magician with staff, book, and gown, might gain an edge and energy he too often lacks. It is even more plausible to see how the clowns can draw on the stock comic turns of the *commedia,* the *lazzi,* for their scenes of fear, touching, beating, and drunkenness; in fact, they often, perhaps inadvertently, do that anyway. And it is surely no great problem to conceive of the lovers, Ferdinand and Miranda, in terms of their familiar *commedia* counterparts. Caliban is probably meant to be more than the *selvaggio* or wodewose, the theatrical wild man. But that a grotesque and vivid Caliban—amphibian, reptilian, or whatever—would fit easily into the kind of stylized production I have tried to envisage, seems a safe conclusion.

Do I need to reemphasize that I am not discussing a slapstick production of *The Tempest*? I am talking about alternatives to the conception of dramatic character that has predominated in this century and the last, and I am pleased to be able to invoke a theatrical tradition and style that is closer to home than, say, those of Japan or India, and thus perhaps more adaptable to Shakespearean productions.

Structure and Atmosphere

The theatrical components discussed above—setting, costume design, makeup, acting style—must of course blend with all other elements of production into an artistic whole. This will mean determining how much emphasis individual parts deserve, a point touched on in the discussion of Leontes. That point can be expanded to note that the need for balance in *The Winter's Tale* indicates that the play's peculiar structure deserves emphasis rather than concealment. Time's speech, and the overt shifts of perception and mood that accompany it, should not be passed over in embarrassment before an inattentive audience; because they give meaning both to what has gone before and what is to come, they deserve pride of place. And the two halves of the play must be shown to have a consistency of effect and a strong relationship. When this sense of the play's overall need has been determined, it should be easier to discover the best means by which to give us the necessary distance to the tragic events of the first half, as well as to make comprehensible the dreamlike, hypothetical, and idealized qualities of the last two acts.

Similarly, the appeal of a *commedia*-style production of *The Tempest* lies ultimately not in the interesting possibilities of staging and acting style, but in the simultaneous releasing of that play from overly solemn approaches and the formulation of an image of the play as a whole that reveals something important about its origins, tone, and meaning. The same kind of point can be made in terms of the other pastorals, but I suspect that in arguing for coherent conceptions of these plays as artistic wholes, I am simply belaboring the obvious, so I shall leave the matter where it must ultimately rest, in the hands of those who labor to recreate Shakespeare's plays for us on the stage, an enterprise whose difficulties and rewards we would be foolish not to honor and respect. Without them, a study of this kind would be greatly reduced in interest, and it is in that spirit that the suggestions in this appendix have been offered.

Index